Best Newspaper Writing 2000

WINNERS: THE AMERICAN SOCIETY OF NEWSPAPER EDITORS COMPETITION

EDITED BY CHRISTOPHER SCANLAN

The Poynter Institute
and
Bonus Books, Inc.

03   02   01   00   99   5   4   3   2   1

International Standard Book Number: 1-56625-157-5
International Standard Serial Number: 0195-895X

The Poynter Institute for Media Studies
801 Third Street South
St. Petersburg, Florida 33701

Bonus Books, Inc.
160 East Illinois Street
Chicago, Illinois 60611

Book design and production by Billie M. Keirstead, Director
of Publications, The Poynter Institute.

Cover illustration by Jeff Papa of Phillip Gary Design, St.
Petersburg, Florida.

Photos for the cover illustration were provided by the Associated
Press and are used with permission. Photo credits: AP photographers
Beth A. Keiser (Amtrak derailment), Charles Krupa (JFK Jr. remem-
brance), Enric Marti (Kosovo refugee camp), Stephen Savoia
(floods), stringer Gianni Schicchi (Bob Dylan), and Omer Sel
(Turkey earthquake). Astrodome photo by unnamed AP staff photographer. Photos accompanying "Choosing Naia," and on cover
were taken by Suzanne Kreiter and provided by Mitchell Zuckoff.
Photos of ASNE winners and finalists were provided by their news
organizations.

Printed in the United States of America

This book is dedicated to the news librarians and researchers whose skills and often-unsung efforts provide the foundation of facts on which the best writing stands; and to our colleague, Nora Paul, who shares the keys to the treasures of the information age.

'Chariots of Fire'
and other torch songs

MAY 2000

Roy Peter Clark's spindly white legs pumped in slow motion as he lumbered across the Great Hall. *Chariots of Fire* theme music blasted from a boombox. Ahead, his chunky torso tilted forward in the classic pose of an Olympian anticipating the relay exchange, Christopher "Chip" Scanlan waited. Clark drew steadily near until at last his arm stretched and—there!—he handed to Scanlan the flashlight tricked up to resemble a torch.

The torch has passed.

At The Poynter Institute we take journalism, but not ourselves, seriously. We understand how good writing can be abetted by a culture in which people pass on understanding to one another. So we vamped a bit when, after founding and for eight years guiding the National Writers Workshops across America, Roy Clark passed the torch of leadership to Chip Scanlan.

Writing for publication is less often a lonely art than a collaborative craft. That's why some of its most successful practitioners donate their time each spring in seven or eight cities to give tips, techniques, and encouragement to anyone who attends a National Writers Workshop. Writers such as Clarence Page of the *Chicago Tribune* or Ron Suskind of *The Wall Street Journal* and editors like Jacqui Banaszynski of *The Seattle Times* or Cynthia Tucker of *The Atlanta Constitution*— many of them winners of ASNE Distinguished Writing Awards and Pulitzer Prizes—give spellbinding performances about their craft. "You don't have to be from the bigs to do big stories," Banaszynski said this year in Indianapolis. "A masthead is not destiny."

The sessions are on weekends. They're cheap. They're usually within driving range of most American journalists. They're instructional, they're inspirational, they're way cool. They're a wonderful introduction to Poynter, a school for journalists where many of these superb writers also have taught, and learned, and where this and 21 previous editions of *Best Newspaper Writing* are prepared.

We nearly stopped producing the book a couple of years ago. The Internet was seducing people from supposed "dead tree" journalism. It took copious time and talent to prepare the ASNE award winners' copy and interview them to gather their insights and create guides for writing teachers. We toyed with the notion that it would be easier on Poynter merely to publish the winners on our website and perhaps produce an anthology of their work every three or four years.

But something odd happened. Sales of *Best Newspaper Writing* increased. A 20th anniversary collection of pieces from the contest, prepared for the ASNE convention in 1998, was so popular that it led to a more polished edition, and that led to an expanded and more sophisticated version that soon will be published by Bedford/St. Martins. *Best Newspaper Writing* thrives.

So, of course, does the competition from which these exemplary writers were selected. You can't know how devoted to the responsibility of selecting them is the committee that judges the competition. It's hard work. Yet members of the ASNE Writing Awards Board are not volunteers; they are appointed by the society's president. Serving is an honor.

Those honored by judging this year were led by Sandra Rowe, editor of *The Oregonian* in Portland. Her colleagues were:

Joann Byrd, *Seattle Post-Intelligencer*
Leonard Downie Jr., *The Washington Post*
Michael R. Fancher, *The Seattle Times*
Robert H. Giles, Media Studies Center, New York
Karla Garrett Harshaw, *Springfield* (Ohio) *News-Sun*
Clark Hoyt, Knight Ridder Washington Bureau
Tonnie L. Katz, *Orange County Register*
Carolyn Lee, *The New York Times*
Gregory Moore, *The Boston Globe*
Michael Parks, *Los Angeles Times*
Robert Rivard, *San Antonio Express-News*
Edward Seaton, *The Manhattan* (Kan.) *Mercury*
Paul Tash, *St. Petersburg Times*
Cynthia Tucker, *The Atlanta Constitution*
Howard Tyner, *Chicago Tribune*

These folks are mentors to good writers. So are many of the award winners. So are my colleagues at Poynter.

One of the important messages from this 22nd volume of *Best Newspaper Writing* is that each of us benefits from having, and from being, mentors. Last year, Mirta Ojito of *The New York Times* paid homage to her mentor, Fabiola Santiago, who guided Ojito at *El Nuevo Herald* and at its sister paper, *The Miami Herald*. Here is how Ojito described Santiago's influence:

"I recently saw notes that she has sent me through the years, and I was reminded that she taught me everything. I remember in particular that she was very good, and is still very good herself, with leads. I remember when I was really young and I was traveling to assignments all over the world, I would call her at whatever hour and I would say, 'You know, I'm trying to say this,' and she would just automatically help me to write the lead. I nicknamed her 'The Leading Lady.'"

For those few moments when they were creating a scene by exchanging the torch, Roy Clark and Chip Scanlan were our Leading Men. They, too, have been mentors for years, including to each other. Roy launched the series of books you hold in your hand, and Chip has been their editor for seven years. Here's hoping you have as much fun learning from them as I do.

Cheers,
Jim Naughton, President
The Poynter Institute

Acknowledgments

To produce this book on a journalism deadline requires the hard work and cooperation of many people and organizations, chief among them the American Society of Newspaper Editors and its member papers. Our special thanks to ASNE executive director Scott Bosley, Sandra Mims Rowe of *The Oregonian*, who chaired the writing awards committee, and her judging colleagues. The Associated Press continued to generously provide the news photos used on the cover.

Once again, the series has been especially enriched by Poynter faculty and staff. Roy Peter Clark, Aly Colón, Karen Brown Dunlap, and Keith Woods each interviewed a winning writer. Kenny Irby provided a conversation with a visual collaborator to one of the winning entries. David Shedden, of Poynter's Eugene Patterson Library, once again assembled the bibliography that is an important regular feature. Billie Keirstead, publications director, supervised the entire effort, assisted by Vicki Krueger, an experienced copy editor who wrote the Writers' Workshop sections. They were aided by Patty Cox and Kathleen Tobin, skilled copy editors, and Priscilla Ely, Martin Gregor, Nancy Stewart, and Joyce Barrett of the Institute staff.

Readers benefit most of all from the stories and lessons about reporting and writing shared by the winners and finalists of this year's Distinguished Writing Awards and Jesse Laventhol Prizes. Our thanks to the writers for the good work that fills these pages and for generously sharing the stories behind the stories.

Contents

Piercing the fog
of personal concern

"Can you remember five things you read in the paper?"

That question was posed by Susan Cheever, the writer and former journalist, in an exchange on *Slate*, the online magazine. "I never can. News," she went on, "has to filter in to me through this fog of personal concern, and not much of it, I have the feeling, gets there. I do read *The New York Times* every day and sometimes the tabs or *The Wall Street Journal*. I watch the news almost every night. Still, my principle concerns seem to be baloney sandwiches, the holes in my kids' clothes, the puppy's whining."

Piercing the fog of personal concern: that's the challenge that faces everyone who hopes to attract a reader. The best stories do that. They drag a reader away from the baloney sandwiches, the whining puppies, and the holes that need darning. They demand to be read.

But how does that happen? If you ask a writer that question, you'll often hear something like this: I don't know. I just have to get my lead and the rest of it writes itself.

Stories that write themselves. Who doesn't want one of those?

But ask reporters what's the most important lesson they learned reporting and writing a story. It stops them dead. "Hmm. Never thought of it that way." "Well, let's see." "Hey, you know what I learned? People like to talk." "I decided to write this one for my mom, so she'd understand it." Sometimes it seems so simple.

But the simplest explanations are usually the best. That's what William of Occam, a 14th century philosopher decided, and to this day scientists are guided by what became known as Occam's Razor—the proposition that an investigator confronted with multiple explanations of a phenomenon can often solve the mystery by focusing on the simplest solution first.

But the best thing about prize-winning stories is the opportunity they offer to teach us how to get better at our craft. It's one thing to read a great story and another to hear how it was produced. In the interviews and essays published here, the writers whose work is featured in this book share lessons they learned producing award-winning work. At ASNE's convention last April, the winners of this year's *Best Newspaper Writing* awards offered these reflections on this question: "What lesson did you learn during the reporting and writing of this story that might be of use to other journalists trying to get better at their craft?"

Many of us view great writing as an unexplainable, mysterious alchemy that requires a combination of genius and luck. But when you view writing as a process, a rational series of decisions and steps from the initial idea to the final moments of revision, then you can begin to discover the keys to the magic: the lessons learned that enable journalists to write stories that pierce the fog of personal concern.

Lesson One: Connect with readers' fundamental concerns. Or what Joel Rawson, executive editor of *The Providence Journal*, once described as writing about "the joys and costs of being human."

Mitchell Zuckoff of *The Boston Globe* won the non-deadline prize this year for "Choosing Naia." It's a chronicle of one family's emotional, medical, and moral roller-coaster ride with genetic testing and the birth and first birthday of their daughter, Naia. In the stories, he combines precise reporting with narrative skill to take readers on a powerful journey that wrestles with some of today's most pressing issues. It opens this way:

> Tierney looks radiant in a new black-and-white striped dress, smiling and chatting as she pulls it up to expose a gentle bulge in her normally flat stomach.
>
> She lies on a table in the fourth-floor obstetrics room at St. Francis Hospital in Hartford. Her husband, Greg, sits in a chair beside her, watching as a technician begins the routine ultrasound test that is their last task before a weeklong vacation on Martha's Vineyard.
>
> The technician, Maryann Kolano, strokes Tierney's belly with a sonogram wand, using sound waves to create a picture of the life inside. Greg

studies the video screen, fascinated by the details emerging from what looks like a half-developed Polaroid. An arm here, a leg there, a tiny face in profile. Then the internal organs: brain, liver, kidneys.

"I'm having a hard time seeing the heart. Maybe the baby's turned," Kolano says calmly. Then it appears, pumping in a confident rhythm. She stops the moving image, capturing a vivid cross-section, and Greg remembers his high school biology.

"All mammals have four chambers in the heart," Greg thinks to himself. "There are only three chambers there..."

The inescapable truth is staring at Tierney and Greg from the silent screen: There is no fourth chamber. There is a hole in the heart. And not just any hole, they will soon learn...

A hole in the heart. In their baby's and, suddenly, in their own.

Zuckoff learned many lessons in the months he worked on this story. Perhaps the most important, he said, was this: "We learned just how hungry our readers were for a story like this. We were overwhelmed. We had over 2,000 responses, people pouring their hearts out to us about their experiences in similar cases....And it made us think about the kind of connection that we could make with our readers. We talk about a lot of the challenges facing newspapers and the different ways we need to reconnect, re-engage our readers.

The lesson I took away was when you write about issues that affect the fundamental parts of their lives, not ever giving up the mandate that we have to do all the other things that we do, we can reinvigorate our relationship with our readers."

Lesson Two: Write while you're reporting.
Leonora Bohen LaPeter of the *Savannah Morning News* won the Jesse Laventhol Prize for deadline news reporting by an individual for a story that took readers into a Georgia courtroom for a dramatic murder trial. Her deadline accounts delivered a riveting portrait of a horrific crime and its aftermath.

MONROE—Tap. Tap. Tap. Tap. Pause. Tap. Tap. Tap.

Ashley Lewis hit the counter of the oak witness box with his index finger, mimicking what he heard through a crack in the bathroom window the night of Dec. 4, 1997, as he got ready for bed.

It sounded like a typewriter. But Lewis, testifying on the first day in the death penalty trial of Jerry Scott Heidler for the murder of a family in Santa Claus a year-and-a-half ago, found it hard to believe his mother, a secretary, would break out her typewriter at almost 2 a.m. Just a half hour before, she had told him to turn the television off and go to bed.

Lewis walked to his mother's room and turned on the light. She was asleep in bed. He walked through the house, turning on other lights. Nothing.

"I got this eerie feeling," Lewis said.

Lewis did not know it yet, but a half-mile away, four of his neighbors lay dead.

"Write while you're reporting." That's the lesson LaPeter said she learned from this story. "In other words, think about how you write the story while you're reporting it. Basically, the second I got to the courthouse every morning I would be looking for my lead, I'd be looking for details, quotes, for the transition, and I'd also be looking for the structure of my story. I'd be thinking about this all day long while I was reporting, and then in the afternoon, I would go into the back of the courtroom and try to tap out my lead while court was still going on. Then at six o'clock when court was out, I would go to the hotel and it wasn't, 'How am I going to write this?' It was, 'What am I going to write, what details am I going to use?' I was able to save time and put out a better story. I was able to go over the story a couple of times and make sure that it read well, and my editor had some more time with the story. Another thing I learned was that it was helpful to have a box on the side of the story that gave the details of what happened that day. For example, when the prosecution closed their case or whatever might have happened that day. I was able to write in a narrative style and not have to clog up the story with details of what happened that day."

Lesson Three: Create a comfort zone for the people you interview.

Leonora LaPeter was one reporter. At the *St. Petersburg Times* there were many reporters. There were photographers. There was a news researcher. There were editors in Tampa and in St. Petersburg. All of them collaborating to cover another horrific crime, and this time recreating the minutes of terror when a hotel worker opened fire in a Tampa hotel and left five dead. They reconstructed the shooting and profiled the victims and the accused shooter in a well-reported and skillfully written package. Their work won this year's Jesse Laventhol Prize for deadline news reporting by a team. Their main story began this way:

> Beside the pool, a man lay shot to death, draped over a blue lounge chair. At the rear of the hotel, near the employees' entrance, lay two more bodies, sprawled in front of a minivan. In the hotel's lobby, near the registration desk, was another body. Elsewhere in the hotel were three more people, shot but still alive.
>
> The stunning scene unfolded in the space of just a few minutes Thursday afternoon at the Radisson Bay Harbor Hotel on Courtney Campbell Parkway.
>
> The dead and the injured were all hotel workers—and so was the gunman, Tampa police said. They identified him as Silvio Izquierdo-Leyva, a 36-year-old refugee from Cuba who had worked at the hotel for only a couple of months.
>
> A fifth person would die before one of Tampa's most tragic days was over....
>
> What had set off the killings? There was no clear answer to that question late Thursday.

To answer readers' questions about the suspect, the *Times* provided a vivid portrait, drawn largely from reporter Kathryn Wexler's exclusive interviews with his nieces. Wexler tracked them down with the help of news researcher John Martin, but she still had to persuade the young women to share what they knew about their uncle.

"I found that it was very important to create a sort of comfort zone for the people I was interviewing," Wexler said. "People who have been touched by tragedy, who have even peripherally been involved in a crime, are often loathe to talk to reporters, and I found myself talking my way into the home of one of the shooter's nieces and then sitting with her and her friend—basically sitting in their living room for about 45 minutes, letting them get used to my presence before I whipped out my notebook, before I started asking questions, just sort of asking how they were, and hoping that with time they would be willing to share some of the shooter's life with me. And it took a while, but they did."

Lesson Four: Care about the subject.

Another Georgian, Cynthia Tucker of *The Atlanta Constitution,* is this year's commentary winner. She challenged her readers with provocative and thoughtful columns that got tough on Jesse Jackson when he visited Belgrade and on the family of Martin Luther King Jr. allying itself with a politician of questionable honesty. One column also gave this reality check to the formerly white-only reunion of Thomas Jefferson's descendants.

As a veteran of family reunions, I can tell you they are often fractious affairs. Folks get their feelings hurt.

"Uncle Junebug hasn't spoken to Uncle Pink in 32 years, and he isn't about to talk to the stubborn old fool now. So who sat the two together at the banquet table? Aunt Lillie Bell never did care for Aunt Coot's sweet potato pie, and she never tires of telling her so. So how did the two of them end up in the kitchen together? The descendants of old Jim Tucker have felt slighted for decades by the descendants of old Jack Tucker—a bossy, elitist crowd. So who allowed Jack's clan to substitute a museum trip for the traditional fish fry and casino night?"

Given my experience with these affairs, I've got a little advice for the members of the Monticello Association: If the first gathering of the black and white descendants of Thomas Jefferson doesn't go all that smoothly, don't give up on it. You're just acting like family.

Tucker said her most important lesson was the value of writing about topics about which "I have some passion and which I know well. In that particular case, I also wanted just to try a different approach. Lots and lots and lots had been written about Thomas Jefferson and the fact that there was this new evidence that, in fact, he had had an affair with Sally Hemings. I had written about it before. But I wanted to approach it in a way that was a little different, a little more humorous, and to approach it in a way that would draw in readers whose point of view might be a little bit different from my own. I'm a Southerner. I know, needless to say, how race is part and parcel of the fabric of the South. I also know family very well. And so it was easy for me to cast it as any ordinary family gathering. In that sense it was a subject that I knew very well.

"Notice I didn't say write about what you know or what you care about. It is nice when you are familiar with a topic. But as we all know, the reporter doesn't have the same freedom as a columnist. Although I guess you could try it. 'Boss, I don't think I'm going to cover that City Council meeting on the new enterprise zone. I don't really know enough about it.'

"We should get smart about a topic as quickly as we can, but in the interim at least we should bring some passion to it. I don't mean bias. In fact, the best passion is that which reflects someone else's fire. Find out why that enterprise zone matters. To the people who want it or don't. If you don't know why people care, then why would anybody care to read your story?"

Lesson Five: Have a conversation with the reader.
Dianne Donovan of the *Chicago Tribune* won this year's editorial award. She won it for well-reasoned, elegant, and graceful editorials on everything from blue moons to a new work by Ralph Ellison, author of *Invisible Man*. She also campaigned about the absurdity of reading Miranda rights to a child. One of her pieces began this way:

Okay, quick: What does "counsel" mean? How about "waive," or "consult"? What's an "attorney"?

Maybe you're not stumped. But maybe you're not 9 years old. And maybe it's not after midnight and you haven't been sitting alone in a room half the night.

It is foolish to think that any 9-year-old child, even a well-rested one, could comprehend the meaning of the Miranda warning explaining his rights to remain silent and to have a lawyer present while he is interrogated by police. And it is absurd to think he could understand those rights well enough to voluntarily relinquish them.

For Dianne Donovan, the lesson learned was this: "When you are writing editorials, it's more important to talk with the reader as if you're in a conversation rather than finger wagging or preaching or being overly didactic, as editorial writers love to be." The challenge with this editorial, she said, was how to make the reader understand the sheer absurdity of it. "I just decided not to overcomplicate the thing and not to get too involved with the legal ins and outs, but just as you would sitting down with your friends or family saying, 'This is goofy. How could a kid understand this?' And I got a copy of the Miranda warning, which I'd been writing about for a while but which I'd never actually sat down and read, and just with that in front of me, the absurdity became so clear. And so I just wrote it in what I hoped was an uncomplicated fashion, just simplifying the argument, and using the whole notion of imagine this kid and how absurd it would be for someone to expect him to understand what waiving his constitutional right is. And I think that's a good lesson for most editorials—that is don't overcomplicate them. Talk to your reader as if you were talking with someone in the same room with you, and it usually gets the point across."

Lesson Six: Talk with your editor.
Michael Dobie of *Newsday* challenged stereotypes about race and sports in a series that examined how athletics can help ethically and racially diverse players form close relationships, yet it can't keep them from wondering how long these relationships will last once the game is over. He's the winner of this year's special award for coverage of diversity. He begins one part this way:

Todd Johnson says he knows the deal. He's a good player. Then again, he has to be.

Because he is black. Because the sport is basketball. Because the Glen Cove High School star knows what would happen if he couldn't cut it on the court. If he lost his starting spot to a white kid, for example.

"I'd be the talk of the town. My teammates, the people who played with me before would be, like, 'Dang, you don't know how to play no more? What happened?'" Johnson said.

Sports can bring kids together. It can also pull them apart by feeding the misconception that race predetermines what athletes can or cannot do.

Blacks are good in basketball. White men can't jump.

Such phrases often are uttered without second thought—or any thought. For players such as Johnson, these labels can hurt in unexpected ways. Stereotypes create expectations. Expectations create pressure....

The message, Johnson says, is clear:

Excel, or you're a failure.

Michael Dobie is a sportswriter. He spends a lot of time on the road or working from his home. "And it's something that's worked very well for me in the past, whether we're talking about a short feature or a longer feature, or even a major project. I've done several of those and mostly worked by myself." This time, however, he learned the value of working with an editor. "And I also discovered that once we did start to get a regular dialogue going, there were things that I hadn't thought of at all that seemed second-nature to him. That's what happens sometimes in projects like this, and it's nice to have another set of eyes to cut through that and help you see more clearly where we were going. So I think the need for constant and early communication throughout a project is something that really came home to me in this one."

Six stories. Six lessons. And I can guarantee you that each writer learned more than the one I've mentioned. Some of them may seem rather simple. But remember the lesson of Occam's Razor: Simple is good. Many years ago, when I was a young kid dreaming of being a writer, I got to meet a real writer, one who'd actually published. I asked her if she'd tell me how to become a writer. Sure, she said. "First, you've got to read. Read everything. Read all the time."

"Uh-huh," I said.

"Then you've got to write. Write all the time. Every day."

"Uh-huh," I said.

"That's it."

"Hmm. Thanks," I said, although to myself I said, "That's a big help."

Today, however, I realize that it's just that simple and that impossible.

But by reading and writing, learning and sharing the lessons of good writing, we can get closer to that dream all of us have: to write stories that connect with readers, that touch their fundamental concerns, that are conversations, that reflect the writer's passion, and engender a reader's excitement.

Sit down and ask yourself, what was the most important lesson you learned as a reporter or as an editor. Write the answer down. Don't keep it a secret. Share it with your colleagues. Every story, especially ones such as those that are honored in this book, can be a workshop that can make you a better journalist.

A NOTE ABOUT THIS EDITION

The discussions with the ASNE winners in this book are based on tape-recorded telephone interviews conducted by myself and my Poynter colleagues Roy Peter Clark, Aly Colón, Karen Brown Dunlap, and Keith Woods. The interview with photographer Suzanne Kreiter was conducted via e-mail by Kenny Irby. For reasons of clarity or pacing, we reorganized some questions and answers, and in some cases, inserted additional questions. The edited transcripts were reviewed for accuracy and, in some cases, revised slightly by the subjects.

Christopher Scanlan
June 2000

Best Newspaper Writing 2000

Mitchell Zuckoff
Non-Deadline Writing

Mitchell Zuckoff didn't know that in pulling together his award-winning work, "Choosing Naia: A Family's Journey," he would be choosing a new direction in his writing.

Though the story of Naia followed a long line of deep, investigative stories that have underscored Zuckoff's career, it was in many other ways like nothing he'd done in his 11-year career at *The Boston Globe*.

After earning a bachelor's degree from the University of Rhode Island and a master's in journalism from the University of Missouri, Zuckoff began his career with the Associated Press, then worked for the States News Service and the *Connecticut Post* before joining the *Globe* in 1989.

He started out as a suburban reporter covering police, schools, politics—"just about everything," he says. After

an 18-month stint with the section, he moved to business and began a succession of notable projects covering currency trading, insider lending, and shady corporate practices abroad. The latter work earned him the Livingston Award and the Heywood Broun Award for a 1994 series on unsavory U.S. corporate practices in developing countries.

He moved on to the *Globe*'s "Spotlight," the newspaper's revered investigative reporting crew. In 1997, he and his Spotlight teammates were finalists for the Pulitzer Prize for revealing fraud and abuse in the state disability retirement system. The team won the 1998 Associated Press Managing Editors Public Service Award for revealing corruption within the Boston Police Department.

Those system-failure stories, Zuckoff says, are clearly important. But in telling the story of a child born with Down syndrome and the choices her parents faced in giving her life, Zuckoff found a new direction for his reporting and storytelling talents. The story, delivered with tightly wound suspense and lyrical writing, profoundly affected the way he and his wife, *Globe* photographer Suzanne Kreiter, came to see their journalistic mission.

"I'm focusing now more on telling the small stories that are really, really important," he says. "It's not that the big sweeping stories aren't important. They are. But I want to tell the intimate, human, small stories that have large reverberations in the lives of people."

—Keith Woods

Choosing Naia, Part 1:
A hole in the heart

DECEMBER 5, 1999

Tierney looks radiant in a new black-and-white striped dress, smiling and chatting as she pulls it up to expose a gentle bulge in her normally flat stomach.

She lies on a table in a fourth-floor obstetrics room at St. Francis Hospital in Hartford. Her husband, Greg, sits in a chair beside her, watching as a technician begins the routine ultrasound test that is their last task before a weeklong vacation on Martha's Vineyard.

The technician, Maryann Kolano, strokes Tierney's belly with a sonogram wand, using sound waves to create a picture of the life inside. Greg studies the video screen, fascinated by the details emerging from what looks like a half-developed Polaroid. An arm here, a leg there, a tiny face in profile. Then the internal organs: brain, liver, kidneys.

"I'm having a hard time seeing the heart. Maybe the baby's turned," Kolano says calmly. Then it appears, pumping in a confident rhythm. She stops the moving image, capturing a vivid cross-section, and Greg remembers his high school biology.

"All mammals have four chambers in the heart," Greg thinks to himself. "There are only three chambers there."

"You know," Kolano says tactfully, "I'm not as good at this as some other people. Maybe somebody else should take a look." She tries to mask her alarm as she leaves the room.

The inescapable truth is staring at Tierney and Greg from the silent screen: There is no fourth chamber. There is a hole in the heart. And not just any hole, they will soon learn. It is a tell-tale sign of Down syndrome, a genetic stew of physical defects and mental retardation.

A hole in the heart. In their baby's and, suddenly, in their own.

The date is July 24, 1998, and Tierney Temple-Fairchild and Greg Fairchild have just entered a world

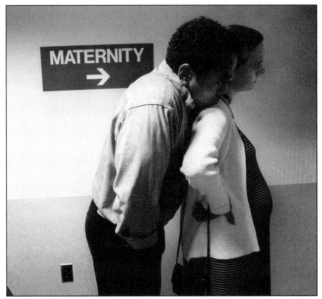

Photo by Suzanne Kreiter

of technological wizardry and emotional uncertainty called "prenatal screening." It is a confusing place where even the name is misleading; abortion screening is more accurate.

Most disorders tested for today—including Down syndrome, muscular dystrophy, and cystic fibrosis—cannot be corrected. That means the most common question prompted by distressing prenatal test results is not, "How can we fix it?" It is: "Should this pregnancy continue?"

Those questions are growing rapidly for countless couples who, like Tierney and Greg, would consider abortion under certain circumstances. Researchers say they are within two years of deciphering the blueprint of human development—the genetic code that acts as the operating instructions for creating life. That achievement is expected to drive prenatal screening into the realm of science fiction. Then what? Does a woman carry to term a baby susceptible to mental illness? Cancer? Obesity? Infertility?

Already, hard science has far outpaced the emotional side of the equation. People can learn a great deal about their unborn children, but no one tells them how to handle that knowledge, or what the future might hold.

That void will be filled in days ahead by the competing and sometimes ill-informed voices of Tierney and Greg's family and friends. Some will urge abortion—the choice made by up to 90 percent of people in their situation—while others will be horrified by the idea.

Complicating matters will be pressures of race, faith, and timing—less than two weeks after the final diagnosis, Tierney's pregnancy will reach the stage where abortion is illegal except to protect her life or health, neither of which is at risk.

All that makes theirs a journey through uncharted terrain, filled with fears and tears. Tierney and Greg will be tested and torn, changing their minds repeatedly as they confront a new reality amid the ache of lost dreams.

* * *

The morning of the ultrasound test dawned with a cloudless pastel sky, custom-made for a couple on course for an enviable future.

Tierney is 31, as smart as she is attractive, with shoulder-length brown hair, large expressive eyes, and an effervescent laugh. She has a doctorate in education from the University of Virginia, where she also received an MBA. Four years out of school, she works in the corporate contributions department of United Technologies, managing education programs.

Greg is 34, model-handsome, with thick shoulders, a strong chin, and a penetrating intellect. He also received an MBA from the University of Virginia, and is now writing his dissertation for a doctorate in business from Columbia University in New York, where he spends several days each week. The dissertation topic: small business in the inner city.

Together for nine years, married for four, Greg and Tierney live with their poodle, Onyx, in a one-bedroom apartment in a pleasant but unfashionable section of Hartford. Greg's bronzed baby shoes and a sepia-toned photo of him as an infant greet visitors from atop a china cabinet near the front door. They have long dreamed of having at least two children and adopting another.

It has been a busy time in their lives, but Tierney's first pregnancy has gone smoothly after some initial difficulty conceiving. Five months have passed with no morning sickness and enough energy for plenty of jogging through the streets of their neighborhood.

A first ultrasound, in late April, showed a healthy fetus due around Dec. 7, Greg's birthday. A second prenatal test for birth defects, called a triple screen, also was negative. In fact, it showed the odds of Tierney having a child with Down syndrome were unusually low, though the test is accurate only about 60 percent of the time. Still, they had no worries about today's ultrasound, scheduled mainly to confirm the due date.

Tierney left home early for a half day of work. Planning to go straight from the hospital to Martha's Vineyard, Greg loaded their Honda Accord, filling the trunk with bags, books, and a cooler with $100 worth of meat, fish, and a homemade marinade.

Greg picked up Tierney at work at 1:15 p.m. and they drove to nearby St. Francis Hospital. As they walked in, Tierney cheerily mused that their next visit would be for the delivery. It seemed fitting and natural: She was born here, too.

But now, an hour after their arrival, Kolano, the technician, has left them alone in ultrasound Room 1. Budding concerns are pushed aside, muted by Kolano's comment that she lacks the skill to properly read the results. Tierney's main worry is that they might miss their 8:30 p.m. ferry reservation.

But then Kolano returns with her boss: Dr. James F.X. Egan, director of maternal/fetal medicine, a vision of authority with silver hair, red cheeks, and blue eyes behind tortoise-shell bifocals.

Egan glances at the screen on the Ultramark 9 ultrasound machine and drops the first shoe: "We're only locating three chambers," he says in a voice that reveals only information, not emotion. He asks them to move two doors down, to Room 3, where he can use a more advanced machine, the Ultramark 5000.

As they begin the move, Tierney starts to cry. Greg takes her hand and says softly, "Stay calm. It's going to be OK. There's not anything to worry about yet."

But the Ultramark 5000 confirms the initial diagnosis in bold color: Their unborn child has a hole between the top and bottom chambers of the heart, a condition that causes a shortage of the oxygenated blood that every cell needs to survive. Also, the heart is situated at a slightly off-kilter angle.

Their baby is fine in the womb, Egan says, because Tierney is providing all the oxygen it needs. But these flaws will require major surgery before their baby's first birthday.

"I'm sorry," Tierney whispers to Greg between rising sobs. "I'm really sorry." She knows it's not her fault, yet she feels guilty. Gently, Greg tells her, "You don't have anything to apologize about."

But "sorry" is more than an apology. Tierney wants to tell Greg she feels sorry for him, sorry for herself, sorry that they won't be having the healthy child they dreamed about. Again, he tells her not to worry.

Then Egan drops the other shoe. This kind of heart defect is associated with Down syndrome, he says. If they want a diagnosis, he could perform a more accurate prenatal test, amniocentesis.

Egan explains he will insert a needle into Tierney's uterus and withdraw a small amount of fluid. Because the fluid contains cells from the fetus, doctors can diagnose Down syndrome with near-certainty by analyzing the chromosomes in the fetal cells. Most people have 46 chromosomes per cell; people with Down syndrome usually have 47. Results take a week to 10 days.

Tierney wants to call her mother. Greg discourages her, saying it would only upset them both, and they still don't know what they're dealing with.

"I feel so bad for you guys," says Kolano, the technician. "This is so tough, but it's better that you find out now."

Greg and Tierney, still trying to absorb the news, wonder what she means and why she seems so flustered. Then Egan offers his sympathy, too, while asking Tierney to sign a release form acknowledging there is a risk of miscarriage from amniocentesis.

Tierney feels rushed and confused—wasn't it just an hour ago everything was wonderful?—but through her tears she signs the form. Her body shakes as Egan inserts the needle. She cries in fear her baby will be jabbed. But the Ultramark 5000 is still on, and they watch the needle pass harmlessly into the uterus and then back out. Greg helps her off the table.

Afterward, there is a brief discussion between Kolano and Egan about whether to administer another, quicker test, called fluorescence in situ hybridization, or the FISH test. But Egan decides they won't; it's not accurate enough.

Tierney doesn't catch the remark, but Greg does. "You can't cure Down syndrome, so he has to mean just one thing," Greg thinks. "He must mean accurate enough to decide about abortion."

Despite Egan's misgivings, Tierney and Greg decide they want the FISH test, using part of the sample taken for the amniocentesis.

Insurance forms are signed and Kolano shows them the back way out, so they can avoid the waiting room. "That makes sense," Tierney says to herself. "If we went that way, people would look at us and think, 'Wow, they just got some really bad news about their baby.'"

They drive home in a fog, punctuated by Tierney's sobs. Greg carries in the cooler; they won't be going to the Vineyard tonight.

For the moment, Tierney focuses on the risk of miscarriage. She lies on the couch, asking, "What does this all mean?" Greg tries to be strong, telling her they'll play whatever cards they're dealt.

They make their first call, to Greg's parents in rural Russburg, Va. "We're really sorry for you both," says Mary Fairchild, whose college major was special education.

She talks of faith and holds back the tears she wants to shed for her first grandchild. "You have to face the situation," she explains. "If you are going to cry, you cry later. It blinds your eyes." Greg's father Bob, a retired Army colonel and bank executive, listens intently but says little.

The next call is to Tierney's mother, Joan Temple, a substitute teacher who lives in Avon, Conn. A devout Catholic, Joan tells them, "You need to relax and not think the worst. Remember, it's God's plan." Privately, she will be praying that a miracle heals her first grandchild. Tierney's parents are divorced. Her father, Ernie Temple, won't be told for another 11 days.

The last call is to a genetic counselor, Alicia Craffey,

who was referred to them by Egan. She promises to as-
semble a package of information, books with titles like,
A Time To Decide, A Time To Heal.

They pick at some dinner, listlessly watch TV, talk
for hours about everything and nothing, then fall into
fitful sleep. Overnight, the ice in the cooler melts. The
food left abandoned inside turns rancid.

* * *

In the morning, Greg awakens in a dark mood. It is
the first of many back-and-forth flips both will make in
the days ahead.

He calls his parents again and unleashes a fury of
thoughts on being black, on the mentally retarded, and
on discrimination against both groups. He knew there
would be problems for their child, born to a white mother and a black father. Now, imagining the added hurdles
of a heart defect and Down syndrome, he pours out a
litany of fears and frustrations.

"I'm just so sick of having to deal with discrimination," he says. "Why couldn't this have been visited on
someone who believes discrimination is not a part of
life? Why couldn't this have happened to someone who
has lived the most privileged life of all?"

He remembers, as a child, watching other boys taunt
a mentally retarded girl, asking her to pull down her
pants and laughing when she did. He remembers her
brother chasing the boys, and now he imagines himself
in that role.

He tells his parents he remembers volunteering as a
teenager for Special Olympics. He was supposed to hug
runners as they crossed the finish line. "I remember my
own visceral reaction when you see a child with what
I would call extreme Down syndrome—very large
glasses, bulging eyes, tongue sticking out of the mouth.
I didn't pull away, but you don't feel as comfortable
reaching over and hugging. Clearly, after you do it, after
you hug the first five, you find out, hey, there's nothing
wrong." Still, his initial response makes him wince.

To himself, he thinks, "When I have people over to
my house and we have dinner parties, what will happen
the moment when the child comes out and the people
won't know what to say and do?" He knows he isn't being completely rational, and he will scold himself later,

but now the world is spinning and so is he.

After the phone call with his parents, Greg tells Tierney they face a frustrating future in which they can never stop being vigilant, educating the ignorant, battling the cruel.

"If we have this baby, just get ready for the onslaught of stupid, maybe well-meaning, but stupid comments. We're going to have to deal with them for the rest of our lives," he tells her. "Tierney, we're going to have to go into our child's school, fighting with administrators, changing this and that. I'm going to have to make sure people aren't abusing my child, putting him in the back of the room or locking him in the closet. This is what we're going to have to do. But I'm mad about it."

He is leaning toward abortion.

But Tierney has awakened more peacefully. For the moment, her confusion and sadness have passed with the night. She tells Greg: "We both consider ourselves to be pretty strong people. If this is going to be a worst-case scenario, then maybe we're the right parents to take this on." She also reminds him they still don't have a final diagnosis—either about the heart defect or Down syndrome—so they should just wait and see.

Tierney leaves to get the information assembled by Craffey, the genetic counselor. Then they read it together, huddled on their living room couch.

They learn that no one knows why Down syndrome occurs or how to prevent it. It appears in all races and in all countries, and is the most common chromosomal abnormality in humans. The only clue to its likely occurrence is the mother's age: women over 35 are significantly more likely to have babies with Down syndrome.

But Tierney is only 31, and that leads them to a surprising discovery. Of the 5,000 or so babies with Down syndrome born each year in the United States, 75 percent are born to mothers under 35. The main reason is that most babies are born to younger mothers. Their low odds of having a baby with Down syndrome are offset by the proportionately larger number of babies they bear.

That helps to explain why the number of children born with the disorder has remained stable for decades, despite the high abortion rate among women who know in advance. Because younger mothers undergo fewer prenatal tests, most don't know their unborn child has an extra chromosome. Also, the number of older women having babies is rising, increasing the overall incidence of Down syndrome.

From the literature, Tierney and Greg also learn that children with Down syndrome are as varied as other children, though they have certain consistent features. All are mentally retarded, most with IQs between 40 and 70 on a scale that considers 100 to be average.

Though often stereotyped as relentlessly happy, they have the same range of emotions as other children. Most have poor muscle tone, upward-slanting eyes, and faces that are broader and flatter than those of other children. Life-expectancy is 55 and rising. Many have vision problems, and heart defects are common, occurring in nearly half of all children with Down syndrome.

Greg and Tierney learn that surgery can correct the type of defect spotted in their unborn child's heart, but success is not guaranteed; some babies are doomed from birth.

* * *

When they awaken the next day it is Sunday and both feel drawn to church. Greg, raised a Baptist, and Tierney, a Catholic, consider themselves religious. And yet, they depart from church doctrine on key matters, most notably abortion rights, which they strongly support.

With no church of their own, they drive to the Church of Saint Timothy in West Hartford, where Tierney's mother sometimes worships. It is a fine brick building, surrounded by tall, strong trees.

Sitting in a pew, bathed in sunlight passing through stained-glass windows, Greg and Tierney hear a sermon about the role of prayer. It resonates so deeply it seems written just for them. "The miracle you pray for," the priest concludes, "may not be the miracle you receive."

From this moment on, there will be no more prayers for the baby not to have Down syndrome. What's done is done, they decide, and such a diagnosis might somehow be a miracle in itself, in ways they cannot yet fully imagine. Instead, Tierney and Greg will pray the heart heals or can be fixed by surgery.

Back home, Tierney begins to feel claustrophobic. With days until the test results come back, she wants to begin their delayed vacation on Martha's Vineyard. Reluctantly, Greg agrees.

Greg spends the ferry ride napping in the car, too tired and depressed to venture out on deck. It is a pattern that continues on the island. The first few days, Tierney goes alone or with Onyx the poodle to Philbin Beach, near the Gay Head Cliffs, to read and reflect under blue skies and a healing sun. Greg stays holed up in their rented house, slowly coming to terms with what their future might hold.

Then, on Thursday, they get a phone call from their obstetrician, Dr. Michael Bourque, with news about the FISH test.

"I'm really sorry to have to tell you this, but it came back positive," Bourque says. Chances for a different result are slim, he says, but the diagnosis won't be final until the amniocentesis results arrive next week.

Greg takes it hard, even though he had expected the news. It's worse for Tierney.

"I was dealing with it and trying to stay strong, and appealing to my better half that I could handle it," Tierney tells Greg. "Now, all of a sudden, it *is* going to be us."

There are tears to shed, more hard news to share with family.

The next day, Friday, exactly a week after the ultrasound, Tierney's sister Tara joins them on the Vineyard. Her visit unleashes new tensions.

Tara is a year older than Tierney, single, a veterinarian in Worcester. The two look and sometimes act like twins. They wear identical necklaces, presents Greg brought home from a trip to Ghana. Each necklace has a single pendant, an African symbol for "hope," that dangles over the heart.

Tara was the first person Tierney told that she was expecting. Tara has been kept informed about the difficult news by phone.

Before heading to the Vineyard with her golden retriever Winnie, Tara spent a night in Boston with their older brother George, 36, an architect and former Air Force captain, and his wife, Allison, an anesthesiologist. Based on a discussion of medical information gathered by George and Allison, the three had reached a consensus: Tierney and Greg should abort.

Tara drops this bombshell when Tierney meets her at the ferry. The conversation fuels Tierney's worst fears. She loves the unborn child kicking inside her, but if the heart defect is irreparable, maybe abortion is the right choice. Still, hearing it from Tara is devastating.

When Tierney and Tara reach the rental house, their reddened eyes are turned from each other. When Tara goes inside, Tierney tells Greg on the porch: "They think this is a big tragedy."

Tara walks back outside and into a confrontation with Greg, whose reading about the heart defect has made him more optimistic. He believes Tara, George, and Allison are overstating their medical fears to justify abortion. He suspects they really want to spare Tierney and Greg—and perhaps, even themselves—the difficulties and discrimination that come with Down syndrome.

"You know," he says sharply, "when this is all said and done, if it turns out more positively than everyone expects, some people will see us as having been pioneers."

Tara shoots back: "And if it doesn't turn out as positively as you expect, some of them will see you as having been stupid."

The next morning, Tara and Tierney have a talk that brings them full circle. After Tara apologizes, Tierney wistfully mentions that the children on Martha's Vineyard all seem so perfect.

Not true, Tara says. On the ferry, a pretty 4-year-old girl with Down syndrome came over and asked to pet Winnie. "She was so cute and so sweet," Tara says.

"Oh, Tara!" Tierney cries. "That's what God wanted you to tell me all along. That's what I needed to hear."

With that, Tara begins to understand how her sister feels, and what she needs.

Writers' Workshop

Talking Points

1) The writer did not observe the scene that opens this story. What reporting techniques did he need to reconstruct the scene? Are there clues that this is based on interviews after the fact?

2) The writer concludes the opening section by providing hints about the decisions to come without giving away the ending. Study how the conclusion is crafted.

3) Examine the language the writer uses: "fears and tears," "tested and torn." Note the word play used in the story and discuss its effectiveness.

Assignment Desk

1) Examine your own reactions to Greg and Tierney's decision. How would they affect your ability to write a similar story?

2) The writer carefully uses details, even in the parts of the story that were reconstructed. Look for ways to mine your interviews for more details.

Choosing Naia, Part 2:
Reaching a decision

DECEMBER 6, 1999

Greg and Tierney sit like defendants awaiting a verdict, their backs stiff, jaws clenched. Holding hands in their obstetrician's office, they brace for the results of the final test that will reveal whether their unborn child has Down syndrome.

Dr. Michael Bourque leans across his desk, tries to meet their eyes with his, and softly begins: "I'm really sorry…"

They were prepared for bad news, but still, tears wash Tierney's face. Greg feels the air rush from his lungs.

The amniocentesis test confirms the preliminary findings: If they continue this pregnancy, their child will be mentally retarded and marked by the distinctive features and ailments of Down syndrome. On top of that, the child will have a life-threatening heart defect.

Greg catches his breath and asks Bourque: "What do people usually do? I mean, in terms of keeping the baby."

Bourque leans back in his chair and considers the question.

It is Tuesday, Aug. 4, 1998, 11 days since Greg Fairchild and Tierney Temple-Fairchild got the first hint of trouble during a routine ultrasound.

They returned home last night from Martha's Vineyard, having spent the last hours of an abbreviated vacation with Tierney's sister, Tara, and brother, George, who came to the island to offer support and advice. George sat with them on Philbin Beach and subtly pressed his case for abortion. Tierney and Greg said they were still gathering information, weighing options.

Once back home in Hartford, Tierney and Greg knew they weren't ready to resume their normal routines. Tierney called her boss at United Technologies, where she manages education programs, to say she needed more time off. She explained only that "complications" have arisen in her pregnancy. Greg made the same call to Columbia University, where he is a doctoral student and instructor at the business school.

Now, as they sit with Bourque at St. Francis Hospital, their every fear realized, they seek guidance that isn't forthcoming.

"People do all sorts of things in this situation," Bourque says. Through a haze of emotion, they hear him ramble through a noncommittal answer. He says some people don't abort under any circumstances, and others abort if the child isn't a boy. He also says an abortion would have to be done elsewhere; St. Francis is a Catholic hospital.

"It's really your decision. It's up to you," he concludes.

Afterward, Greg is irritated, feeling he gained little useful information about Down syndrome, the heart problems, or how to respond. He wonders why Bourque doesn't seem to know more.

Tierney, who has known Bourque since she was 19, suspects the doctor knows more than he's saying. She thinks: Is he worried about being sued? Does working in a Catholic hospital limit what he can say about abortion? Is he going overboard trying not to influence us?

They drive several miles to Connecticut Children's Medical Center to see a pediatric cardiologist, Dr. Harris Leopold. There, for the first time, they get an upbeat assessment from a medical professional: Leopold's nurse, Karen Mazzarella.

"Everything will be fine," she tells them. "Your biggest worry is going to be whether your child wants to ride a motorcycle or get a tattoo." In the hallway outside her office are bulletin boards covered with photos of children who have undergone successful heart surgery. They are babies, little kids, and teenagers, in a rainbow of colors. Some have Down syndrome.

Leopold is as encouraging as Mazzarella, even in his body language. Rather than separating himself with a desk, he cozies up close, pulling his chair forward so their knees almost touch. With detailed charts he illustrates the heart defect, explains its effects, and shows how it would be repaired.

He saves the best for last: "The success rate for this surgery is better than 90 percent." And, for reasons involving the shape and development of the heart valves, the prognosis is best among children with Down syndrome.

Greg feels vindicated. His reading about the heart defect had led him to believe the odds were promising. He refused to be shaken from that belief, despite the bleak scenario Tierney's brother presented of a brief and painful life for their child. But Tierney is oddly unsettled.

On the beach at Martha's Vineyard, she had told her brother she would only abort if she learned that the heart defect meant certain death. But now, despite hearing an encouraging assessment from Leopold, she is gripped by doubt.

She wonders if Leopold is downplaying the effects of a damaged heart on a child with Down syndrome. She probes for a darker response: "Will there be some kind of interaction between the two, so having the heart defect will stunt development and make it even harder for this child?" She asks it several times, in several ways. Each time, Leopold says no.

On the way home, Greg is fuming.

"Do you really want this child?" he demands. "What's wrong here? You've got doctors telling you that everything is going to be OK. Why don't you believe them?"

"I don't know," she says, the hope that had sustained her ebbing away. "Maybe it's their job. Maybe they only tell you the good parts because this is what they do. I'm not sure they're giving us the right information, or maybe he doesn't really know about Down syndrome. I just don't know."

She wants to see another doctor, a genetics expert who is an authority on Down syndrome. That appointment is in two days.

Tonight, though, there is unfinished family business.

* * *

Greg and Tierney still haven't called her father, Ernie Temple, an engineer as solid—and at times, as unmoving—as the granite of his home state of New Hampshire. Tierney was in the eighth grade when her parents split up.

"We've had some bad news about the baby," Tierney

begins. When she finishes, Ernie says, "Well Tierney, that's really too bad. But you know, the way medical services have improved, with technology, there's a lot that can be done."

The phone call ends, and only then does Tierney catch his meaning. He didn't mean medical services and technology to help a disabled child. He meant abortion. She calls him back.

Ernie elaborates: "Do you understand what having a child with these disabilities is going to bring to your life, to both of you? You've got career goals, you're both professionals."

Then he shifts focus. "Do you understand the baby is going to be in pain? Do you want to put the baby through that?

"This child will cause trauma and tragedy from the first breath," he says.

Tierney is stunned but she tries again, telling Ernie about state-funded programs that promote physical and mental development among disabled children. She mentions it to suggest that there are resources available for their child. But Ernie sees it through the eyes of a staunch fiscal conservative.

"Do you really think it's fair to keep the baby?" he asks.

"What do you mean, 'fair'?" Tierney responds.

"Knowing what you do about this child, is it fair for you to take state money, resources?" Ernie says.

Tierney lets the comment pass, but it is the harshest thing he has ever said to her.

There is little else to say. Tierney promises to consider his points, but tells him she hopes he will be involved with their baby if they decide not to abort. Ernie says he will, but he's hardly convincing.

Tierney is deeply disappointed, realizing only later that she had been seeking approval, not advice. Greg is angry.

He thinks it's possible Ernie is repelled by the idea of a grandchild with Down syndrome. But maybe it's something else: lingering race issues. Greg's thoughts rush back nearly a decade, to Ernie's reaction when he heard the two were dating.

Greg and Tierney met while working as managers at

Saks Fifth Avenue in Manhattan, Greg in the dress department and Tierney in women's coats and suits. They were recent college graduates, Tierney from the University of Pennsylvania and Greg from Virginia Commonwealth University. Lunchtime chats evolved into heated debates on politics, society, and race. Romance bloomed.

When Ernie first met Greg and thought he was only Tierney's coworker, the two got along famously. But after Ernie learned the truth, he refused to speak to Greg for a year. Only with time and the inevitability of their relationship did he relent.

Still, neither Greg nor Tierney considers Ernie racist; Greg says he is on good terms with his father-in-law, and Ernie has grown close to Greg's parents, often visiting them in Virginia.

"I've come to believe his concern is about protecting his daughter, helping you avoid a life of discrimination," Greg tells Tierney. "As your father, he would prefer you not have to deal with it. When we met, his attitude was like, you could just stop dating me. And now, he's saying technology can help us avoid the problem, the discrimination, that comes with Down syndrome."

Ernie's opinion clouds an already difficult situation. And time is fast running out—Tierney's pregnancy is approaching the 24th week, the point at which a fetus is considered "viable" and abortion is illegal except to protect the mother's life or health.

A decision looms, and still Tierney and Greg are shifting positions repeatedly.

* * *

Two days after the talk with Ernie, Greg and Tierney return to Children's Medical Center to see Dr. Robert Greenstein, a geneticist and authority on Down syndrome. Greenstein is as encouraging as Leopold was, explaining the strides being made in helping children with Down syndrome lead full and happy lives.

More good news, but Tierney is still struggling.

"What more do you need to know?" Greg asks.

Tierney is still worried about the heart, and also about the chance their child will be in the minority of Down syndrome cases with profound mental retardation. "Maybe we should do the termination," she says, avoiding the word abortion. "But I'm really conflicted. Even though I'm feeling good about all the information we've received, maybe we're trying to do too much."

Soon, Greg is beset by new doubts of his own.

"Is having a child with Down syndrome going to present all sorts of complications with other children?" he wonders aloud. "What about the younger children being required to take care of their older sibling, possibly for the rest of their lives from a financial perspective? Would keeping this child mean we aren't able to adopt a child later?"

The case for abortion seems to be growing stronger.

Greg calls his parents to voice his fears. At first Bob and Mary Fairchild listen quietly, as they have throughout these past two weeks. But Mary can hold back no longer. She blurts out: "So, you're just going to go with the abortionist?"

Bob, quiet by nature, decides it's time to speak up. "Gregory," he says to his beloved only son, "this is not a tragedy. This is not the end of the world. All of us are born with defects. If you and Tierney give this child the love you have for each other, this child will be all right."

The call helps, but Greg and Tierney want more answers.

Tierney asks their genetic counselor, Alicia Craffey, for phone numbers of people whose children have Down syndrome. The calls yield uniformly heartwarming stories of prom dates, family vacations, and sleepaway camps, of joyful children overcoming obstacles and enriching the lives of their parents and younger siblings.

There is some talk of financial strain, but—unlike many prospective parents in their situation—that issue plays little role in Tierney and Greg's decision. Both have already made career and educational choices that put personal goals ahead of monetary concerns. Instead of starting a college fund, they decide, they would open an "independent living fund" for their child.

Still there are nagging doubts. Using another number supplied by Craffey, Greg calls A Kids Exchange, an organization that helps arrange adoptions for children with Down syndrome. If the problems overwhelm them, they wonder, could an adoptive home be found for their baby?

"No problem," says Janet Marchese, who runs the matchmaking service from her home in White Plains, N.Y. "I have a long waiting list for these babies."

Greg asks, "What if it takes three years or more to determine how severely mentally retarded the baby is?"

She repeats: "No problem."

"OK then," Greg says, "How about finding a home for an interracial child, with Down syndrome and a heart defect?"

"No problem."

Now there are no more questions to ask, only a decision to make. After all the twists and turns, all the changes of mind and heart, that is the final piece of information they need.

Tierney and Greg talk about the encouraging medical outlook, the upbeat stories of children with Down syndrome, and the possibility of adoption. They talk about the mechanics of abortion. They talk about their sense of themselves and each other. They talk about their families. They talk about love.

They remain anxious about the heart, about severe mental retardation, and about the long-term effects on their lives.

But when there are no more words left to say, it doesn't add up to abortion. They look at each other and know they have decided: They will have this baby.

They call it a leap of faith.

"If I had to terminate, I could bring myself to do it," Tierney tells Greg through tears. "But to terminate in a circumstance where I was afraid of taking on a challenge, I just don't think I could live with the repercussions it would have on my life. On our life together.

"Why wouldn't I allow God to take this pregnancy where it needs to go? And if my baby is going to die in heart surgery, my baby is going to die in heart surgery. My dad might say, 'Tierney, why do you have to go through that, or why does your baby have to go through that pain?' But I have to trust."

* * *

Five days later, Aug. 14, the legal deadline for abortion comes and goes. Greg doesn't give it any thought. Tierney has a twinge of doubt, but it passes.

Now that a decision has been made, they have to

share it with their families. The hardest calls are to Tierney's father and brother because they were the biggest proponents of abortion.

Unwilling to confront Ernie, Tierney is brief and to the point. "I'll be there to support you," Ernie says.

Several weeks later, during a visit to Ernie's house in New Hampshire, Greg goes a step further. "I know you said you're going to be supportive, but you also said some things that indicate maybe you're not going to be," Greg tells him.

Ernie repeats his pledge of support, but doesn't waver from his original stand. "I'm supported in what I believe," he says of his contention that continuing the pregnancy would be a tragedy.

"Whether you agree or not with our decision," Greg says, "it's important that you be involved with your daughter. She needs you and wants that." Ernie says he understands.

Tierney is tougher on her brother. She tells George the information he shared with them was frightening, often wrong, and reflected his personal biases. George grows defensive, saying he was only trying to help. But in his own way, he eventually acknowledges her point. A few days later, a bouquet arrives, with a card from George and his wife, Allison: "We love you and look forward to meeting our new niece or nephew."

As it turns out, an unintended byproduct of all the prenatal tests is an answer to that question: It will be a niece. To their delight, Tierney and Greg are expecting a girl.

With the decision made, Greg returns to school. Tierney goes back to work after role-playing with Greg about what to say when people ask about her absence. "I say, 'I'm doing fine.' That's true. My baby's not fine, but I'm fine. I'm not lying, and I really don't need to go into it any more," Tierney says.

Over the next few weeks, Tierney and Greg slowly explain the situation to a select group of colleagues and friends. Some take it in stride, some cry, some pray, some offer sympathy. Tierney and Greg tell them there's nothing to be sorry about.

"Please don't be upset for us," Greg tells friends who take it hardest. "We're going to do what we have to do.

It's serious, but it's not the end of the world."

Two acquaintances express surprise that it was genetically possible for an interracial couple to have a child with Down syndrome. On the flip side, Greg suspects some others think the mixing of races played a role, based on the flawed assumption that his and Tierney's genes were incompatible.

In fact, no link to race has been found in the 133 years since the syndrome was identified by an English doctor, John Langdon Down. The only known genetic link involves a tiny number of people who are hidden carriers; tests show neither Greg nor Tierney is one. To the best of anyone's knowledge their unborn child's condition was a fluke, a missed signal at conception.

As summer turns to fall, there are baby showers to attend and preparations to make. Tierney shops for baby clothes with her mother and sister. Greg's father, Bob Fairchild, refinishes an antique bassinet and ships it north. In it is a pillow embroidered with the words: "Anybody can be a father, but it takes someone special to be a Daddy."

In mid-November, with just weeks until the due date, the nesting instinct takes hold. Greg and Tierney buy an apartment in the complex where they have been renting. It has only one bedroom, just like their unit, but the price is too good to pass up. "It has a wonderful view of Taco Bell," Tierney jokes. "We'll have a new place, a new baby, new everything."

Bourque, Tierney's obstetrician, monitors the pregnancy closely. In November, her ninth month, there are signs that growth of the fetus has slowed. Bourque decides to schedule the birth for Dec. 3. Tierney will be induced to deliver, so specialists can be on hand to deal with any emergencies.

The slowed growth renews Greg's fears, which are compounded by the knowledge that the risk of stillbirth is higher among fetuses with Down syndrome. It is much too late to change course, so he decides not to share his thoughts with Tierney.

"If they had found some other kind of defect, like a limb missing, you know what you're getting into," Greg thinks. "They could tell you where the limb ended and where it began. They can't tell us how mentally retarded she'll be, how severe the effects of Down syndrome will be, and that's hard."

* * *

It is Sunday, Nov. 22, and Tara has come to Hartford to spend the day and see the new apartment. After her initial doubts, Tara now sees her unborn niece as a blessing and a gift.

Greg plans to make a chicken dinner, but first they have a leisurely lunch at the Prospect Cafe in West Hartford. Greg and Tara talk animatedly about work, but Tierney sits quietly.

They come home and pop a movie into the VCR. As night approaches, Tierney grows increasingly certain something isn't right. She grabs her copy of the pregnant woman's bible: *What to Expect When You're Expecting*. She rustles through the well-thumbed pages, searching for information on fetal movement.

"I can't remember the last time the baby kicked," she tells them both. Turning to Greg, she says quietly: "I'm worried."

Writers' Workshop

Talking Points

1) The writer uses several techniques to tell this story: direct observation, recreated scenes based on interviews and research, and the internal thoughts of Greg and Tierney. Study how he weaves these together.

2) Study the story and the interview with the writer to determine which scenes were observed by the reporter and which were reconstructed. Is there a difference in voice between these two kinds of scenes? What, if any, clues does the writer provide?

3) The story ends with a dramatic cliffhanger. Are there clues to what will happen in the next section? Discuss whether the amount of information the writer reveals is adequate.

Assignment Desk

1) Note the use of similes in this story: "as solid as granite," "sit like defendants awaiting a verdict." How can you use vivid similes and metaphors in your stories?

2) The narrative is organized chronologically. Make an outline of the series and study the use of scenes to build the narrative.

Choosing Naia, Part 3:
A difficult birth

DECEMBER 7, 1999

Tierney curls herself up into a fetal position on a hospital gurney. She is shaking, praying, drawing air with shallow breaths as a doctor inserts a needle into her spine.

Her eyes are wild. As the needle slides between two bones of her lower back, a strange, piercing sensation shoots down her leg as though she has stepped on a live wire. She feels alone and afraid; her husband, Greg, has been told to wait outside the operating room.

Tierney's mind races. She thinks of the day four months ago when a routine ultrasound foretold her baby's future, her husband's, and her own. The memory makes her shiver more, and the doctors who surround her take notice.

"There's nothing to be nervous about," says her obstetrician, Dr. Michael Bourque.

She nods, but says to herself: "Oh yeah. I'm having this emergency delivery, my baby has all these problems, but there's nothing to worry about."

It is Nov. 22, 1998, 11 days before Tierney was originally scheduled to deliver a baby girl with Down syndrome, a major heart defect, and uncertain prospects.

The day began leisurely enough, with a visit from her sister, Tara, and plans for a roast chicken dinner. But as the hours passed, Tierney grew increasingly aware that her unborn child—on most days an active kicker—was unnervingly still.

Tierney had seen Bourque just four days earlier, and everything seemed fine. He even warned her to expect less kicking as the due date approached, because the baby would be taking longer naps. But this nap was lasting too long.

When Tierney shared her worries with Greg, he went to a drug store and bought a stethoscope to listen for a heartbeat. All they could hear was a gurgling sound, so Tierney called Bourque's office. He told her to drink fruit juice and eat a candy bar, to see if they could stimulate the baby with sugar.

An hour later, as day turned to night, still nothing.

Another call to Bourque prompted action: He instructed her to go immediately to St. Francis Hospital so he could check the baby's vital signs. Tierney and Greg rushed out without packing a bag, leaving gifts and baby clothes strewn across their bed, scared but fairly certain they'd be home soon.

At first, the fetal monitor strapped by a nurse around Tierney's middle picked up a steady heartbeat. Their anxieties started to ease. But the heart monitor was set for 45 minutes to track the beats over time. Soon the beats grew further and further apart. "I better get Dr. Bourque," said the nurse at Tierney's side.

Along with Bourque came an ultrasound machine, which showed that Tierney and Greg's unborn daughter wasn't moving. The amniotic fluid that normally bathes a fetus in the womb had dried up; Tierney's body apparently had stopped producing it. Bourque asked a medical resident to assess the situation.

"Since she has no fluid, I'd give her a zero for that. And I'd give her a one for movement," the resident said. On a scale of 10, Tierney and Greg's unborn child was failing badly. The chance of a stillbirth—already higher than usual as a result of the Down syndrome—was increasing with each passing minute.

"Your daughter wants to be delivered tonight," Bourque said.

With Greg running alongside, a birthing team rushed Tierney to an operating room and began preparing for an emergency Caesarean section, in which an incision is made through the abdomen and uterus to quickly remove a baby.

Now, not two hours since arriving at St. Francis, Tierney is curled on the gurney and the anesthesiologist is injecting her spine with drugs that will numb her lower body.

As he waits outside, Greg dons blue-green hospital scrubs and calls Tierney's mother and sister. After a few minutes, the anesthesiologist pinches Tierney's leg to test if the drugs are working. When Tierney can no longer feel the doctor's touch, Greg is admitted to the operating room.

He sits at Tierney's side and watches Bourque work.

Bourque calls to them, just moments after making the incision: "We can see the baby's head." He moves with a single, practiced motion, like a father lifting a child who has fallen. Bourque pulls from Tierney's uterus a baby covered with the muck of new life.

It is 10:16 p.m. and Tierney Temple-Fairchild and Greg Fairchild have just become the proud and nervous parents of a 5-pound-12-ounce, 17 3/4-inch, brown-haired, not-quite-healthy baby girl.

* * *

Quickly the umbilical cord is cut, ending not only the baby's physical attachment to Tierney, but also cutting off the rich supply of blood that her own damaged heart cannot provide. If she survives, she will need major surgery before she turns one.

Tierney's face is screened by a drape, and she hears only the faintest noise from her newborn daughter. She knows the baby is alive, but she is frightened by the absence of a hardy cry. Tierney prepares herself for the worst.

"Did I do something wrong?" she asks Greg.

"No, nothing," he tells her. Setting aside his own worries, Greg smiles and says she did great. He doesn't mention that their baby's skin seems to have a blue cast and her movements are sluggish. On the positive side, Greg notices she has relatively good muscle tone, in contrast to the "floppy" body they were told to expect from a newborn with Down syndrome.

A team of neonatal specialists swings into action, taking the baby into an adjacent room with Greg following close behind. They suction fluid from her nose and mouth. They clean, dry, weigh, and measure her, speaking to her in dulcet tones.

They give the baby a dangerously low score of 2, out of a possible 10, on a newborn health scale that measures heart rate, breathing, muscle tone, color, and reflexes. After five minutes, the score rises to 5; at 10 minutes, it is 7, a hopeful sign but no guarantee of survival.

Tierney is still on the operating table, dazed and anxious. She begins to shake again as Bourque closes the incision. As he sews, he comforts her, praising her for recognizing the danger: "Nice call. You saved your daughter's life."

Still, Tierney is doubtful, wanting to see for herself.

Greg returns minutes later, wheeling the baby toward Tierney in a plexiglass bassinet. He lifts their swaddled daughter and puts her close to Tierney's ashen face. She brightens, marveling at the delicate life they have created.

"Oh! She's beautiful," Tierney says.

But then, the combination of anesthesia and stress catches up to Tierney; she starts throwing up. For the first time, Greg is forced to juggle his roles as husband and father. He trades the baby for a bedpan, and holds it for Tierney.

When everyone is cleaned up, they head off in separate directions. Tierney is taken to the recovery room. The baby is brought to the neonatal intensive care unit. Greg goes searching for Tara and Tierney's mother, Joan Temple.

When he finds them outside the maternity ward, Greg says, "You have a granddaughter. You have a niece." Joan kisses him. Tara grips him in a long, strong hug.

"My baby had a baby," Joan says over and over.

Greg leads them to the intensive care unit. It is dark and quiet, yet a buzz of smooth efficiency saturates the filtered air. Nurses glide silently among seven bassinets, four of them containing babies who barely crease the crisp white sheets.

Around each bassinet is a maze of high-tech machinery and intravenous feeding tubes, oxygen tanks, and monitors that glow and hum and keep watch like worried parents. Not all these babies will be going home.

A nurse leads them to their daughter, granddaughter, and niece, who is napping in bassinet No. 5 from the exhaustion of birth. They marvel in unison at the baby in the tiny knit cap with tufts of hair peaking out. They admire her long fingernails and rosebud lips.

"Hello sweet baby," Joan says. "Hello."

Left unspoken are the doubts about her survival. Her serene countenance notwithstanding, the baby's bloodstream has a dangerously high level of acid—an indicator of insufficient oxygen in her system. She has a frighteningly low number of platelets, which are neces-

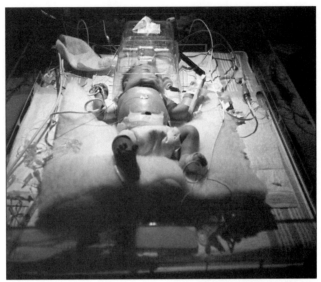

Photo by Suzanne Kreiter

sary to stop bleeding. She will get at least one transfusion in the next two days. She requires supplemental oxygen from a tube in her nose. Later, it will come from a transparent tent over her entire face.

Her blood pressure is low, her kidney function is questionable, her lungs don't seem to be working quite right. She still hasn't had a good cry. She shows signs of an infection, though the doctors aren't certain about that.

Then, of course, there's the hole in her heart. It's not clear how many of the ailments are linked to that, but most appear to be the result of her difficult last hours in the womb.

Later, Bourque explains that Tierney's placenta—the organ that links the baby to the mother—had begun shutting down early, depriving the baby of nourishment. It is a relatively common occurrence among babies with chromosomal defects like Down syndrome, and he suspects the baby would have died within a day if not for the emergency delivery.

At 1 a.m., his daughter now three hours old, Greg stands over her, trying to digest a torrent of information about the monitors that surround her. He furrows his brow and studies the heart rate, the blood pressure, the oxygen saturation level. It is as though he is trying to move the numbers to their proper levels through sheer will and new love.

"Can I touch her?" he asks a nurse. She explains he will need to thoroughly scrub his hands and arms. He wants to, but knowing that Tierney is alone and waiting, he declines.

When they are reunited in the otherwise empty recovery room, Greg shares with Tierney what he knows of their baby's condition. Tierney feels pleased she realized there was a problem. But she wonders if her active lifestyle was partly to blame, and she wishes she had called Bourque sooner.

"Did I reach too high? Did I do something? Did I not rest enough?" she says. "What would have happened if I didn't call at all? Would the baby have died?"

Both Tierney and Greg wonder: Will she die anyway?

* * *

It is after 2 a.m. when they drift off to sleep in Tierney's hospital room, she in the bed and Greg scrunched on a fold-out chair. But first, they formally give their baby a name they had settled on.

Like most expectant parents, Tierney and Greg had spent the last months of pregnancy puzzling over names, adding and deleting prospects on a list posted on their refrigerator. Both were drawn to unusual names, and something clicked when Greg spotted Lake Nyasa —a huge body of water in Malawi—while scrolling through a computerized encyclopedia.

Fiddling with the lettering and dropping the "s," they came up with Naia, which they pronounce "Nye-uh." Only later will they learn it is more appropriate than they ever imagined. With a slightly different spelling, their baby's name is a Swahili verb that means "decide." As a noun, it means "purpose."

For a middle name, they chose Grace. For Tierney, it evoked the hymn "Amazing Grace" and had the added benefit of honoring a relative of her father's who died young. For Greg, it reflected a desire to heal the wounds that surrounded their decision.

"For me, grace is the concept of forgiveness," he told Tierney. "This has not been easy on our family. I believe, or I wish, that the baby will do more to raise people, to change people's expectations and beliefs. She provides an opportunity for people to have grace, to mend bonds that were strained."

* * *

When day breaks, Tierney sleeps late while Greg goes home to walk their dog. When he returns, they are eager to see Naia Grace and learn more about her condition.

When they enter the intensive care unit they meet one of several new doctors in their lives, cardiologist Seth Lapuk.

In a small conference room away from the bassinets, Lapuk elaborates on what Greg and Tierney already know about the heart defect, the low blood pressure, the lack of pressure in the lungs, the whole array of problems facing Naia.

Then Lapuk tells them a more personal story.

One day when he was a boy, he was playing in his family's garage, trying to reach a wall-mounted button that would open the electric garage door. He arranged a teetering stack of boxes under the button and began climbing. He was halfway to the top, when his younger brother came in. Without a word, the younger boy went over to a car parked in the garage, reached in and hit the remote. The door rose while Lapuk watched in astonishment.

Lapuk's younger brother has Down syndrome.

"Don't underestimate what your daughter might do. Expectations with these children are often lower than they should be," Lapuk says. "You don't know what can happen."

Lapuk's story heartens them as Greg pushes Tierney's wheelchair toward Naia's bassinet.

Tierney leans her head against Greg's side. "That's our baby," she says. It is the first time Tierney has seen their daughter outside the delivery room.

Greg touches Naia, his hand as big as her entire torso. "It's OK little girl. It's OK," he says.

"She looks good," Tierney says in a quiet, hopeful voice, her eyes half-closed from painkillers and lack of sleep.

Later, back in Tierney's room, there are three books

on a table by her bed: *What to Expect the First Year*, a memoir on race called *Life on the Color Line*, and the Holy Bible. Martha Stewart is on the television, on mute.

A bouquet from Joan brightens the room. A camera sits on a rolling table, waiting for a happy moment to record.

For now, the joy at the arrival is tempered by fears about Naia's health, prompting reflections on their decision.

"You know, the baby might not make it," Greg tells Tierney, his voice choked with emotion. If Naia dies, he says, some people will think: "You see, you should never have had this baby. It was tragic for the baby, it was tragic for you, and you should have terminated months ago and saved everybody this huge problem.

"And as traumatic as that will be for us, I think, yeah, it will make those people feel better because it will confirm what they were thinking all along," he says.

Tierney nods in understanding, but no matter what anyone else might say, she is convinced they made the correct choice.

"The baby is doing well enough that she deserves a fighting chance, and she deserves her own opportunity," Tierney says, slumping in her hospital bed. She wears a pink bathrobe over a white nightgown. Around her neck is her "hope" necklace, which she hasn't removed since arriving at the hospital.

"It's not like she's on a respirator. She's breathing on her own. Yes, she's got some challenges and she might not make it, but this was the right thing to do. I'm convinced of that."

Tierney's beliefs were reinforced by the sight of one of the other babies in the intensive care unit, a baby that looks like Naia in miniature. The baby's grandmother was holding her in a rocking chair, whispering encouragement to the frail infant. The woman's focus was complete; she never looked up.

The baby's mother was in a car accident that triggered premature labor. The baby was born at 26 weeks—14 weeks premature—and weighed just 1 1/2 pounds. Tierney realizes that's roughly the same size Naia was when they were deciding whether to continue or abort.

"They are spending a ton of energy saving this baby," she tells Greg, "and this baby is worth saving." For a moment, it isn't clear if Tierney is talking about the other woman's child or her own. Then, gulping air between words she'd rather not speak, Tierney adds, "We had to give her the chance to make it. And if she...can't...she ...can't."

* * *

As the days pass, Naia clings ever more fiercely to life. Responding to intense, around-the-clock care from the St. Francis staff, she begins to show slow but steady improvement.

Her kidneys begin to work and the oxygen level in her blood rises. The acid in her blood is tapering off. She has begun to shed some of the IV's, monitoring devices, and other medical appendages that had sprouted from her tiny body like tentacles.

Yet problems remain, including a persistently low platelet count in her blood.

On her fourth full day of life, it is Thanksgiving, and Joan delivers dinner to the hospital. Before eating they say grace, which has special meaning now that the word is Naia's middle name. Their prayer includes an offer to help those in need.

It occurs to Tierney their wish has been granted. "I'm really supposed to be helping somebody less fortunate, and it's going to be my baby," says Tierney, as she prepares to go home without Naia.

When Naia is six days old, her condition has improved enough to supplement intravenous feedings with breast milk. Until now, Tierney has been using a pump to collect her milk, storing it for later use. On her first try at the breast, Naia doesn't take much, and tires quickly, but it pleases Tierney just the same.

The next day, Sunday, Nov. 29, Naia gets her first visit from Tierney's father, Ernie Temple, who had argued against her birth but now is trying to live up to his promise of support.

Beforehand, Ernie and Tara went shopping so he could buy a changing table for Naia. They also tried out rocking chairs, and Ernie seemed ready for a grandfatherly role.

On their way to the intensive care unit, Greg tells

Ernie about his granddaughter's medical problems and prepares him for what he will see. When Greg picks up Naia, Ernie says she looks good. Then Greg asks Ernie if he wants to hold her.

"No. Not this time," Ernie says. The visit ends.

Afterward, Greg and Tierney think Ernie's reluctance was innocent, reflecting his fear of detaching one of her tubes or otherwise harming such a fragile baby.

"Or, you can go with Option Two," Greg says, "and he's uncomfortable with this baby, period. We don't really know."

* * *

Five days later—Dec. 4—Naia has beaten the worst of her most immediate problems and is ready to go home. She has been in the hospital 12 days, eight more than planned.

It's a surprisingly warm December day, with temperatures topping 60 degrees and the roses outside St. Francis still showing off their rich red petals.

Greg's parents, Bob and Mary Fairchild, have taken a train up from Virginia to meet Naia and escort her home. Both were firmly in favor of continuing the pregnancy. Now that the baby is here, Mary gives voice to their hopes for the future. It sounds like a promise and a prayer.

"I think a lot about how the world will treat Naia," she says. "But the people who love her will be so heavily weighted on her side that how the world perceives her will be totally irrelevant.

"I know it will be challenging for Greg and Tierney," Mary says as Bob nods in agreement. "I wish more than anything they could have had the healthy child they were hoping for. They didn't, and that hurts a lot. But I admire them, and I know they will always want the best and do the best for Naia. That will never change."

After a final briefing from doctors, Greg and Tierney emerge with Naia. They are beaming. Just a few days ago they didn't know if she would ever leave the hospital.

Naia is bundled enough for a blizzard, tucked under a crochet blanket that was a gift from the hospital. At her side is a black-and-white stuffed dog. She yawns and looks around, at the lights on the ceiling, at her parents.

A nurse pushes Naia's bassinet, but Greg keeps one hand gripped on the side, as if to keep it from rolling away.

On the short drive home, Naia falls asleep. Greg carries her into the apartment, still buckled in her new car seat. He gingerly sets her down on the floor and looks to Tierney.

"OK. Now what?" he asks.

"I don't know," Tierney answers.

Writers' Workshop

Talking Points

1) Study how the writer provides background to readers in this dramatic opening scene. Is it enough information for readers who start the series with this installment? How does it affect the pacing of the scene?

2) The use of numbers traditionally is thought to bog down a story. What details here make the use of numbers necessary?

3) The writer describes Greg "trying to digest a torrent of information," and then lists the monitors that keep watch over Naia. How does this objective list convey Greg's emotions?

4) The story ends with quotes from a conversation between Greg and Tierney: "'OK. Now what?' he asks. 'I don't know,' Tierney answers." Discuss possible reader reactions to this conclusion.

Assignment Desk

1) Research and write about an evening in an emergency room. Practice using the reporting and writing techniques employed in "Choosing Naia" to describe the scene.

2) "A camera sits on a rolling table, waiting for a happy moment to record." The writer uses a telling detail that captures the mood. Look for other examples of the ways that writers use details to convey mood in their stories. Include such details in future stories you write.

Choosing Naia, Part 4: Struggling to grow

DECEMBER 8, 1999

Naia latches onto Tierney's breast, her eyes rolling back in sleepy serenity, her body more relaxed with each sip of milk.

"Yes. You're a good eater, Nai-nai," Tierney whispers, cradling her baby on their living room couch.

Greg is setting the table for a takeout Chinese dinner. A small Christmas tree waits expectantly nearby; snow flurries brush against the apartment window; a jazz CD plays softly.

But this is no blissful family tableau.

Naia's skin has a distinctly yellow cast. Tierney's mouth is a tight line. Her eyes are red and her neck muscles dance under the collar of her white turtleneck. Greg is unshaven, funereal in all black clothing.

During the 10 days since she came home from the hospital, Naia has stubbornly failed to thrive.

It is Dec. 14, 1998. Naia is 22 days old and weighs 5 pounds 14 ounces, just 2 ounces more than her birth weight.

Her damaged heart is struggling to pump enough oxygen to the rest of her body. Her liver isn't working properly. She's brewing a urinary tract infection. She is sleeping too much, eating too little. Her system is so fragile that a cold could kill her.

Having decided to continue the pregnancy knowing their child would have Down syndrome and a heart defect, having soldiered through the difficult birth and frightening first days of Naia's life, Tierney Temple-Fairchild and Greg Fairchild are finding that the problems keep piling up. More even than they had allowed themselves to imagine.

"We're in that grind of always worrying that there's something else we need to worry about," Greg tells Tierney.

And there is good reason to worry. With each passing day, Naia's body is in a more urgent race with itself.

Despite weakness and lethargy, Naia needs to quickly gain enough weight to survive the heart surgery she needs for a chance at a healthy life. If she gains the weight, she can win the race. But if her heart begins to fail before she is strong enough for the operation, the surgery itself might kill her.

* * *

The first goal in Naia's life is deceptively simple: 8 pounds. That is how much doctors believe she should weigh before they risk opening her chest to repair her heart.

Eight pounds is within the normal weight range for newborns, but it seems months away for Naia. Now, with Naia's growth rate stalled, Tierney and Greg face difficult new choices.

First among them is whether to end breast-feeding and switch exclusively to a bottle, using breast milk Tierney collects with a suction pump. Already, when Greg feeds Naia breast milk from a bottle, she finishes more quickly, is less tired afterward, and seems to drink more than when she nurses directly from Tierney.

Naia's pediatrician, Dr. Della Corcoran, has even begun dropping hints about ending Naia's reliance on breast milk altogether, switching her to a high-calorie formula more likely to hasten weight gain.

Greg and Tierney want to do what's best, but it seems odd that breast-feeding—usually the best choice for babies—might be placing Naia at greater risk. It is particularly hard for Tierney. She was eager to breast-feed, believing it would help Naia flourish, despite the mental retardation and physical disorders of Down syndrome.

"She's getting a bonding experience from me, which I love and I'm sure is good for her," Tierney says. "But why am I doing this if it comes at the expense of her gaining weight, which I know is the most important thing right now?"

Sighing, she adds, "It's just all so hard."

The question of breast milk or formula will haunt them for several more weeks. But it is not the only challenge that Naia, Tierney, and Greg face on the road to 8 pounds.

* * *

Eight days later—Dec. 22—Naia is one month old. A visit to the doctor takes the place of a celebration.

While waiting to see their pediatrician, Greg and Tierney sit with Naia in the waiting room and listen to a mother laughingly complain about how big and heavy her daughter was at birth. Her baby is the same age as Naia, but twice the size.

Greg and Tierney offer the woman wan smiles but say nothing. Comments about Naia's size—"Is she a preemie?"—are common on the infrequent occasions when Tierney and Greg expose Naia to the world, where the winter cold and potential for illness must be avoided at all cost.

Things only get worse inside Corcoran's office. The doctor delicately places a squirming Naia on a counter-top infant scale. Greg and Tierney watch intently, barely breathing.

Naia is 5 pounds 14 ounces. No change in more than a week. Tierney throws her hands up in frustration.

This means the end of pure breast milk. Tierney can nurse Naia twice a day, Corcoran says, but four other feedings must be from a bottle of breast milk mixed with a formula called Pregestimil.

Corcoran explains that Naia's slow growth is most likely a result of her heart's failure to pump enough oxygen-rich blood, without which her body lacks the fuel it needs to gain weight. The formula should boost her growth despite the heart defect.

Tierney is upset but tries not to show it. She realizes the most important thing is that Naia get those calories. She dutifully records Corcoran's instructions in a small brown notebook she has begun carrying to keep track of Naia's lengthening list of medical problems.

Corcoran also notices that Tierney and Naia share a common yeast infection called thrush—on Tierney's breast and in Naia's mouth. She prescribes an antibiotic called Nystatin. Naia needs it four times daily; twice a day for Tierney. Again, Tierney writes it down in her book.

Since last week, on orders from her cardiologist, Naia also has been taking a heart medication called Lasix. Defects such as Naia's—a hole between the chambers—can lead to a buildup of salt and fluid in the body, which compounds heart problems. By encouraging urination, Lasix helps to improve heart function.

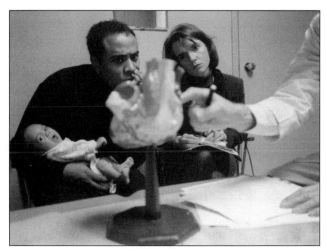

Photo by Suzanne Kreiter

During the examination, Corcoran adds an unintentional insult to the injury of Naia's newly diagnosed ailments. Corcoran refers to her as "my little peanut," and Tierney recoils.

"What's the matter?" the doctor asks.

"We don't use the word 'peanut' for her," Tierney says, calm but cool. She tells Corcoran the word has negative racial connotations, particularly in the South, where Greg grew up.

Corcoran says she calls all her infant patients peanut, but apologizes and says she won't refer to Naia that way again.

The doctor punctuates the visit by saving the worst news for last: Naia is jaundiced, a clear sign of liver problems and the cause of her yellowish skin tone.

Jaundice is not uncommon among newborns, regardless of whether they have Down syndrome or a heart defect. Sometimes it's related to breast-feeding and clears up on its own. But there's another kind of jaundice that is potentially lethal.

Instead of returning home as planned, a discouraged Tierney and Greg drive to Connecticut Children's Medical Center. There, Naia must undergo blood tests to check her liver function.

Before the tests, Greg and Tierney go to the hospital pharmacy to fill her new prescriptions. While they wait, a little boy walks over to them. He has an awful, hacking cough, but his mother does nothing to draw him away from Naia.

Tierney looks to Greg with pleading eyes, fearful that—on top of everything else—Naia will catch a deadly germ.

"Don't worry," Greg says softly, shielding Naia as best he can until the boy leaves. "He was far enough away."

Tierney nods, but her face betrays her stress.

Medicine in hand, they go to a small room on the hospital's second floor that is gaily decorated with hanging mobiles and cartoons of Barney and Tweety Bird. A nurse has trouble finding a vein from which to draw Naia's blood. Naia screams. Tierney winces.

As they wait for Naia's cries to end, they notice a poem pinned to the back of the door, placed there by a hospital worker whose son nearly died. Shoulder to shoulder, Greg and Tierney read its rhyming couplets. The closing lines read:

"We'll love him while we may...
But shall the Angels call him
Much sooner than we planned,
We'll brave the bitter grief that comes,
And try to understand."

Finally, Naia's blood drawn, they scoop her up, hold her close, and bring her home.

* * *

Since Naia's birth, medical problems and routine care have dominated Greg and Tierney's time and thoughts. Naia's first Christmas is a low-key affair. Gifts run along the functional lines of baby clothes and a bottle sterilizer.

Yet in the quiet moments between feeding, diapering, medicating, and sleeping, they reflect on the decision they reached nearly five months ago. The discussion is triggered when Greg finds a *Newsweek* magazine lying around the house. It's long out of date, from March 22, 1997, but they had never read it.

Deep inside Greg notices an article on birth defects and prenatal screening. It contains this line: "Down syndrome in theory is completely preventable, in the sense that there is a reliable test for the extra chromosome known to be its cause, after which the pregnancy can be terminated."

Greg and Tierney know that, but the next line comes as a shock: Among women who learn they carry a fetus with Down syndrome, about 90 percent abort. At last, they have an answer to the question Greg had tried to ask their obstetrician, Dr. Michael Bourque: "What do people do?"

"There's no changing our decision, not that we'd even want to," Greg says. "But 90 percent? It's human nature when you do something to look around and see what other people have done. But to hear that you're so in the minority...."

"You have to wonder," he adds, "what do the other nine people know that we don't?"

It dawns on Tierney that, based on the 90 percent figure, nearly everyone they've told about their decision would have made the opposite choice. It's also possible that some people they've told actually faced the decision and chose abortion.

"That shouldn't surprise you," Greg says. "You probably wouldn't do the same thing that 90 percent of other people would do in most cases, anyway."

Tierney smiles and thinks about their decision to marry across racial lines. "Well, I guess that's true about both of us." Greg smiles back.

* * *

It is Jan. 14, 1999. Naia is nearly eight weeks old and weighs 6 pounds 8 ounces. She has gained 12 ounces since birth, 10 in the past three weeks, the result of orders by Corcoran to add even more formula to her feedings. Eventually, the formula will be mixed as thick and rich as a milk shake.

Still, Naia is a pound and a half away from her goal, and time is growing short. Surgery is needed sooner than expected.

Naia's heart is barely keeping pace with her body's hunger for oxygen. To compensate, she takes deeper and deeper breaths. With each one, her skin sucks up and under her ribs, making her chest look like a child-size xylophone.

Naia's cardiologist, Dr. Harris Leopold, has been teaching Greg and Tierney to look for signs of congestive heart failure, in which the heart is unable to pump blood with enough force to the body. One sign is a bluish tint to the skin.

Greg and Tierney always expected they and their child would be aware of black and white. Now, they also have to worry about the yellow of jaundice and the blue of heart failure. To top it off, a fifth skin color has entered the mix: pink.

Just before Christmas, Tierney took a picture of Naia to a photo shop across the street from their apartment to order reprints for faraway family and friends. A few days later, Greg picked them up and brought them home.

"Greg, they lightened Naia's picture!" Tierney fumed when she saw the results. "She looks a lot whiter than she did in the original." She marched across the street with the original photo and confronted the man who had taken her order.

"I don't understand why you did that," she said.

"I'm sorry," he said sheepishly. "I just looked at your complexion and figured that she would look like you. It's just that most babies are pink, so I made her pink."

"She's not pink," Tierney said.

He agreed to redo them. No charge.

* * *

During the early weeks of the new year, Naia's heart remains a priority, but her liver problems have begun causing even bigger fears. The source of her jaundice remains a mystery.

Two weeks of near-daily visits lead Naia's liver specialist, Dr. Jeffrey Hyams, to conclude that Naia has one of the more dangerous types of jaundice. He suspects it's either a blockage in the tubes that connect the liver to the small intestine, or an inflammation of the liver called neonatal hepatitis.

Hepatitis can be treated with drugs, but a blockage likely would require surgery. There also is a possibility that Naia's liver will fail completely, requiring a transplant. In the meantime, Hyams tells Greg and Tierney there's a good chance Naia needs a liver biopsy, a surgical procedure in which cells from the liver are removed for extensive tests and microscopic analysis.

When added to the looming heart surgery, the prospect of liver surgery, a transplant, or even a biopsy frightens and depresses Tierney and Greg.

Hyams also diagnoses the urinary tract infection, which requires Naia to take another antibiotic, amoxycillin. He prescribes vitamins K and E, and a multivitamin called Polyvisol. It fills another page in Tierney's medical notebook.

After days of fear and uncertainty, Tierney and Naia go to Hartford Hospital for a procedure in which a chemical is injected into Naia's body then traced as it moves through her system. If it doesn't pass from her liver to her intestine, a life-threatening blockage would be the most likely culprit.

To perform the test, a technician places Naia on a padded gurney, using straps to immobilize her under a machine that tracks the chemical. She screams and struggles, but eventually surrenders to sleep. Tierney also succumbs to stress and exhaustion, nodding off in a chair at Naia's side, her head down on the gurney just inches from her daughter's.

When they awake, the technician has the first bit of good news in what seems like a long time. The chemical passed into Naia's intestine; she doesn't have a blockage. "Our prayers were answered," Tierney tells Greg when she and Naia come home.

Naia's jaundice remains an issue, but from that and other tests, Hyams concludes she most likely suffers from neonatal hepatitis. It is an ailment of uncertain cause—possibly an infection, possibly some link to Down syndrome—that will resolve with medicine and time.

No surgery, no biopsy, no transplant needed.

And soon, Naia's skin will begin to lose its yellow tint.

A casualty of their worries about the heart, the weight, and the jaundice is Tierney's effort to breastfeed. By mid-January she is no longer even collecting her milk and mixing it with the formula. "I did the best I could," Tierney tells herself.

Left in the freezer are 15 glass bottles, each filled with four or five ounces of breast milk. Tierney doesn't want to dilute the thick formula, yet she can't bear to throw them out. So they remain in the freezer, until they spoil.

* * *

Back in August, when Greg and Tierney were choosing to have Naia, the most vocal opponents were Tierney's father Ernie and brother George. Now, both are trying in their own ways, with varying degrees of success, to heal the rift.

On his first visit with Naia, in early January, George steps into the role of favorite, and only, uncle. He holds Naia, smiling and laughing. When bedtime comes, he kneels by her cradle, rocking her gently and telling her it's time to sleep.

"I'm sorry," George tells Greg and Tierney. "I wish I had never said anything." They embrace and forgive him.

Ernie, meanwhile, has expressed himself mostly with gifts, sending Naia a playpen for Christmas along with pants, booties, a yellow sweater, and several body suits. Tierney assumes the clothes were the work of Ernie's girlfriend, whose daughter runs a company that sells clothing for undersized babies.

When Ernie drops by on a business trip, he keeps his distance from Naia. He seems interested when Greg and Tierney describe her ailments, but he won't hold her. There is no change of heart, no apology for saying her birth would be a tragedy.

Ernie's rigidity makes Greg and Tierney wonder if his attitude reflects something more than race, something more than what he said about having a baby that burdens society and themselves. They wonder if her problems are stirring up painful memories of his own past.

Ernie's only sibling, his younger brother Norman, suffered from a severe birth defect. A kind and funny man, Tierney's uncle and godfather, Norman Temple was handsome. But only from one angle. The other side of his face was deformed, his nose and eye crushed like kneaded dough.

When Norman was a teenager, a surgeon attempted to repair some of the deformities by sewing his hand to his face. It was one of several painful attempts to grow new skin, and they met with limited success.

Ernie had looked out for his kid brother when they were boys, and he cared for Norman before he died of cancer in 1989.

Early in Tierney's pregnancy, before they knew about Naia's Down syndrome, Ernie made a comment that struck them at the time as strange but unimportant. It began when Greg asked Ernie if he had any advice or concerns about his unborn grandchild.

"Well, you're both physically fit, and you both have good genes," Ernie said.

Thinking back, Greg and Tierney are certain the message was: "You don't want to suffer through our experience with Norman."

"It's like that was the ultimate test for him, his ultimate fear," Greg says. Finishing his thought, Tierney says, "And now it's come true, like a self-fulfilling prophecy, and it's difficult for him to accept."

* * *

Slowly but surely, the heavy diet of formula takes effect. By Jan. 28, Naia weighs 6 pounds 13 ounces. On Feb. 11, she is 7 pounds 4 ounces. On Feb. 26, she is 7 pounds 8 ounces. Finally, by March, she reaches 8 pounds.

Still, her growth rate is troublingly slow, and her heart defect continues to tax her body. Hope that surgery could wait until late spring is cast aside. It will happen by April 1.

In the meantime, despite all her challenges, Naia has been growing into an individual in her own right.

She seems to recognize her name. She is starting to like baths, especially when someone sings "Rubber Ducky." She has a favorite toy, a stuffed red Elmo doll, from *Sesame Street*. She follows objects with her eyes, particularly ones with bright colors and bold patterns. She sings out in little yelps. She smiles an innocent, toothless smile. Greg melts every time she gives him one.

A few days before Naia turns four months old, Greg tells Tierney: "I think Naia is beginning to look a lot like me."

"She's cuter," Tierney says, and they both laugh.

Tierney returns to work, having received a promotion and arranged a schedule that will allow her to work from home some days. Greg works at home on his doctoral dissertation and oversees daytime care of Naia—with some unexpected help.

Just before Tierney's maternity leave ended, Greg's mother, Mary Fairchild, moved to Hartford from her home in Virginia. While Greg and Tierney remained in their old apartment, Mary settled into the new place Greg and Tierney had bought just before Naia was born. Greg's father will join her when Naia has surgery.

* * *

It is March 16, and Naia's growth has stalled again. The operation will be in two weeks. Today Greg and Tierney tour the surgery suite at Children's Medical Center.

Despite the growth problem, Tierney has been feeling confident about Naia's prospects. "I am ready for Naia to be the Naia that I know she's going to be afterwards. Only occasionally do I think that maybe something will go wrong," Tierney tells Greg.

Greg, on the other hand, has grown increasingly worried. "It's major surgery," he says. "And then it's the idea of her having all that stuff attached to her. It's depressing."

At the end of their hourlong tour, as they walk into the intensive care unit, Greg and Tierney notice a commotion at the end of the hall. Five doctors huddle, talking in low tones with grave looks on their faces. Just outside the doctors' circle, a young couple stands limp, sobbing and rocking and making feeble, futile efforts to comfort each other.

The tour guide hurriedly turns Greg and Tierney the other way.

Writers' Workshop

Talking Points

1) Underline the numbers in this story that describe Naia's age and weight. How important are these numbers. How would the story differ if it were less precise?

2) Discuss the degree of intimacy the writer has reached with the family. How do you think he did this? How important is it to select a source for a story like this? What qualities do you look for?

3) Study the description of skin colors. Note how this writing vividly paints images with simple language. How is the writer able to do this? Do you agree with this approach?

Assignment Desk

1) The use of numbers, Tierney's notebook, and skin colors are used as themes to give this story its structure. Look for themes that will provide structure for your stories.

2) If you were writing this story, would you show it to the family before publication? What are the benefits? What are the drawbacks?

Choosing Naia, Part 5:
Mending a heart

The doctor in blue surgical scrubs holds out Naia to her worried parents. "Give her a kiss," he says.

Tierney and Greg take turns touching their lips to Naia's soft cheeks, then looking at each other with watery eyes and a shared thought: He's telling us to say goodbye.

Dr. Craig Bonnani, an anesthesiologist, says nothing. He either doesn't sense their anxiety or doesn't want to make it worse. Bonnani leaves with a bouncy walk, holding Naia in one arm, like a football.

Doctor and patient are headed down the hall to an operating room at Connecticut Children's Medical Center.

Over the next five hours, if all goes according to plan, Naia's plum-sized heart will be stopped, her blood will be circulated by machine, her breathing will be done by mechanical lungs. Her chest will be sawed open, and her malformed heart will be rebuilt to support her growing body.

And, barring a catastrophe, her life will begin anew.

It is March 31, 1999, the day of the surgery Tierney Temple-Fairchild and Greg Fairchild knew would be needed ever since they decided eight months ago to bear a child with Down syndrome and a major heart defect.

For a few difficult days last summer, fears that the heart problem was a death sentence made them strongly consider abortion. They went ahead with Tierney's pregnancy only after learning that the odds of successful surgery were good.

Now, as they watch Bonnani walk away with Naia, all they can do is wait, and wonder, and pray they made the right choice.

"She'll be OK," Tierney says to no one in particular.

"She'll be OK," Greg repeats, wiping his eyes.

* * *

Last night, Greg's mother, Mary Fairchild, gave Naia a leisurely bath, letting her splash around on her stomach as though she were swimming. Tierney gingerly clipped Naia's fingernails and placed her in a battery-powered swing.

Before Naia fell asleep, Tierney read to her from a children's book of prayer. On one page was a pastel drawing of a little bear in bed, a blanket pulled up to her chin. Next to it was the "When I'm Afraid Prayer":

"I'm scared, God,
So please help me,
And keep me in your care.
I always feel much safer,
Just knowing you are there.
Amen."

Then Tierney tucked the book into Naia's cradle and kissed her goodnight. Greg came over and did the same.

With surgery just hours away, Naia was the only one who slept peacefully. Greg sat bolt upright at 3:30 a.m., having dreamt that they overslept and missed the operation. Tierney awoke three times just to check the alarm. It was working fine.

They dressed at dawn and arrived at the hospital at 6:30 a.m. A half-hour later they settled into the pre-operation holding area, a hive of activity among doctors, nurses, and parents.

While the adults scurried around, most of the children remained quiet—little ones in cribs, big ones in beds—all wearing hospital gowns adorned with cartoons of Bugs Bunny and Tweety Bird. One father rode his toddler son around the room on a miniature all-terrain vehicle. The mother sat on the boy's bed, trying to muster a smile. Her sad eyes made an unavoidable point: For all the effort to make it seem like a children's playroom, there is no denying the fear here.

Twenty-six children are scheduled for operations today. "For the most part, they're healthy kids coming in for day surgery, pretty minor stuff," said nurse Fran Macoomb.

Naia, facing major open-heart surgery, is the exception. She is also the smallest child in the room. Though more than four months old, she is 8 pounds 8 ounces, smaller than some robust newborns. In fact, Naia is in the bottom 5 percent for growth among children her age with Down syndrome.

At 7:30 a.m., technician Debbie LaBelle came to

Naia's metal crib to draw blood, to match her type for a transfusion, and to complete routine presurgery tests. Naia's cries rang through the room as LaBelle tried repeatedly to find a vein. Greg gripped the bars of the crib. Tierney closed her eyes.

When LaBelle finished, Greg sat with Naia in a rocking chair, whispering all the things a father says to a daughter when he's scared and she's too young to understand his words. He held one of her hands. In Naia's other hand was her Elmo doll.

It is 7:45 a.m. when Bonnani arrives, picks up Naia, asks Greg and Tierney to kiss her, then takes her away to Operating Room 3.

* * *

It is a 20-by-30-foot room bathed in artificial light. All around are trays of gleaming steel surgical tools covered by sterile blue cloths. There is a bank of flashing monitors, one of which shows Naia's oxygen saturation—the level of oxygen in her bloodstream. It reads 84 percent. "Normal would be in the 90s. It's a good thing she's here," says Cookie Eckel, one of two nurses assisting Bonnani.

A backlit screen on one wall displays X-rays of Naia's chest, front and side view, taken two weeks ago. To a trained eye, the X-rays reveal an enlarged heart. It's a side effect of Naia's malformation, called a complete atrioventricular canal defect.

In a healthy heart, oxygen-rich blood and oxygen-depleted blood are kept apart by walls that separate the four chambers. But like the hearts of many children with Down syndrome, Naia's heart has a hole between the upper and lower chambers. Also, it has only one valve, where there should be two, to regulate the passage of blood through the chambers.

As a result of the hole and the valve problem, blood in Naia's heart that is saturated with oxygen mixes with blood that is not. Mixed blood acts on the body like watered-down gasoline in an engine, causing it to sputter and stall. The heart also has to work overtime to supply the oxygen the body craves, adding extra stress to an already weakened system.

Near the X-ray light board is the machine that will breathe and pump blood for Naia during the operation.

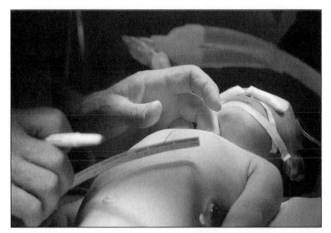

Photo by Suzanne Kreiter

And right in the middle of the room is a padded table where Bonnani places Naia.

Surrounded by all the equipment, all the activity, Naia seems even tinier than usual.

She lies on her back, naked, content at first to watch Bonnani and the nurses. Eckel briefly pulls down her face mask and kisses Naia on the cheek. "I just can't resist," she says.

But Naia's calm is shattered when Eckel and another nurse pin down her arms for Bonnani to cover her face with a plastic mask, through which flows an anesthetic gas. Naia cries, fighting to get free. "Hey, you *are* strong," Eckel tells her.

Fifteen seconds later Naia is asleep, a blue pillow supporting her motionless head. Bonnani puts a breathing tube down her throat. He tapes her eyes shut. A nurse inserts a catheter. Warm air is blown over her body to ward off a chill. A pad under Naia's back forces her chest to arch upward, giving the surgeon the best possible angle to work.

"How're you doing, sweetcakes?" Eckel asks Naia. "You sure look comfortable." In fact, she looks anything but.

At 8:02 a.m., in walks Dr. Lee Ellison, pediatric cardiac surgeon. Tall and lean, he wears scrubs, white clogs, and a thoughtful expression. He carries himself with none of the stereotypical bluster of some surgeons.

Rather, there is a quiet confidence, a low-decibel voice of authority.

He starts by measuring Naia's bony torso. To guide his scalpel, Ellison carefully draws a four-inch line down the center of Naia's chest.

As he works, a song begins to play on a radio speaker overhead. It's the 1960s hit, "Never My Love."

There are now nine people in the room with Naia: Ellison, Bonnani, and a second surgeon, Dr. Chester Humphrey; one scrub nurse; one circulating nurse; a nurse anesthetist; one physician's assistant; and two technicians who run the pump machine that will keep Naia alive while her heart is immobilized. They move quickly in pairs and threes.

Just before the operation begins, Ellison paints Naia's chest with brown antiseptic liquid, then covers her with blue cloths. Only a candy bar-sized patch of skin on her chest is exposed.

At 8:44 a.m., Ellison makes the incision. He takes pride in making a particularly fine line, especially on girls. The scar, in time, will become almost invisible.

The incision made, the blood wiped away, Ellison takes a small power saw and cuts through Naia's breastbone.

* * *

While Ellison works, Greg and Tierney take refuge in the hospital cafeteria. It's a round room with 40-foot walls painted to resemble a fantasy galaxy of planets and stars. One of the painters was a *Star Trek* fan; a tiny *Starship Enterprise* soars through space in an inconspicuous spot.

They talk about the weather, the war in Kosovo, the coffee, the sunlight that pours through the cafeteria's glass ceiling. But now and then, the conversation turns back to a recent discussion about Naia's future if the surgery goes as hoped.

Lately, Greg has been thinking that as prenatal testing becomes more routine, and as the tests become more sophisticated and less risky, the number of people with Down syndrome will fall. The prospect worries him.

"There's safety in numbers," he says. "When there are other children in the school system who are different, when Naia isn't the only one, it makes it easier in terms of advocacy."

Greg also wonders if advances in genetic therapy might eventually allow doctors to remove or repair the extra chromosome that causes Down syndrome.

"As I sit here now, I'm not sure I'd want that," he says. "I'll bet money that 12 years from now if someone walked up to me and said, 'Would you change who Naia is?' the answer would probably be no. Part of what I love about Naia might be directly related to the fact she has Down syndrome."

Yet Tierney is intrigued by the idea of correcting genetic flaws while a baby is still in the womb.

"In the papers last week there was a story about a child who had spina bifida corrected to some extent in utero," she tells Greg, referring to the debilitating spinal disorder. "If it's fixable, then why not? Why wouldn't we want every opportunity for everything to go right?"

"It's not that I wouldn't appreciate Naia for exactly who she is," Tierney adds. "But it could become similar to whether or not my child has polio. Of course you'd fix that."

Greg agrees, as long as nothing changes the Naia they love.

At 10:50 a.m., a woman with a familiar face enters the cafeteria, smiling and heading toward their table. It's Karen Mazzarella, the cardiology nurse who eight months ago spoke the first encouraging words about their unborn child's prospects. She arrives with an update from Operating Room 3.

"Everything is going fine. Smooth as silk," she says. "You always like to have a very dull surgery."

Greg's shoulders relax. Tierney sighs. They touch hands. There's a long way to go, but signs are good.

At that moment Naia's grandmothers enter the cafeteria. Greg's father, Bob, is en route from Virginia. Tierney's father, Ernie, is home in New Hampshire. He offered encouragement by phone two days ago, but he won't be coming.

When they hear Mazzarella's report, Mary Fairchild and Joan Temple bask in the news, making grandmotherly plans for Naia's future. First, though, Joan voices mock frustration with her granddaughter.

"I didn't get my kiss from Naia this morning," she says. "I want to get it."

* * *

After sawing through Naia's breastbone, Ellison carefully spreads it apart to expose the pericardium, a leather-like sac that surrounds the heart. With a practiced hand, he cuts through it, setting aside a piece the size of a half-dollar for use later during internal repairs.

With the calm that comes from 25 years of holding life in his hands, Ellison prepares to put Naia on the heart-lung machine.

He inserts plastic tubes with metal ends into the veins that bring blood to her heart. The blood is diverted to the heart-lung machine, where it is oxygenated then returned to Naia's aorta for distribution to her body, bypassing the heart altogether.

Throughout the operation, Ellison and his team take care to prevent air from entering Naia's circulatory system. Even a tiny amount could travel to her brain and cause a paralyzing stroke.

Ellison's next step is to stop Naia's heart, so he doesn't have to work on a moving target. He injects a solution into her coronary circulation system that paralyzes the muscle. At the same time, he cools Naia's heart with ice.

The maneuvers work; Naia's heart grows eerily still. In precise medical jargon, Ellison calls it "an excellent cardiac arrest." In any other circumstance, it would mean death.

Now, 20 minutes after the incision, the only thing keeping Naia alive is the heart-lung machine. In addition to its work as a pump, the machine cools Naia's blood, lowering her body temperature to 82.4 degrees Fahrenheit. Just as people can survive relatively long periods at the bottom of a frozen pond, the cold brings Naia's system to the point of suspended animation, limiting the risk of brain damage.

His preparations complete, Ellison begins his repairs by opening Naia's heart. He cuts through the right atrium, the chamber where depleted blood enters the heart to begin the process of being saturated with oxygen and pumped to the body.

Through tiny magnifying lenses attached to his glasses, Ellison peers inside. With the blood drained and the beating stopped, he can clearly see the hole in Naia's heart.

To fix it, Ellison cuts a piece of white Dacron cloth to roughly the size of a Chiclet. That's how much he needs to patch the lower half of the hole, between the left and right ventricles.

He sews the Dacron patch into place, then picks up the piece of Naia's pericardium that he had set aside. With it, he patches the upper half of the hole, between the left and right atria.

As he sews each patch into place, Ellison uses deft suturing techniques to convert the single large valve Naia had at birth into two separate valves, each of which must open and close thousands of times each day.

As the internal repairs are nearing completion, Ellison begins warming Naia's body. Then he sews closed the heart and allows blood to return. He watches proudly as the rebuilt muscle grows pink with warm blood. It shivers for a moment then starts to pump on its own, quickly falling into a normal rhythm.

Ellison's next concern is whether the hole is closed and the new valves work properly. He tests with an echocardiogram, a machine that uses sound waves to monitor heart function.

It shows that Naia's hole is closed completely. However, as Ellison suspected, the rebuilt valves allow a small amount of blood to flow backwards from whence it came. Ellison calls it a "trivial leak" that won't affect Naia's recovery or health.

Overall, Ellison is satisfied, calling it "an excellent result." He believes there is little chance Naia will need future heart surgery.

Ellison sutures closed the pericardium, then uses stainless steel wires to rebuild Naia's breastbone. Then he sews her skin back together, taking care to make the scar as straight and small as possible.

* * *

At 11:35 a.m., while Ellison is still patching and sewing, Greg, Tierney, and their mothers move from the cafeteria to a waiting room near Operating Room 3.

Toys are scattered around, along with poignant memorials to children who didn't survive. A wall plaque is engraved with a lost child's name and a passage from a favorite children's book: "In memory of Jason Michael Cianci. Love you forever, love you for always. As long as I'm living, my baby you'll be."

As they wait, no one mentions the memorials. The grandmothers chat about how wonderful Naia is. Tierney recounts the first stroller ride she gave Naia, only last week, when the weather warmed enough to risk taking her outside. Greg says little.

At 12:55 p.m., Ellison walks in. Everyone stands. He smiles.

"She's all done," the surgeon says warmly. "We did exactly what we talked about, and so far everything looks just right." He explains her need for a blood transfusion and more sedation, describes the breathing tube still in her throat, and mentions that the rebuilt heart valves show small signs of leakage.

All Tierney and Greg hear is that their daughter is OK.

"That's great," Greg says. The tension drains from their faces, their bodies. They embrace.

"Yay for Naia!" Tierney calls out. "Naia the great!"

As he leaves, Ellison turns and warns them not to be alarmed by how Naia looks. "Just treat her like you're at home," he says. "Just smooch her."

* * *

A half-hour later, Naia's parents and grandmothers are escorted to Room 306 of the pediatric intensive care unit.

Naia lies on her back, motionless, her eyes closed. She has lines attached to all four limbs, her torso, and her head. She looks like a crumpled marionette.

A breathing tube brings air to her lungs. A drainage tube removes blood from her chest. An intravenous line supplies nutrition to her depleted system. A nasogastric tube is in her nose for future feedings. A catheter takes away her urine. An arterial line in her wrist checks her blood pressure. A pulse oximeter measures the oxygen level in her blood. It reads 96 percent, just where it's supposed to be.

It makes them cry to see her like this. Greg fingers Naia's fine hair. Tierney follows doctor's orders and kisses her.

A nurse, Wendy Lord, comes in to check Naia's pupils and adjust the monitors. Mostly for modesty's sake, she puts a doll-sized diaper on Naia. Lord wears a

Black Dog T-shirt, the unofficial symbol of Martha's Vineyard. For Greg and Tierney, it sparks rueful memories of the day last summer when an ultrasound test changed their lives, just hours before they planned to leave for a Vineyard vacation.

Nurse Cookie Eckel comes by to see how Naia is doing. "She's one feisty little lady," Eckel tells Greg and Tierney. Eckel says the surgery was flawless, and necessary. "She had a big hole in there. You got your money's worth."

Greg and Tierney can't help but smile.

Eckel leaves and Tierney's mother takes care of her unfinished business. Tears streaming down her face, Joan bends low and kisses Naia on the forehead.

"Grandma loves you," she whispers.

* * *

It is April 4, Easter Sunday, four days after the operation. Naia's recovery has gone slowly.

She's still in the pediatric intensive care unit, two days longer than Greg and Tierney expected. She'll be here at least one more day, breathing with help from a ventilator. She's fighting a fever, and her blood pressure is low. She remains sedated with morphine.

Naia has resisted attempts to get her to breathe on her own. When the doctors turn down the respirator—hoping her own breathing system will kick in—she barely responds. Today, though, they hope to wean her from the respirator entirely.

The day begins with a visit from a nearly six-foot Easter Bunny who leaves a basket of toys and a blue-and-yellow quilt sewn by Girl Scout Troop 988. Naia sleeps through the visit.

At 11:30 a.m., Ellison removes the drainage tube from Naia's chest. Then, at 4:30 p.m., he returns to remove the breathing tube. Naia is deep in a morphine-induced sleep.

Greg and Tierney expect Naia to scream when the tube comes out, but there is only silence. They fear the worst. "It's like her birth, when she didn't cry," Tierney says.

Ellison calms them, telling them to "look at the big picture." In fact, though she remains asleep, Naia has begun breathing for herself.

As the hours drag on, Naia confounds expectations and continues to sleep. The doctors order an antidote for the morphine, called Narcan, and she finally begins to stir. Then she starts to thrash, pulling at the tubes in her nose and on her foot. After a few scary moments, she settles down.

At 11:30 p.m., Greg and Tierney go to a nearby parents' room for a dinner delivered by her mother. Like the Thanksgiving after Naia's birth, their Easter dinner is another holiday meal eaten in the sanitary confines of a hospital. Exhausted, they quietly savor lamb, Swiss chard, mashed potatoes, and black olives, a family favorite.

The days go slowly. A planned five-day stay stretches to 10. But with the extra time and extra care, Naia's strength gradually begins to return.

Now, on April 9, it's time to go home.

Greg and Tierney are buoyant. Naia is snuggled in pink-and-green pajamas. There is something different about her.

It's partly the silky ribbon a nurse has tied to a lock of her hair. And it's partly the smiles she showers on passersby like rice at a wedding. Most of all, though, it's her coloring.

Now that her heart is working well, Naia's skin has taken on a healthy glow. It's not the white of her mother, nor the black of her father. It's not the yellow of jaundice, nor the blue of heart failure, nor the pink of a photo clerk's baby ideal.

It's her own unique color.

Writers' Workshop

Talking Points

1) How does the writer build tension in this story. What techniques make this story effective?

2) The writer switches back and forth from the operating room to the cafeteria where family members wait. How does this set the tone for the story? What effect does this have?

3) This story includes a great deal of scientific and technical material. How does the writer keep the story moving while providing the medical background? What is the effect on the pace of the story?

4) How does the writing in the last three paragraphs differ from the rest of the story? Do you like this effect? Why does the writer use this approach?

Assignment Desk

1) The writer is meticulous in describing the surgery without using too much technical language. Observe another technical process—a mechanic working on a car, a house being built—and write a story.

2) The writer uses a matter-of-fact voice that still builds tension. What are devices you can use to build tension in your stories?

Choosing Naia, Part 6:
Life with Naia

DECEMBER 10, 1999

His basket filled with food and diapers, Greg ambles toward the Stop & Shop check-out line. The store isn't crowded, and he could choose any line. But he is drawn to one in particular.

He places his groceries on the moving belt and looks past the cashier to a smiling young woman.

"Hello," Greg says, and the young woman looks up from her work as a bagger.

"Hi," she says sweetly.

Greg wishes he could tell her all the things in his heart. He wishes he could ask a hundred questions about her life, her job, her family. About the friends he hopes she has. He wishes he could tell her about his 6-month-old daughter at home.

He says none of that. It would seem odd, intrusive. When her work is done and his groceries are neatly packed, Greg says, "Thanks." He gives her a warm smile. She smiles back.

The bagger's name is Sarah and she has Down syndrome.

It is June 3, 1999. After all the uncertainty, all the fears, all the medical problems from an emergency birth through open-heart surgery, Greg Fairchild and Tierney Temple-Fairchild have begun settling comfortably into life with Naia.

Still, a day rarely goes by that doesn't include reflections on the choice they made. Not that there are doubts. Greg's grocery store encounter merely reinforces his and Tierney's certainty that they made the right decision 10 months ago about carrying Naia to term.

"In retrospect, it doesn't seem like a big deal. This hasn't crushed us or demolished our relationship or affected anybody in our family in a negative sense," Greg tells Tierney.

Of Sarah, he says: "It felt really nice to see she's not closeted in a facility someplace. She's out working, in a productive way, as a member of society. Maybe this is evidence that the days when you didn't see any adults with Down syndrome in the community are at their end."

They know there will be unforeseen problems ahead, obstacles that cannot be corrected by doctors, prayer, effort, or time. But with Naia growing stronger, more active, and more inquisitive every day, Tierney is equally undaunted.

"It's important for us to have high expectations," she says firmly. "I'm preparing myself that there will be developmental delays. It's our job to help Naia through her challenges. How well we do that will determine how she pursues life as an adult."

* * *

For all their willingness to tackle the hard work ahead, Tierney and Greg know it's too early to predict how independent Naia might be. It will be years before anyone can fully gauge how the extra chromosome in every one of her cells will affect her mental and physical development.

And yet, there are reasons for optimism.

Two months have passed since the surgery that repaired Naia's damaged heart, and the results are as visible as the tender rolls of fat that have sprouted on her once-frail body.

In addition to the high-calorie formula she still drinks, Naia has begun eating mushy cereal from a spoon. Soon she'll graduate to squash and mashed carrots. She has the energy to laugh more often, and with more vigor. On the other hand, her cries are no longer the weak mews of a kitten. When she's upset, they're full-throated yells.

With each passing day, Naia seems to come more into her own as an individual. She has begun playing a flirtatious game of peek-a-boo with visitors, staring at them until they make eye contact, then quickly turning away. She has begun rolling over and using her pudgy arms to propel herself forward while on her stomach. She uses this precrawl to pursue her new favorite diversion: Onyx the poodle. Naia can't catch her yet, but she's getting closer.

Naia's developmental leaps are partly traceable to state-funded visits from therapists with Connecticut's Birth-to-Three System, which provides early intervention for children with disabilities. Similar programs exist in Massachusetts and many other states.

Mary Halloran, a developmental therapist, has been thrilled by Naia's performance during their weekly sessions. "Naia is doing beautifully," she wrote on a May 9 progress report. "Today she rolled, played with her feet and played with her hands at her midline. She's experimenting with sounds and is *very* aware of what's going on around her."

Between visits, Greg and Tierney supplement the work being done by Halloran, occupational therapist Wilma Ferkol, and physical therapist Bonnie Herrin. They do exercises to improve Naia's mobility and strengthen her muscles, which aren't as taut as they should be.

"It might just be that's what parenting is all about, for us or for anyone with children. There's always something else to be working on with your kid," Greg says. "It's not that we're going to be able to work our way out of these deficits, but we'll do whatever we can to be further down the road."

The improvements extend to Naia's medical outlook. Tierney's little brown notebook has taken on a decidedly different tone.

When cardiologist Harris Leopold listened to Naia's heart on May 14, he said, "Sounds good." Tierney happily wrote that down. Two weeks later, gastroenterologist Jeffrey Hyams examined Naia for lingering signs of jaundice. "Looks great," he said, and Tierney wrote that down, too.

One by one, the medicines that once sustained her become unnecessary. By her first birthday, she will need just one, Captopril, which lowers her blood pressure, making life easier for her rebuilt heart. And just as cardiac surgeon Lee Ellison intended, the scar on Naia's chest is fading to a faint white line.

That isn't to say Naia will be free from medical concerns. Sight and hearing problems are common among people with Down syndrome; Naia might need glasses by the time she turns two. More ominously, children with Down syndrome are 15 to 20 times more likely than other children to develop leukemia, and more than 25 percent of adults with Down syndrome develop

Alzheimer's-like symptoms of dementia after age 35.

But overall, almost from the moment Tierney and Greg brought Naia home after surgery, their focus has changed. No longer fearful about Naia's survival, they are introducing her to the world. After being kept safely inside nearly all winter and early spring to avoid potentially deadly colds, Naia has become a girl about town, visiting parks, stores, restaurants, and the homes of family and friends.

Naia's public appearances prompt regular cries of "What a cute baby!" from strangers on the street. In the parking lot outside a bagel store, one woman goes on at length about how beautiful she looks in brown. "What a wonderful skin tone she has!" the woman says. Greg smiles. "Thank you," he says.

Some people notice Naia's petite size and ask if she was premature. Rarely does anyone ask about Down syndrome. Some may wonder about it and not want to seem impolite. But Greg and Tierney suspect some people either don't realize she has the disorder or think she has only a "mild" case.

Even Naia's pediatrician, Dr. Della Corcoran, wonders aloud during one visit if Naia might have a rare, less severe form of Down syndrome called Mosaicism, in which not all cells are affected by the extra chromosome.

"No," Tierney told the doctor. "We've had it tested. She has full-blown Down syndrome."

"Well, she doesn't look it," Corcoran said.

In fact, the facial features common among children with Down syndrome are somewhat more subtle on Naia. For instance, her eyes don't slant sharply upward, and they don't have pronounced skin folds at the inner corners. Her tongue only rarely juts out of her mouth, unlike some children with the disorder whose mouths are small and whose jaws are slack, giving their tongues the appearance of being large and protruding.

There's no link between the severity of Down syndrome-related features and the extent of a person's mental retardation. However, Greg and Tierney believe the less Naia exhibits those features, the less discrimination she might encounter. The notion leaves them with mixed emotions.

"I know she's cute, and I think she would probably be just as cute if she had those features. But would she?" Tierney says. "Would she be as cute to other people? I don't know."

Greg sees the issue through the prism of race.

"It's like the difference between being a visible minority versus an invisible minority. I have no doubt that people who don't like black people will let me know very quickly, one way or another," he tells Tierney. When that happens, he reacts accordingly, deciding whether to steer clear or confront them.

"But when you're part of an invisible minority you don't always have that knowledge of where they stand, and that's not always an advantage," he says. "People might have unreasonable expectations of Naia, based on her appearance. When they talk to her and find out about her condition, they'll have to readjust, and that might be difficult, for her and for them."

* * *

With Naia's medical crises resolved, Greg and Tierney decide it's time to formally include her in their spiritual lives.

And so, on June 12, an idyllic day that holds the promise of summer, Naia and her family drive to the Church of Saint Timothy in West Hartford for Naia's christening.

They don't worship regularly at the parish, but the choice is both appropriate and symbolic. Tierney and Greg had come here last July, two days after learning about the problems facing the fetus in Tierney's womb. As they sat together that Sunday morning, sad, frightened and confused, they heard a sermon about prayer and miracles.

Only now can they fully appreciate the message.

"Naia is a miracle just as she is," Tierney tells Greg, her eyes welling up. "That's something I feel every day."

As they walk from the parking lot to the church, Naia lets out a stream of happy gurgles. Angelic in a white satin dress with puffy sleeves and a scalloped hemline, she stares at the trees and sky. Nestled in Tierney's arms, she plays with her feet, tugging at tiny green-and-white rosettes on her socks.

Naia's godfather will be Kyle Rudy, a friend from Tierney and Greg's days working at Saks Fifth Avenue in New York. Naia's godmother will be Tierney's sister Tara, whose initial doubts about continuing the pregnancy have been replaced by heartfelt support and endless shows of affection for her niece.

Inside the church, Greg holds a white candle, Tierney holds Naia, and the Rev. Henry Cody blesses her with sacramental oil and water. "She is now called a child of God, for indeed she is," says Cody, who has known Tierney since she was small.

Cody reads from a prayer book that seems written just for Naia. "The parents have generously invited the child into this world by giving a share in the life of their own bodies," it says. "This invitation will be prolonged with every mouthful of food, every drop of medicine, and every inch of shelter they provide."

Naia's grandmothers take pictures. Greg beams. Tierney cries, for joy.

* * *

Just when life seems to be calming down, Greg, Tierney, and Naia are forced to confront an unexpected new challenge.

It's June 23, and Greg and Naia are relaxing in their apartment, waiting for Tierney to come home for dinner. Since March, Greg's mother, Mary Fairchild, has been living in the nearby apartment they purchased shortly before Naia was born. Mary and Naia spend most days there while Tierney goes to work and Greg writes his doctoral dissertation.

At 5:30 p.m., the phone at Greg and Tierney's apartment rings. It's Mary.

"Greg, the back porch is on fire," she says before running outside.

A spectacular fire has engulfed a six-story factory building down the street. Embers from the blaze have taken flight, landing on the building housing Greg and Tierney's future home.

No one is hurt, but the new apartment is destroyed, much of it from smoke and water damage. They also lose their good stroller, a baby swing, a playpen, and lots of toys, as well as a computer and several pieces of furniture.

Most of the losses are covered by insurance, but it will take nine months to rebuild. Mary is returning next week to her home in Virginia, and Greg, Tierney, and Naia had planned to move into the new apartment next month. The lease on their current apartment is expiring and cannot be renewed.

They'll have to move in with Tierney's mother, in nearby Avon.

"Last July we found out about Naia. Then the emergency c-section. Then the heart surgery. And now this," Tierney says with a rueful laugh. "I'm at the point now where I think we could handle just about anything."

In a way, she tells Greg, maybe all the trials have been a good thing.

"We've learned that we really are the people we thought we were when we married," Tierney says. "Sometimes it takes a long time to learn how you'll react together in a crisis. I think it's safe to say now we know exactly who the other one is, how we'll react together, how we'll work it out."

For Greg, the key to their future is the way they worked through the decision about Naia.

"Some couples could go through something like this without ever having really agreed," he says. "One person forced their will and the other capitulated. That wasn't the case with us.

"You learn quickly that as long as you're right with the person you're with, even if other people around you don't agree with what you're doing, it's OK. They can hop off the train, because we're going on without them."

In the months ahead, that sentiment will be put to the test, in the form of a confrontation with Tierney's father.

* * *

As summer turns to fall and Naia's first birthday approaches, Greg and Tierney are increasingly troubled by Ernie Temple's continued standoffishness. He sends gifts, but during his visits he remains distant from Naia. He still hasn't held her.

It's a sharp contrast from Greg's father, Bob, who gravitates to Naia whenever he sees her, hugging her, playing with her, letting her tug on his beard.

Tierney and Greg's frustration reaches a boiling

point when Ernie's girlfriend casually mentions during a phone conversation that he's bouncing her grandson on his knee. They wonder why he doesn't do that with Naia.

On Ernie's next trip through Hartford, on Oct. 20, Tierney asks him that question over pizza at a Bertucci's restaurant.

"I just want to understand what you're willing to do, how involved you're willing to be, how you're going to interact with Naia," she says. "I want to know what your issues are with her."

"I thought they should have been apparent to you," Ernie answers flatly.

It's not the Down syndrome, Ernie says. It's race, the same problem he had a decade ago when he first met Greg. Despite having walked Tierney down the aisle at her wedding, despite the good times he has shared with Greg and Greg's parents, Ernie still disapproves of interracial marriage.

He considers it a betrayal of Tierney's heritage, and his discomfort colors his relationship with his granddaughter.

Tierney is shocked and saddened, a bit sickened as well. Yet she keeps her tone level and tries to point out the illogic of his words, the hypocrisy of his behavior. She uses reason and science to contradict his points, including his suggestion that mixing races might cause physical problems or "sickness," a comment Tierney takes to mean Down syndrome.

But she knows there's no convincing him, and she'd rather be back home with Naia and Greg than hear any more of this.

When he hears about the dinner, Greg is disgusted and shocked by Ernie's comments. "This guy has done such a good act around me, my parents, that I thought maybe he had gotten over those views. I feel duped," he says.

At the same time, Greg and Tierney see the bitter irony: Naia is a victim of garden variety discrimination. Ernie would reject any child of theirs, not just one whose genetic disorder once made them consider abortion. Perhaps the "tragedy" Ernie had envisioned last summer had nothing to do with Down syndrome.

Photo by Suzanne Kreiter

In a phone conversation nearly a week later, Tierney spells out a set of new rules to her father. "I can't have my daughter in an environment where she is going to be discriminated against, especially by her grandfather," she says. "If you can't tell me how long it will take for you to warm up to her, then I have a problem."

Two days later, Ernie calls back with an apology. He was too blunt, cruel even, and the comments he made at Bertucci's don't reflect how he really feels, he says. He might not agree with Tierney's choices, but he says he will respect them.

"Respect is absolute," Tierney says. "It's black and white. It's not gray. If you want to have a relationship with us, what's most important is that you respect my child, and that you demonstrate that with your actions."

Ernie says he understands. Tierney and Greg, hurt by his words and protective of their daughter, are skeptical.

But they will give him a chance, knowing that only time will tell.

* * *

It's Sunday, Nov. 21, Naia's first birthday party. Tierney has baked a cake using her grandmother's recipe, and Joan's house is awash in presents. There's plenty to celebrate.

This week, Naia received an encouraging one-year assessment from the Birth-to-Three therapists. "Naia's strength has improved greatly over the past few months," it says. "She visually explores and takes in much of what is happening in her surroundings…Naia is a very friendly little girl who greets her visitors with a broad smile and vocalizations, often 'hi.' "

Even better, for several months she's been calling Greg "da-da." And just days before her party—at long last, as far as Tierney is concerned—Naia looked to her and said, "ma-ma."

Still, there are signs of developmental delays. The therapists estimate she is at the level of a 9-month-old without Down syndrome in terms of gross motor skills; a 7- to 8-month-old for fine motor skills; and a 10-month-old for "expressive language."

More upbeat is Naia's one-year medical report. After routinely depressing visits to doctors early in Naia's life, this one is remarkably different. Greg jokes around, wearing Naia on his head like a hat. Naia laughs, pulling his hair. Then Corcoran, her pediatrician, bursts into the room with outstretched arms and a hearty "Happy Birthday!"

Corcoran says she's "astounded by Naia's development," including Naia's newly acquired ability to pull herself to a standing position, a precursor to walking.

"If I didn't know she had Down syndrome, I wouldn't make a referral to Birth-to-Three," Corcoran says. When Tierney suggests that Naia's progress is probably a result of the therapy sessions, Corcoran says there's more to it.

"This isn't Birth-to-Three. This is Naia," she says.

Adding to their delight, Naia weighs 17 pounds 10 ounces, and is 28 1/4 inches tall. She has gained nearly 12 pounds and grown more than 10 inches since birth.

This baby who flirted with death, who arrived for

surgery eight months ago near the bottom of the Down syndrome growth chart, has made a stunning reversal. She is now in the 50th percentile for weight and the 75th percentile for height among children her age with Down syndrome. Naia has even grown her way onto the standard growth charts; she's on the low end, but she's there.

As they look back over the past 16 months, Tierney and Greg remember the painful knowledge gained from prenatal testing. But now that pain has been replaced by pleasure. When they think about the summer of 1998, there's a sense of confusion, a shared bewilderment: "How could anybody not want Naia?"

Still, they are grateful to have learned about Naia in advance. "The diagnosis she got in utero is exactly what happened," Tierney says. "Being prepared for her to have special needs allowed us to adjust our expectations, to deal with the grief and to reach acceptance. When she was born, we were ready. We were ready to celebrate Naia."

As the birthday party gets under way, Naia positions herself in the midst of her presents, pulling at the shiny wrapping paper and taking an occasional lunge at Onyx the poodle. Using the couch for balance, she pulls herself to a standing position.

Tierney and Tara stand close together, wearing their matching "hope" necklaces. Lately, Tierney hasn't worn hers quite so often. She has traded hope for something more concrete, an amber locket that opens to reveal tiny photos of Greg and Naia.

She soon might have to buy a bigger locket. Undaunted by all they've been through, she and Greg have begun making plans for another child, hoping Tierney will be pregnant again by spring. They think Naia will be a great big sister.

Greg takes Naia's hand, and she lets out a squeal of "DA-DA!" She takes one tentative step, then another.

Writers' Workshop

Talking Points

1) Reread the opening anecdote. How does it symbolize the story of Naia? Is it an effective lead? Would a different summary be appropriate?

2) The writer says "re-creations are incredibly valuable when used with tremendous care." Review the series and discuss the use of re-creations.

3) Do you think this story caused pain for any family members, especially Tierney's dad, Ernie? Are his views handled fairly by the writer?

4) Can you determine the emotions of the writer in this series? How well does he convey his feelings or keep them in check? Which is appropriate?

5) The series was accompanied by a box that gave readers information about the way the story was reported. Why do you think the box was published? What is the value of such information—to readers, to the writer, to the newspaper?

Assignment Desk

1) Compare the introductions and conclusions to each segment of the series. Discuss how they are woven together to build the series. Look for ways to use these techniques in stories of any length.

A conversation with
Mitchell Zuckoff

KEITH WOODS: Tell me what the story of Naia and the story of Greg and Tierney evoked in you?

MITCHELL ZUCKOFF: You can't spend as much time as Suzanne [Kreiter, Mitchell Zuckoff's wife, and photographer for the series] and I spent together with them without the story deeply affecting you. We're parents. We obviously gained a great affection both for Tierney and Greg and also, as we got to know her, Naia, and so their story now means more to me than I think any story I've ever worked on. We really got at some of the most fundamental issues that anyone could face. And I think whenever that happens, you can't help being affected as well. It affected us very deeply.

You talk about getting to the heart of the matter and getting to the way that we think about ourselves, about other people. Why do you think that's important to a newspaper audience?

I'm not the first one to recognize that newspapers have challenges. There are a lot of other ways people get information and get the news and get told what's going on around them. If newspapers can use the form to its fullest extent, getting at issues that you can't touch on a click, on a news site, or on even a 15- or a 30-minute TV program, then we will continue to refine our role in people's lives and continue to define our role as essential to people's lives. When you write in a narrative form, when you write in a way that is gripping for readers, as I hope my story is, you connect with them, and so editors see that that's happening. They see that these kinds of stories gain tremendous currency with readers and tremendous feedback from readers. So they encourage more and more.

As I read through the story, I feel that you are operating in the minds of the people about whom you

write. There are clearly times when you're observing and writing what you hear and what you see, and that's a fairly objective process. But there are quite a few times throughout the story when you are telling me what they're thinking.

I was nervous about taking that approach at first, but I know what I knew and I was confident in the end in doing it because of the interviewing. Going back again and again, asking Greg or asking Tierney or asking them both together and sometimes separately, "What were you thinking when he said that," and "What made you think that?" I was also incredibly fortunate to have found subjects who are extremely articulate, extremely intelligent, and have the kind of emotional accessibility to their own feelings to be able to communicate these things.

They seemed very reflective from the beginning of the story.

Exactly. And once I got to know them and was able to see how reflective they are, I knew that I could trust them and trust my own reporting to honestly portray what was going through their minds as this was happening.

You move fairly seamlessly between three different ways of telling the story. One is from inside of the heads of the subjects. Another is from the moments when you are observing. And then the third is when you're re-creating. I guess I may be able to know intuitively where you are making the switch from one to the other, but sometimes I can't tell whether you were there or not.

Thank you. That means it worked.

I've heard from many people who say it's either a great way of telling a story or not a particularly honest way of telling a story. Did you struggle at all with that question?

Absolutely. It's not something I've done a lot. We all do some re-creating in our writing. When you write a police story and you describe what happened, you weren't there but you use an attribution at the end: "police said." But you still just re-created based on somebody else's recollections or knowledge. Now that's all we're doing here, and we're asking the reader not to expect us to have "Greg said" or "Greg said later" at the end of each passage.

I've reached the conclusion that re-creation is not as good as actually being there, but there are certain times when there's no alternative. I think this story would have suffered without the re-creation of certain things. We could not have been at the moment of discovery for Greg and Tierney. It's just not practical. And yet if this story's going to work, you really do have to start at their beginning. I say re-creations are incredibly valuable when used with tremendous care and when a clear and conscious decision has been made that this is the only way and the best way under the circumstances to tell the story. I agree that we sometimes overuse it, and it's never an excuse for lazy reporting. If there's a way to be there, you be there. But there was no alternative here, and I would never have given that up.

Tell me how you connected with them.

I called Down syndrome groups. I called geneticists. I called genetic testing labs, genetic counselors, OB-GYN groups—just everybody who I could think of—who might be able to find me someone. Ultimately I linked up with a woman who trains genetic counselors in New England who is based here in Boston.

How did you find her?

We had written a story in the *Globe* about this woman named Judith Tsipis who had her own experience with a son who had a genetic condition and later started training counselors. So there was a story there and I was just searching clips like everybody does. I came across her name, called her, and she mentioned that there was an Internet listserv of genetic counselors in New England,

and if I would write a memo about what I was looking for, she would post it. She did, and very quickly—within a matter of weeks, I guess—Alicia Craffey, the genetic counselor who Greg and Tierney were using, saw it and said, "My God, if ever there were a couple who are equipped to do this, it's Greg and Tierney." And that was only a couple of weeks after they had found out and so it was very fresh in their minds.

Were you making decisions throughout this piece about how much to tell about Greg and Tierney? I wonder what struggles you had about revealing their feelings on abortion, their relationships with siblings, and in Tierney's case especially, her relationship with her father.

I did struggle a great deal with it. But to their credit, they understood, and the struggles were made much easier by their commitment to telling the truth and their understanding that there would be certain things that might be painful and uncomfortable for both of them and for the other people around them. But my struggles, I have to say, were made just immeasurably easier by the fact that—on just the deepest, most fundamental level—they understood the value of telling the whole story. This is something we talked about from the first day we met: that it's not just a story about you. It's about the people around you and society, and it's the ever-widening concentric circles around your baby, Naia. And if it can't be about those things, then we really shouldn't do it. And since we had laid down the ground rules early and they understood it completely from the very get-go, it made those struggles easier. But having said that, it was still hard when I was writing things in the privacy of my computer that I knew would cause pain and would cause discomfort for them and their family.

And Ernie (Tierney's father), not having agreed to do this story, is going to be shown with some serious stains on his humanity when this is all done.

Although the portrait of him is not flattering by any stretch, I saw Ernie in the context of the 90 percent out there. We say right at the outset that 90 percent of people who find out that this is their diagnosis choose to terminate their pregnancies. And, yeah, it turns out that Ernie has race issues as well; but at the outset he's just saying, "Look, this is not something you want. You guys are young. Start over." And although that comes across to a lot of people who've read the story and talked to me about it as just incredibly harsh, I reconciled it by saying, "Ernie is the voice of society. He's the majority." And so in that sense, while it's not necessarily flattering to him, it's what people are really saying out there.

There were times when you appeared to be two places at the same time. Was Suzanne doing reporting for you?

Suzanne absolutely did reporting for me. I was also the *Globe*'s roving national reporter last year at the same time I was reporting this, so I might be out of town. And so we just realized it made sense. If there was a doctor's appointment or something good going on that Suzanne thought might be visual, she would go. And then I would debrief her afterward. She would download to me all kinds of things, and then I would go back over to Tierney and Greg and ask them a load of questions just to flesh it out.

Give me an example of where that shows up in the story.

When their pediatrician calls Naia a "peanut," and she says it very innocently, and Greg and Tierney obviously take it differently, that was an appointment that I wasn't at. Suzanne heard all that and witnessed it and then told me the whole story. She had taken some notes—she got into the habit of taking notes because she knew I was going to pepper her with questions when she got home. And then I called Tierney and Greg about it and I called Dr. Corcoran just to confirm that that is how everybody else also interpreted it.

You foreshadow the race issue very early in the sto-

ry. Tell me about your thinking from the time you met Tierney and Greg.

When Tierney called and said they'd be willing to meet with us, I had no idea they were an interracial couple. I didn't know until we were walking into the house and, frankly, my first reaction was negative. Not in the racial sense, but because of what the implications were for the story.

What do you mean?

We had so many plates spinning on sticks with this story—there were so many things in the air. Would the racial issue complicate it to the point where it was just too much for readers to deal with? Maybe I was fearful that it was too much for *me* to deal with as a writer. Because you knew that they would have all these other issues at the same time they were dealing with this enormous issue that I was really focused on: Do we want to have a baby who has these challenges? And so my initial reaction was, "Is this the one extra plate that brings the whole thing crashing down?" But almost immediately upon talking to them and upon getting to know them, it was so clear to me that their decision to marry informed so much of their decision to have Naia. They had been through unpopular decisions. They had been forced, because of the nature of their relationship, to really, really get to know the other person and to know the other person's heart and to know what they were made of. And could you make unpopular decisions and how do you deal with that? How do you stand up? And so that started becoming so clear to me that it was just wonderfully natural and wonderfully organic to the story. I agonized over the balance that this story needed because of that issue. Because there were people thinking that race should have been even bigger up front. It was one of the hardest parts of the writing. How much play do you give to any one piece of this?

How did you know that you had put it into the right perspective?

I think two ways. One, it was my gut. Having met so many times, having spent so much time with Greg and Tierney, I had a really good sense of them, and I had a really clear idea how much they were talking about it. I knew what books were on their bookshelves. I knew how much race played into their daily lives. So in that sense, I had a good baseline to judge it against. And my second test was Suzanne. Suzanne read all the stories in draft form, and I would run things by her, and she also became just incredibly involved with Tierney and Greg and really knowledgeable about them. So if it sounded right to me and it sounded right to her, I figured we were pretty close to having it on target.

You've got to tell me about platelets; you've got to tell me about weight and blood levels and the chambers of the heart. But I sense as I go through the story that these pieces of information are kind of slipped in on me without a lot of fanfare and maybe even hoping I don't notice that I've just learned something.
    Did you go back and say, "How am I laying out for readers the things they need to know?"

That was one of my biggest fears. It's so easy to lose readers with technical or medical information. You've got to deal with this stuff—and they had to deal with it even more than I did—but you've got to do it gently and you've got to do it in a way that it's almost incidental or accidental. You want people to feel like, "Oh, yeah, that makes sense." There should be no place at which you get stopped, where you get confused. That, I think, is the biggest danger. Because once a reader starts getting confused, it's very easy for them to lose the thread of the narrative or start skimming or start looking elsewhere. I think a good example is the details of the operation. I wrote and rewrote that section five times, minimum. Maybe 10 times even. I just fine-tuned and fine-tuned and cut out anything that wasn't absolutely essential and absolutely clear. Then I went back again and again to the surgeon, Dr. Ellison, who was wonderful about letting me read it back. I read it over to him again and again to make sure that my changes weren't making it

incorrect. Because there's that balance between simplifying and obfuscating and really losing the reader because you've just given them bad information. You
know, we've got a real medical community here in
Boston. If I got the operation wrong, I'd have about 500
calls on my answering machine when I got into work
from the folks at Children's Hospital.

I take it you witnessed the operation.

I did not. Thank you. It means it worked. I witnessed it
up to the point where Ellison makes the incision in
Naia's chest. The only request that Greg and Tierney
made of Suzanne and me, the only real request of any
import in the entire 16 months, was they didn't want us
in the room during the operation once he started opening her heart. They felt very strongly that they didn't
want anyone to record Naia's death. And so once the incision was made, Suzanne and I left and joined them
down in the cafeteria. The rest of the operation from that
point was re-created using several methods: In every
operation that's done, the doctor dictates very specific
notes about what he did and the sequence of events. So I
had the typewritten notes that Ellison had made on
every detail in the operation. They're unbelievably
complex, down to the length of incision and what he did
and what kind of sutures he used to tie things off. So I
had that in front of me. Then I actually got a video of
this very same kind of operation, and I watched the
video. And then I had Ellison walk me through it.

**Let me ask you a broader question about those two
pieces of this story, what you saw and what you re-
created. Tell me what the most compelling moment
of being there was for you.**

I think the most compelling thing, something that actually brought me to tears, I'd have to say, was just after
the operation. We were all led to the recovery room,
post-op. And seeing Naia there, lying with all these
tubes coming out of her, and Tierney was crying and her
mom was crying and I think Greg was as well. And it
was an incredibly powerful moment to be there, to be

part of that, because it was, I think, painful to see her like that. But it's also this incredible release of emotion after this daylong—and actually it was months-long—anticipation of this day, that she had come through it. And having survived this operation it opened up this whole other set of issues and possibilities. They had gotten her through her failure to thrive, her jaundice, all these issues to this operation. And this operation was, for Greg at least, more troubling in some ways than the Down syndrome. She might die on the table. And when she didn't and we were all there around her in this room, it was just an incredibly powerful thing to witness.

I see what you're trying to tell me: "A breathing tube brings air to her lungs. A drainage tube removes blood from her chest. An intravenous line supplies nutrition...A nasogastric tube is in her nose...A catheter takes away her urine. An arterial line in her wrist...a pulse oximeter measures the oxygen level."
In the itemizing of those things, you've shown me all that you've been trying to tell me about the impact of finding this child when you got there. Is this in any way Mitch Zuckoff emoting in that paragraph?

Very much so. Very much so. Because the emotions were so strong, I found myself trying to deal with it by just focusing on the mechanics. But then I realized in the writing that that was my way of dealing with the emotion of it, and so I thought that by listing all this litany of tubes and wires, it would be hard for a reader to miss the effect that this would have on parents or on anyone seeing a baby like this.

Tell me something about your decisions on organization. How do you think about management of the story?

I knew from the very outset that if I was going to try to follow these people for this long, I had to be incredibly diligent about how I managed the information, how I kept track of everything. I'm a list maker. So as I was reporting it, the organization of the information started from the very outset. After every interview I transcribed the notes as quickly as possible. I never allowed myself to fall behind on any of the transcriptions because I knew I would never be able to find the notebook where this great first interview was, or the third interview was, if I didn't have it really closely organized. I just knew it would make the writing so much easier if it was all neatly and sort of chronologically organized. Everything was dated. I worked out a form for the date, the place, the weather at the start of each interview so I could help get myself back into the moment a year later when I had to write about it. Once I had all that in terms of managing the information, it was reading that briefing book so many times that I knew where everything was.

When you talk about Tierney's (journal) book, I assume that at one point you have it in your hand and you're looking at it. Tell me some of the other material you had that allowed you to build the details in the story.

I have Tierney's medical book. I have all the records of Naia's "Birth-to-Three" development visits, the home visits. I have her entire medical record and her entire surgical record. I have a journal that I asked Tierney and Greg to keep when we started. They did it sporadically. They were understandably quite busy with all this.

Are there other practical things about doing a story like this that a journalist ought to know?

I'd say first and foremost is support from a key editor. You don't want to undertake something like this if your editor is saying, "Well, let's see how it goes. Let's see what you come up with." You're committing so much of yourself, so much time, so many nights of driving to somebody's house and spending two or three or four hours with them. You want to know right up front that your editor believes that you can do this story, that you *should* do this story. And when it comes down to the crunch time, when you're asking for 15 clear pages inside the paper, he or she is going to really go to bat for you.

Who was the editor?

Ben Bradlee Jr., who's our deputy managing editor for projects. Ben and I go back a long way and we've done a lot of projects together. From the moment I approached him with this and gave him a two-page memo saying what I wanted to do, he was four-square behind it.

Now tell me anything of any great relevance about the editing of this story. Are there moments that stand out that made this piece as good as it is?

When I talk about editing I think of it in two levels. The first level was Suzanne, who was my first reader and in many ways my first editor. So what stands out for me is that she didn't divorce me when I would let her read something, and she would have an issue or a problem or a concern, and I would then rant for the rest of the night and go sulk. So that's the first thing that stands out—and I'm only half-kidding. I think Ben's support throughout the project stands out. But then in the actual line editing, what really stands out was how much trust he had in me to take a really gentle hand to this. The kind of editor-reporter rapport that you always hope for was there. He knows me, he knows my writing, he knows my style, and the changes he suggested were invariably improvements in my voice. So that was wonderful. And sometimes Ben's greatest contribution was just pulling me back, not adding something, but just taking a line out at the end. Actually we dropped a kicker on Day One. He said, "You know, you ended this twice, and your first one was better." I think that was almost word-for-word what he said. And he was right.

What did you get from the writers you've read? Where can you see direct ties between something that you've read and something that you've written?

I mentioned Tom Hallman (Portland *Oregonian* reporter), and Tom French (*St. Petersburg Times* reporter), and Ken Fuson (*Baltimore Sun* reporter). Before I started writing this, I read Fuson's series "A Stage in Their

Lives." [Non-deadline writing winner, *Best Newspaper Writing 1998*]. I learned so much from him in terms of how to move the ball forward each day without losing readers, with just the right amount of reference points to the day before while not boring the continuing reader with background. And that was a technique that I had really wondered how I was going to do. And when I read his work, it helped enormously for me to say, okay with just a line or two you can bring people back to where we were yesterday. That was a design very much based on having read Fuson before and having read the 1998 ASNE interview before I started writing. I didn't want to let that go unmentioned because it was an enormous help to me.

I think my biggest hero is John McPhee, and not that I have for a second compared what I do to what he does. I think the rest of us are still figuring out stuff that he knew 30 years ago. I've read about how he organizes and how he very carefully decides where things are going to go. I've read how he uses index cards and will actually map out an entire story, section by section and point by point, while having his overarching themes run through them like a piece of string that truly pulls them together. When I read his work and see how he will keep coming back to that theme and how it looks like he's digressing but he really isn't, and how he pulls it back in, that's something I hope in some way comes through in what I do.

I read Tom French and I read "Angels and Demons." He just never lets you go, and there's just nothing extraneous in there. Although you know from the first words that these women are dead—there are going to be surprises but you know the general outline before you begin—he doesn't allow the story to go slack anywhere. It's just taut all the way through. There's no fat. And then you realize, "Ah, I just read, in his case sometimes, 30,000 or 40,000 words, and I feel like I didn't take a breath."

You start at the end of a moment and linger there for a minute, and then you go back to the beginning of that thought and take me back to the point that we started. Is this something that you are consciously putting into the story?

Very much so. That was by design. I think it happens on three or four of the days. It's an amalgam of classic newspaper style. If you just stick with the chronological story here, and if I just end at one point and start the next day with the next moment, you're not going to draw readers in, unless the next moment is the most dramatic possible moment. But I think this story needed to re-establish itself with drama at the beginning. Tierney curled in a fetal position. I mean, when we left them the day before she was nervous, she was thinking about what was about to happen, and not feeling the baby moving.

And now she's on a gurney.

And I hoped the reader's begging, "Well, how'd she get there? What happened? What's going on?" And by doing that as a technique, I know that if I get through that very dramatic scene quickly enough, then re-establish how they got there, within a matter of 60 typewritten lines or so you can have everything you need to get people fully re-engaged in the story. So it was very much by design.

What sort of interviewing did you do to get to the level of detail in the opening scene and other moments like that?

Well, it was a combination of interviewing and physically re-creating, and I'll take them in order. You ask, "Well, where were you? Okay, you were at this hospital." That's how people usually answer the question: "We were at the hospital." And you let that go by, because you want them to get into the content first. And when they give you the basic outline, and Greg and Tierney were very good at giving more than a basic outline to start, I did go back and say, "Well, okay, where were you in the room. Greg was sitting in the chair? Okay, Tierney you were there. Well, Greg, was the chair facing Tierney? Was it next to the gurney?" And so I did that again and again when it was so clear to me that that moment, that place, was going to occupy an enormous, significant place in their psychic lives from that moment on. It was so clear to me that I needed to know everything about that place, to the point of almost boring them to death with the drilling. "Okay, well, what do you remember from the walls? What did you see?" Because I didn't just want to know what was there. I wanted to know what he remembered seeing. "Did you remember what it smelled like? Do you remember who you saw?" And they had forgotten at first, for instance, that they had moved from one room to another. But in going back over, they remembered, "Oh, no, we moved from room 1 to 3."

Did you go to these rooms yourself?

I did. That was the second step, saying okay, the way to really report this now is to witness it. And I actually sat in the chair and was lying on the gurney, and the wonderful people at St. Francis, they put on disk all these ultrasounds. They popped the disk in, so while I was sitting in what I call Greg's chair, I actually saw what he saw on the screen as it was happening. They have a system set up where you can do that, both on tape and on disk. And so being there and trying to imagine, and remembering exactly how they described it was enormously helpful. And then I went back to them and told them about it and they said, "Hey, I remember when I was sitting there I noticed this," and that freed up a whole bunch of other memories for them.

Now it would be my natural inclination to feel very silly asking people those kinds of questions. How do you get past that?

Well, I thought when you said you'd feel silly you were talking about when I put my legs up in the stirrups. Now, if you really want to feel silly…you know, it's the fear of the writer. I knew how afraid I was that I would get to the point of actually sitting down to write this and feeling even more silly if I hadn't found something out; if I didn't ask this question; if I was wondering as I was writing, "Did he see this or do this? Well, damn, why didn't you ask that?" I would feel even worse, and that always gets me over the hump, because I think we all feel that way at times. And sometimes you ask questions that you know—especially knowing somebody well—the answer's obvious, but you still need to hear him say it. Sometimes you feel like a reporter at the scene of a tragedy, holding a microphone in front of somebody and asking, "How do you feel?" It's obvious, but you still need to hear it sometimes, because you just can't assume, and you can't reach in your own mind to figure out what he must have been thinking. That's the only way you get Greg saying, "Hey, there are only three chambers there. Mammals have four." That doesn't come out the first time you ask.

How much of this did you explain to them ahead of time?

A lot. A lot. We kind of made a joke of it on the first interview that there are times when I'm going to be really annoying and there are going to be times—just please bear with me—when I'm just trying to get it right. And again to their credit, they're teachers by nature. They're both Ph.D.s, they're both really also just very, very understanding people, and they got it immediately and they understood that if we put up with this guy, he's going to get it right. No matter how much he tries to screw it up, if we tell him five times what the room looked like, he's probably going to get it.

A conversation with
Suzanne Kreiter

KENNY IRBY: When did you get involved in the planning process?

SUZANNE KREITER: Mitch and I conceived of the story together, so you could say I was present at its birth.

When did you take your first pictures?

The first time Mitch and I drove to Hartford to inteview Greg and Tierney. After about an hour and a half, when they agreed to let us document their lives for the next 16 months, I started shooting Greg and Tierney at their dining room table. This was only three weeks after they had made their decision to continue the pregnancy.

What was your biggest challenge in covering this story?

My greatest challenge was keeping my own emotions in check. It was an emotional roller coaster for me as well.

How did Greg and Tierney react to your being around at such vulnerable times?

They were very gracious in letting me be around during hard times. They had very important things to concentrate on, so my presense was easy to ignore. Greg once told me that I was often "there, but not there." I took that as a huge compliment.

More importantly, there were times I chose not to be there. Knowing when to step away makes it easier to be there in tough times.

Were Mitch and you there at the same time?

Sometimes we were together, sometimes apart. I physically had to be there more often.

How often did you record images?

I visited Greg and Tierney roughly once a week. During the birth and heart surgery, I was there three or four days in a row.

I scanned a generous number of images into a dedicated project file after every shoot during the 16-months.

What equipment did you rely on most of the time?

I am a very low-tech photographer. I used an ancient Nikon FM2 with a 20-35mm zoom. I also used a 80-200 zoom. I shot Fuji 800 film often pushed to 1600 ASA. I often had shutter speeds as low as an 8th of a second. I used a strobe for only one image—Naia's birthday.

What was the key to working so closely with Mitch?

Probably a strong marriage. It was a stressful story, but we were both equally invested. The story definitely came home with us, but that was okay.

Did you record pictures that you later decided should not run?

No.

What was the key ingredient that caused this story to gel?

Greg and Tierney's willingness and belief that sharing their story would benefit their daughter.

How did you feel about the presentation of the story?

The Boston Globe gave an enormous amount of space to this story. Thirty-five photos ran over a six-day period, some of which were five columns. I was thrilled by the *Globe*'s support.

How did you edit this project?

It was often difficult. I had the help of a very talented, and equally invested picture editor, Leanne Burden. The opinions I heard from her, Mitch, and the chief designer, Janet Michaud, helped me choose the final photos.

There were an additional 35 images published on the web. I heard about people who went to the website in order to see more photos.

I think the series as told in words and still images in a serial narrative was a very powerful medium. I believe that viewing the photos in the newspaper was a more powerful way of seeing them, as opposed to on the website.

St.Petersburg Times

Anne Hull

Finalist, Non-Deadline Writing

Anne Hull is a national correspondent for the *St. Petersburg Times* in Florida.

Born in 1961 in rural Florida, she joined the *St. Petersburg Times* in 1985 as a feature writer and in 1995 moved to the national desk, where she has covered welfare reform, immigration, hurricanes, and presidential politics. Hull attended Florida State University. She was a 1995 Nieman Fellow at Harvard University. In 1994, she won the ASNE Non-Deadline Writing Award for "Metal to Bone," a story about a 14-year-old accused of trying to murder a Tampa police officer.

Hull's work displays her ability to see the world through the eyes of others. In "The Smell of Money," the second part of her three-part series, "Una Vida Mejor: A Better Life," Hull explores the world of Mexican women allowed into the United States as "guest workers," crab picking in the swampy wetlands of the Carolina coast. Her riveting narrative connects readers to the world of these women who are searching for success on their own terms.

The smell of money

MAY 10, 1999

When Mickey Daniels Jr. ordered his Mexican workers for the blue crab season, he expected a certain type of woman. Humble. Compliant. Focused on supporting her poor family in Mexico. Thrilled by the American dollar. He was right on one count.

* * *

Delia Tovar tried to warn her younger sister about the smell.

It would linger on their skin, in defiance of lemon-water baths and rags doused with bleach. It would burn into the shine of their dark hair, inhabit their sheets and seep into their dreams.

Wandering the aisles of the Food-a-Rama, they would stink of crabs. Everyone would know they'd been brought from Mexico to do the work Americans refused.

"Think of it as the smell of money," Delia told her sister.

With the desert sand of Palomas still in the cuffs of their jeans, Delia and Ceci Tovar finally reached North Carolina, exhausted from riding a bus for three days. They were dropped at a darkened gas station in Elizabeth City, and a Daniels Seafood employee drove them another 90 minutes down the windswept coast. They reached their trailer at midnight.

Six hours later, they were awakened for their first day of work. The moon was still out. Delia's hands trembled.

When they pushed open the door to Daniels Seafood, hundreds of cooked crabs were heaped on silver tables, waiting for them. The clock above the sink read 6:45 a.m. Delia and Ceci stood on the concrete floor, blinking against the fluorescent lights.

They were issued aprons, hairnets and knives. No gloves. The crabs were so sharp that Latex wouldn't last 10 minutes.

Only Delia had worked at Daniels Seafood the previous season. She knew speed was everything. Slow pickers could be sent back to Mexico, defeated and poor.

A Daniels Seafood employee gathered the newcomers around a table piled with crabs. She swept her arms around to draw them near.

She didn't know Spanish, and they didn't know English.

So she spoke loudly.

"This," she said, "is a crab."

Then she disappeared.

Orientation was over.

The four elderly black women who still picked crabs for Daniels Seafood pretended not to notice. They turned their backs on the Mexican women struggling behind them.

They sat at their own table, turned toward each other, as they had for the last 40 years.

"I saw some pretty hamburger yesterday."

"He had whole chickens for $2."

"I heard about Miss Mollie Fearing died."

All four of the women needed eyeglasses to see. Each used a 6-inch stainless steel knife, its tip bent or bowed to personal preference, its weight and feel unique. Bits of meat and shell flew against the walls in the fury of their butchering.

The awful work of crab picking was woven with the gossip and the tragedies of Roanoke Island. The women spoke with the peculiar dialect of all Roanoke Islanders. It was a brogue left over from the English settlers of the 1600s, seasoned with black vernacular, and formal flourishes from the King James Bible. Tourists would stop in their tracks when they heard it.

It was their own lost language, from their own lost world.

Roanoke Island was a floating emerald between North Carolina's Outer Banks and the creeping coastline. It was moist and green, with a salty breeze that jiggled the lines of the shrimp trawlers.

Dates here were remembered not by distant events— declarations of war or moon walks—but by hurricanes and nor'easters.

"Wasn't it the Ash Wednesday Storm that Ginny was born?"

"Yes, I believe it was 1962, surely was."

Red-mesh crab pots were stacked in yards, and fishing nets were strung across porches. Anchors were thrown down like gauntlets on lawns, in case anyone wondered.

This place drew its life from the water.

Mary Tillett began working in a crab house in 1929. She was 15, wiry and strong, with a high forehead, the daughter of Ephfraim, a fisherman. She'd set out at dawn each morning, walking through the pine and juniper woods of Roanoke Island to reach the crab house.

In 1929, Mary earned 5 cents for every pound of meat she picked. Almost 70 years later, in 1998, Daniels Seafood paid her $1.70 a pound. She was 84 years old.

White women generally did not pick crabs. When an outsider would ask why, the question hung in the air as if it were an unsolvable mystery.

"I don't know why to save my life, I surely don't," Mary Tillett said.

The racial history of coastal North Carolina was different from the rest of the South. Slavery was not as widespread as it was inland, where tobacco plantations had large slave holdings. Freed men and runaway slaves wandered to the water's edge, where all they needed to survive was a net and a boat.

But whites still ruled the local fishing economy, before and after the Civil War.

Black men crewed for white pilots, chasing shad or menhaden. Their wives and daughters took jobs in the fish, oyster and crab houses.

The women spent their days covered in brine and shell. Hemmed in by the water, cut off from major roads and commercial areas, black women at midcentury had few employment choices.

At least crab picking offered freedom from standing over an ironing board in a white woman's house.

But as time passed, hacking away at crabs for pennies seemed like serfdom to a younger generation. By the late 1980s, the chairs around the crab tables began to empty.

The owners—in a panic over their disappearing labor force—laid the blame in one place.

"We can't compete against the welfare programs of

the United States government," said Jimmy Johnson, president of the National Blue Crab Industry Association.

The truth was not so simple. Growth and development brought new jobs. Even unskilled women were choosing a Burger King heat lamp over a crab knife. Others pursued education. Some did draw welfare.

The crab house owners said raising wages wouldn't help. There was just some work Americans weren't willing to do anymore.

But their theory of higher wages was never tested.

The "labor shortage" allowed them to import poor women from Mexico for the annual crab season. Within three years of their arrival, crab meat production in North Carolina increased by 21 percent, according to the Division of Marine Fisheries.

Daniels Seafood was among the smallest of 31 crab processing plants in North Carolina's $38-million blue crab industry. It was also one of the last—in 1995—to import Mexican women to pick crab.

The gray building with white trim sat at the edge of Roanoke Sound, just off the Nags Head Causeway. Nothing about the place looked cutthroat.

But it was here, beneath the hand-painted sign that swung in the wind and read "Daniels Crab House," that the whole global marketplace came tumbling together.

The Mexicans had created a grueling standard for themselves. If they didn't work fast enough, they could be returned to the border.

The local black women who'd given half their lives to Daniels Seafood wondered whether they'd be replaced by the newcomers.

And somewhere, someone in New York or Philadelphia was ordering an $8 crab cake, oblivious to the lives behind it.

* * *

That first morning, the Mexican women struggled just to hold their crab knives. They sliced their fingertips. The crabs pierced the soft palms of their hands. Ceci had trouble even grasping the shells. They shot off the table and clattered onto the floor. She tried again. She turned to her sister, her voice breaking. "Like this, Delia, like this?" she asked in Spanish.

Delia tried to remember. Not only was Ceci relying on her, but so were two other Mexican women who were also starting their first day at Daniels Seafood.

Using a paper towel, Delia showed the rookies how to wrap the wet knife handle so it wouldn't slip. "Look," she said, demonstrating. The paper would also cushion the steel handle.

With two strokes, Delia severed the crab's legs and pried open the body with the tip of her knife. She was rusty and unsure of herself.

In Spanish, she told the new girls, "You learn how to hold them softly so they don't hurt your hands so bad." She grimaced.

Each crab was like a sharp cage, containing barely two or three tablespoons of meat in the hidden compartments.

The first step was scooping out the yellow "mustard" or "butter," the organs and eggs that were thrown into garbage cans.

The premium lump meat was at the base of the crab's swimming legs. A picker had to remove it carefully to preserve the value. The meat in the rest of the body was less delicate and scraped out in flakes. The claws were also shucked.

The average picker went through about 1,000 crabs a day to produce 27 pounds of meat. At $1.70 a pound, her daily gross earnings were about $46.

The Mexican women were annihilating their crabs. What meat they managed to extract was littered with bits of shell.

"This is a mess," said Ruth Daniels, the meat packer and a distant relative of the Daniels Seafood family. "I don't think any of these girls ever seen a crab before."

Daniels Seafood sold half of its meat to local restaurants and distributors; the other half was loaded on overnight trucks to Baltimore, New York and Philadelphia.

The blue crabs were harvested from local waters and delivered live to Daniels Seafood six days a week. A pressure cooker in a back room could steam 1,200 pounds at once.

The crabs kept coming. As soon as the pickers finished one pile, another pile was shoveled on.

"I'm so tired and sore," Delia said to her sister, in Spanish. The floor was littered with shells, claws and orange paste. Bits of shell and meat clung to their cheeks and forearms.

Quitting time was 3:30. They had watched the clock all day. Ceci went to the sink to wash off. Her legs ached. Her back ached. Her neck felt pinched and immovable from bending over the crab table. She let the water run over her hands.

One of the black women came up behind her. It was Annie. She was 77, with gray hair and a spine that curled over like a drooping flower. She reached out for Ceci's arm, her voice tender.

"It's hard work, ain't it, honey?"

The words were foreign, but Ceci understood the tone. She smiled.

Delia tried to exude excitement. She had watched her mother do the same thing the previous season. Act thrilled by the prospect of the American dollar. Be hungry. Be unstoppable.

She held up her yellow ticket. There in blue pen: 25.3 pounds. "My first day!" she said, in Spanish. "Tomorrow, more!"

The others said nothing, piling into the van that smelled of dead fish. One fell asleep.

It was a custom of Daniels Seafood to provide transportation to the pickers. Ruth Daniels drove.

First on the route were the black women, who all lived in the same neighborhood of shaded streets on Roanoke Island. The van wheeled up to a trailer. Annie slowly stepped down, calling over her shoulder, "We'll see y'all tomorrow then."

Ceci lifted her head. "*Mañana*, Annie."

"*Mañana*, baby," Annie said, as she began her slow gait to her front door.

Ruth stopped at Food-a-Rama so the Mexican women could buy their groceries. Before dropping them at the trailer, she tapped her watch, pointing to the six and moving her finger to half-past. "Six-thirty, six-thirty. *¿Comprende?*"

Delia understood perfectly. *Sí, sí*, she said.

For dinner, they warmed store-bought tortillas and made frijoles in a cast-iron skillet. They slumped over their plates.

The crab knives had done their damage. Delia showed the others how to soak their hands in warm water. They wrapped their fingers with surgical tape, like defeated boxers, and then slipped on nightgowns.

* * *

The fastest picker in the history of Daniels Seafood was a woman named Juana Cedillo. On a good day, Juana could shuck 40 pounds. There was just one problem. She was stuck in Mexico.

Of all the women Daniels Seafood had "ordered" from Palomas, a small ranch in Central Mexico, only Delia and Ceci Tovar had been issued the necessary visas to cross the border.

The job recruiter had instructed the other women to report back to the U.S. consulate in Monterrey for interviews.

Juana Cedillo had staked her financial hopes on one more season of work at Daniels Seafood. The 1998 season would have been her third. The decision was wrenching. Juana was a mother of eight.

Every family in Palomas had someone who worked in the States. The coming and going was a part of life, fueling a million Mexican songs about separation and wandering.

But until the crab houses came along, the women in Palomas never left home.

The crab houses were stealing the mothers away from their children, yet the children were wearing new shoes because of the crab money.

When Juana Cedillo had not been immediately granted a visa in Monterrey, she returned to Palomas, arriving at night, suitcase in hand.

Her youngest son, Eduardo, who was 6, was asleep. Juana sat at the edge of his bed. When he woke and saw his mother, he began to cry. He thought he was dreaming.

Juana made a decision. She told her children the next morning.

"I am not going after all," she announced at breakfast. "I will be here to see you grow."

Juana's instincts were good. The other women from Palomas who made the nine-hour bus ride back to the

U.S. consulate in Monterrey were not given the interviews they imagined. They answered questions through a glass window.

All but one were denied visas.

When Mickey Daniels Jr., the owner of Daniels Seafood, learned that his most experienced crab pickers had never made it across the border, a full assault was launched.

There was a reason the crab house van was slapped with a Helms '96 campaign sticker.

"Jesse will straighten this mess out," said Ruth Daniels.

But not even an inquiry from U.S. Sen. Jesse Helms' office in Washington could fix things.

According to an aide in Helms' office, the women from Palomas were denied visas because they didn't show enough proof of their permanent ties to Mexico.

"What do you mean, the consulate needs proof?" Ruth Daniels shouted to the Helms aide. "Ma'am, they got nine young'uns apiece in Mexico. What are they s'posed to do, bring 'em all in and line every one of 'em up?"

Mickey Junior stared at the phone. This was a disaster. The crab season was under way.

"We're gonna have to get us some more."

"More," meaning Mexican women.

A single visa had been granted. Ana Rosa, Juana's 19-year-old daughter, was already on a bus for North Carolina.

Juana's parting words to her daughter:

"Read your Bible."

One more thing. The most important thing.

"Remember, you are not an orphan. You have a family in Mexico."

* * *

Three days later, Ana Rosa stepped off the bus in North Carolina with her Bible wrapped in plastic and what was left of the gorditas her mother had sent along. Dark circles shadowed her eyes. The next morning she took her place at the crab table next to her cousins, Delia and Ceci Tovar.

A few days later, three more women from Palomas arrived, including Delia and Ceci's 23-year-old sister,

Guadalupe.

Of the newcomers, Ana Rosa was the most valuable addition. She was an excellent cook. With her bandaged hands, she made pork chuletas.

They dubbed themselves *Las Chicas Jaibas*. The Crab Girls. Their legs ached. Their backs ached. While the black women were allowed to sit in chairs around the crab picking table, the Mexican women were forced to stand.

The concrete was unforgiving during an 8 1/2-hour shift. They devised tricks. They bought padded socks for their sneakers. They shifted their weight from one foot to the other, or leaned their hips into the table. Just squatting, bending the knees briefly, offered relief.

"What do we do, go on strike?" Delia said one night. "He'd just send us back."

Reality set in. What had they gotten themselves into?

As little girls in Palomas, they had walked to school together, carrying their madras book bags as they kicked their way along the dusty streets. They had often imagined America. Everything new, fresh from the assembly line. Large houses with green grass, blonds carrying shopping bags.

A job recruiter in Mexico who sent women to work in the crab houses had even said, seductively, "Maybe you'll get to see New York City."

Here was their America:

Six mornings a week, they stumbled from their trailer at 6:30 with their Eggo waffles or their mugs full of Cocoa Puffs. Ten hours later, the van brought them home.

Their trailer was 7 miles from town, across a 3-mile bridge that separated them from Roanoke Island. The closest store was a marina that sold bait and beer. Rottweilers from the trailer next door prowled the street.

At night, the county mosquito truck released clouds of white fog to ward off the insects that swarmed the wet flats.

Nine women shared the double-wide trailer, furnished with secondhand plaid couches and single beds. A wall-unit air conditioner pumped against the summer heat. One windowless bedroom occupied by a worker named Esmerelda became known as *El Horno de Esme*. Esmerelda's oven.

For this, the nine women paid Mickey Daniels Jr. $1,080 in rent.

Mickey Junior had the mistaken impression that in Mexico his workers lived in wooden houses or huts with dirt floors. He figured the trailer, which he bought to house his foreign workers, along with the property, was a step up.

To him, charging nine women a total of $1,080 a month didn't seem like gouging. He looked at it this way: weekly rent for each worker was $30, which included transportation to work, the grocery store, the bank and other errands. It also covered basic phone service, utilities and cable TV, "and me havin' to run over there every time they pour hot grease down the sink and stop up the plumbing."

On weeks when the availability of crabs dipped and the women didn't work every day, he knocked their rent down. If one week they worked only three days, he didn't charge rent.

The women hated the trailer. The smell of crabs came home with them on their hair and clothes. They stuffed their dirty laundry in plastic garbage bags to contain the odor. They used gallons of sweet Pantene shampoo.

They pasted air fresheners to the walls of their bedrooms, six, seven to a room, but nothing worked.

Only one event broke their misery.

Payday.

Ceci brought almost $200 home the first week. Although Daniels Seafood paid by the pound, the Fair Labor Standards Act made sure the women earned the minimum wage of $5.15 an hour.

The money was intoxicating. The women stashed their cash around the trailer, keeping the hiding places secret even from each other. They counted and re-counted it. Sometimes, they took it out just to look. More than anything, they wanted to spend it.

That was the trap.

One of their fathers had warned his daughter against squandering her earnings in the land of temptation.

"They will have your sweat and you will have nothing," he told his daughter.

* * *

"Guest worker"—which is what the Department of

Labor called the 3,000 or so Mexican women who came to work the blue crab season—was a cruelly ironic term.

The guests paid their own way to the United States. They weren't allowed to switch employers once they arrived. Many lived in fenced encampments.

Unlike immigrant farmworkers, these guest workers were prohibited from seeking legal assistance from the federally funded Legal Services Corp.

One final indignity. Social Security taxes were deducted from their paychecks. They would never see a penny of it.

Complaining would only bring a one-way bus ticket back to the border, where thousands of replacements waited.

One North Carolina crab house owner was sued by the American Civil Liberties Union for taking 50 percent of his workers' paychecks for rent. Another owner kept his workers' passports and visas under lock and key, holding them hostage.

Cheating the Mexican women out of overtime pay was common. Most were unfamiliar with the time-and-a-half formula used to figure overtime pay.

Despite the rip-offs and the captive nature of their employment, the Mexican women still begged and bribed their way into jobs in the crab houses.

But it meant they placed their lives at the mercy of whoever had bought the rights to their work.

* * *

The fate of the women who worked for Daniels Seafood rested with a born-again, anti-government tightwad.

Every decision Mickey Daniels Jr. made was guided by two forces:

What would Jesus do?

How can I increase my profits?

Mickey Daniels Jr. grew up in Wanchese (pronounced WAN-cheez), a 300-year-old fishing village on the south end of Roanoke Island. Since boyhood, he fished, he crabbed, he threw trotlines; anything he could do to relieve the water of its creatures, he did.

But never on Sunday.

The Daniels family were Assembly of God people. No music, no dancing, no movies, no immodesty.

Before their church was built in Wanchese, prayer meetings were held in the fish houses, where preachers shouted Scripture from atop crates of frozen flounder.

Mickey Daniels Jr. rose before dawn six days a week, ventured out in his boat alone, diverted from his duties neither by hurricanes nor 102-degree fevers. His sober ways set him apart from other fishermen who celebrated the week with a suitcase of beer down at the dock.

Mickey Junior and his wife had raised their five children in a crowded two-story house with one bathroom. They had no medical insurance. When the children were older, Linda Daniels waited tables to bring in extra money. The family had no pension plan.

"Around here, you work till you drop," Mickey Junior said.

With his tousled hair and faded blue jeans, Mickey Junior looked like a 50-year-old lifeguard. He considered sunglasses an affectation, so his pale blue eyes were constantly red.

He had a slow-drip pattern of speech, and leaned in doorways, his hands jammed in pockets.

One thing that managed to rile him was government regulations. There were wage laws, worker's comp, bans on crabbing in environmentally protected areas, regulations on discarding his bait; he felt there was no limit to the government's squeeze on his business.

In the 1980s, a group of Vietnamese immigrants tried setting up fishing operations in Wanchese. "They got everything free," Mickey Junior said. "The government set them up with (crab) pots and boats. We struggled and strived all our lives and didn't get nothin' free. Some of them would fish our pots. So some of the locals cut their buoys off the ropes. I guess that's why they moved away."

Mickey Junior took less enjoyment from his work than he used to. He said he wasn't in it for the money, but who could tell? Poor-mouthing was a local hobby. Most of the fishermen drove rusted-out trucks that smelled of wet dog.

Mickey Junior said he was "too private" to discuss his income. "One year you're up, the next you're down," he'd say.

The marketplace was not highly scientific.

Daniels Seafood bought its live crabs from 17 commercial crabbers, including Mickey Daniels Jr. A pound of crab meat costs Daniels Seafood about $5. Add $1.70 to pay the pickers. Daniels Seafood wholesaled its meat for between $7 and $12 a pound, which accounted for 85 percent of its business.

Mickey Junior might be out on his boat when his son would radio him from shore. "Dad, the account's only willing to go $7." To which Mickey Daniels Jr. would mutter, "That's too low." After stewing a few minutes, he'd pick up his radio. "All right, but no more than 40 pounds at $7."

Retail sales accounted for just 15 percent of Daniels Seafood's business, but it was the most profitable. Walk-in customers paid $17.75 for a pound of lump crab meat.

Mickey Daniels Jr. said he was lucky to make 50 cents profit on each pound of meat he sold, after expenses.

His business was vulnerable to weather and the availability of crabs. But the most ferocious threat was foreign competition.

"Our government allows foreign crab meat to come in and be sold way cheaper for what we can sell ours," Mickey Junior said. "And we're supposed to compete with the foreign crab house that pays their workers 20 cents a pound, with no inspections, no Social Security, no workman's comp. That's not fair competition."

Five miles from Daniels Seafood, a supermarket sold pasteurized crab meat from South America. It cost half of what Mickey Junior sold his for.

But that same fierce new global market also allowed Daniels Seafood to hire crab pickers from Mexico.

There was no question that replacing the older women with Mexicans would have increased production. When he watched Mary Tillett, he could see how much she'd slowed down.

His father had hired Mary Tillett in 1958 when he opened Daniels Seafood. Carmichael Daniels had an unusual relationship with his pickers. When one died, he was often the lone white mourner in the brick church.

Years later, when his son took over the business, some in Wanchese would say with bemusement or irritation, "Mickey Junior caters to the blacks, same way his daddy did."

A final gesture, maybe, Mickey Junior's allowing the older women to stay on.

In the off season, he left fish or collards on their porches, wrapped in newspaper. They had an understanding, welded in history, but fading, almost gone.

"That family's been good to me, sure have," Mary Tillett said.

And yet because three of the women suffered from age-related maladies—diabetes, arthritis—Mickey Junior filed a permit to pay them special handicapped wages, which meant he was exempt from paying them minimum wage.

If Mary Tillett sat at the table for eight hours and picked only 14 pounds, he paid her $24.

"You will always have a place here," he told the older women.

Production at Daniels Seafood was up. Mickey Junior was thinking of expanding to accommodate more pickers.

His decision to make the Mexican women stand at the crab picking table instead of giving them chairs was purely business.

"That way, I can get more around the table," he reasoned.

When Mickey Junior "ordered" his Mexican workers for the 1998 blue crab season, he had a certain type of woman in mind: compliant, focused on earning money for her impoverished family, and ultimately, a temporary figure on the landscape of Roanoke Island.

He was about to learn how wrong he was.

The women from Palomas were young, single, curious, wanting something beyond just money.

One night on an excursion to Kmart in the crab house van, they saw a Ferris wheel twirling in the sky. There was a boardwalk, and colored lights, and calliope music.

They could not take their eyes from it.

* * *

Their revolt began in the smallest of ways.

Delia found a Spanish-speaking interpreter. She had a question she wanted to ask Mickey Junior. Why were the black women allowed to sit in chairs?

"When you're their age," he answered, "then you can sit down."

To which Delia replied, in Spanish, "When we are their age, we won't be here."

In late July, Roanoke Island was a summer postcard. Crape myrtles wept their blossoms on smooth bicycle paths. Tourists descended, rubbing their wet hair with white motel towels on the dunes.

Like the black women before them, the Mexican women were separated from this world. They could see it, but they were apart from it.

One afternoon, a salesman appeared at their trailer. His tipsy truck of merchandise was heaven on wheels: chorizo, corn meal, white queso like Delia's grandmother made fresh from goat's milk in Palomas, and CDs by Mexican heartthrobs in leather pants.

The salesman made his living finding out where Hispanics lived, driving along the swampy reaches of the rural coast. He began making stops at the trailer. He mentioned the Mexican dances being held on weekends in towns like Swanquarter. They would last through tobacco season.

But the women from Palomas had no car. They couldn't drive. They were exiled in their trailer. Trapped.

Their one escape was the grocery store. Mickey Junior was driving them home from the crab house one afternoon when Delia called from the back seat of the van.

"Mickey Junior, Food-a-Rama, Food-a-Rama, five minutes."

He pulled into the parking lot of the grocery store. "All right, all right, but *andale*," he said, flexing his minuscule Spanish.

He couldn't see that the women had left the grocery store and ducked into Family Dollar, where they peeled through racks of blouses and shoes, leaving him to sweat in the van for 35 minutes.

The language barrier worked both ways. What could he say, when they returned to the van with shopping bags and smiles? He pointed to his watch and said, "Too long." By then they were lost in their fashion show, holding up skirts in the stinking van.

Not long after, they requested a trip to the beach. The beach!

The next Sunday, Mickey Daniels Jr. found himself ankle-deep in the surf of the Atlantic Ocean.

When their mothers had worked for Daniels Seafood—Ana Rosa's mother, and Delia and Ceci's mother—they never saw the open water, though it was less than 2 miles from the crab house. They worked all day and washed out their clothes at night. In the trailer, they hung photos of their children above their beds. One tore pages from a catalog and taped up pictures of microwaves and washing machines.

"But these new ones," Mickey Junior said, shaking his head in frustration.

"This batch seems more American."

Lessons Learned

BY ANNE HULL

An editor can set the tone for a story early on. For this story about a group of women from a windswept village in Central Mexico leaving home to work in North Carolina's seafood industry, my editor, Chris Lavin, suggested I read *One Hundred Years of Solitude*. Great, I thought, Gabriel Garcia Marquéz is our standard. But the advice was liberating: My editor was signaling that it was okay for us to stretch on this one. He was giving me permission to wander beyond the normal fences that stop many reporters.

Of course, the down side to this strategy is the terror it stirs in a reporter. Possibilities can be frightening.

"Una Vida Mejor" published as a three-part series. It followed a group of women from a remote village in central Mexico who pinned their fortunes on six months of work inside a North Carolina crab house. The crab houses of North Carolina were switching from a local labor force of American black women to a commuter society of women from Mexico. I suppose this was a global economy story. Technically, it was about the U.S. guestworker program known as H2-B. But it was ultimately a tale about America: the merciless glorious bully. It's okay to keep asking yourself, "What is this story about?' and to have the answer keep shifting slightly.

Here are a few lessons learned during this story, but they are surely universal.

Lesson one: Certain stories require a time investment. When I first started reporting "Una Vida Mejor," my editor and I thought I would go to Mexico, travel by bus with the women to North Carolina, and then hang around for a week or two to observe their indoctrination as crab pickers. We quickly realized this story would be all the more powerful if we could follow an entire six-month crab season. All stories need endings, and "Una Vida Mejor" begged for one: Would Ana Rosa and the other women from Palomas ever fit back into their traditional lives in Mexico, their pockets full of cash, their suitcases stuffed with Wal-Mart jogging suits? How could we tell this story if we didn't know how it ended?

Lesson two: Read. I read and re-read passages from Melissa Fay Greene's *Praying For Sheetrock* to see how she paid attention to small details, and to try to break myself of conventional journalistic structure.

Lesson three: Organize notes throughout the reporting process. I had a tower of notebooks, not counting documents and stats from federal agencies. Figure ways to remind yourself what's in each notebook. (For example, scribbled on the front of one notebook: "night Ana Rosa got kissed/Mickey at church/crabbing with Mickey on cold day.") To really organize, number each page in a notebook and make an index of key moments, facts, and quotes within that particular notebook.

Lesson four: Find off-camera "experts" who will likely not appear in the story but will act as your guardian or teacher. It's tempting to put these sources in the story, but their role is often much more valuable backstage.

Lesson five: Witness as much as possible. Experience what those you are writing about experience. This can mean uncomfortable accommodations, no toilets, or four-day bus rides across 2,500 miles. Suffering by proxy is no good; besides, you miss all the details, and later, the license to really tell the story.

Lesson six: On long stories or projects, allow—beg for—time to re-draft . Do not leave yourself four weeks to write a story you have spent five months reporting. Start writing as early as possible. Signal to your editor you want time to have the story superbly edited so there's no hysterical crunch at the 11th hour. (There will be anyway.)

Chicago Tribune

Robert L. Kaiser

Finalist, Non-Deadline Writing

Robert L. Kaiser is a general-assign-
ment and projects reporter for the
Chicago Tribune. Before coming to
the *Tribune*, Kaiser was the Kentucky columnist for *The
Cincinnati Enquirer*, roaming the state and chronicling
its events and characters. He also served on the paper's
editorial board. Before that Kaiser was assistant city editor and writing coach for his hometown paper in Kentucky, the *Lexington Herald-Leader*, where he started in
1986 as a reporter. He began his career at *The News
Enterprise* in Elizabethtown, Ky. In 1996 the Kentucky
Press Association named him best columnist in the state.
He received the *Chicago Tribune* Writing Award for
1999.

Kaiser combines detail-driven reporting and spellbinding writing in his account of two police officers
whose lives changed forever in one fateful night on
patrol. His riveting narrative shatters the stereotypes of
police to reveal the humanity and frailty of the men and
women behind the badges.

'Man, we are the real police'

AUGUST 15, 1999

Joe Ferenzi pulled a black T-shirt on over his protective vest and cinched his wide, black police belt tight around his waist. He pulled his gun out of his backpack and put it in the holster. It was a 9 mm SIG-Sauer P22—black and silver with a 13-shot magazine—never fired on the job. He had chosen it while at the academy because it felt good in his hand.

Ferenzi checked out a radio from a storage room near the front desk. He grabbed a laptop computer. He got the keys to the unmarked car he and his rookie partner, Michael Ceriale, would be driving.

Then he saw Ceriale.

The big cop grinned ear to ear. His hair still was wet. His face was freshly shaved. Under his gray T-shirt, Ceriale wore a St. Christopher medal on a thin gold chain.

"Man, I overslept," Ceriale said.

"That's OK. It's only the weekend," Ferenzi replied facetiously. "We shouldn't be busy."

They hit the road about midnight, Ferenzi at the wheel of their Ford Crown Victoria, which had been designated a CD, or civilian dress car. Tonight they would be free to roam the streets of Chicago's troubled Wentworth District.

Working in plain clothes, Ferenzi and Ceriale— along with every other young patrol cop eager to make arrests, get experience and win a promotion—would be doing the work of seasoned officers. The police union suggests that a cop have five years of experience before joining a plainclothes tactical team. The department requires three years. Ceriale and Ferenzi had been in the department 15 months, including six months as cadets.

Their boss, Lt. Michael Byrne, had every confidence in the two rookies. Neither Ferenzi nor Ceriale had worked in the Wentworth District more than four months. But the way Byrne saw it, the Deuce, as Wentworth was known, provided more experience in four months than many officers get in years on the job.

Ferenzi and Ceriale had asked to work midnights partly because of Byrne. Word had it he was a good boss, with an impressive résumé.

Byrne took an interest in Ferenzi and Ceriale, giving them good assignments and engaging them in friendly banter that often started with jabs about each other's ethnic heritage.

In contrast to the rookies, Byrne had been in the department for two decades, having worked in the narcotics, gangs and organized crime units.

He had transferred to the Wentworth District a little over a year ago.

Byrne's career had taken him through some of the city's toughest neighborhoods, where he was known as a street-smart cop, whose aggressive tactics were sometimes called into question.

Byrne shrugs off the handful of lawsuits filed against him.

"If you put yourself out there working fast areas and doing lots of police work, you're going to get complaints," he says.

Byrne thought Ferenzi and Ceriale had just the right mind-set. They wouldn't drive around chatting and killing time.

As they rode in the big silver Ford, Car 293, Ferenzi felt good.

"Man, we are the real police," he said.

They settled on a simple formula. If they scored a good arrest that night, maybe they could lock into a CD car whenever they wanted.

"Half that stuff's luck, though. You just gotta be in the right place at the right time," Ceriale said.

The car purred along State Street in the dark, rumbling over bumps and manholes. Up ahead were Miracle Food and Liquor and Harold's Chicken Shack No. 9. To the left, row after row of high-rises of the Robert Taylor Homes and Stateway Gardens glided past like tombstones.

The Crown Victoria was brand-new and smelled good. You could push back the seat as far as you wanted because there was no cage between the front and the back. It was a clear summer sky, what you could see of it above the glow of the city.

"Maybe we'll get a homicide tonight," Ferenzi said.

* * *

The night unfolded slowly until the police radio crackled with news of a shooting near 43rd and State Streets.

Ferenzi mashed the accelerator with his size 9 boot and headed north. The orange globes of street lamps flew toward them.

A crowd had gathered by the time they reached the scene of the shooting yards away from an Amoco station. Paramedics had arrived ahead of Ferenzi and Ceriale.

The victim, a man in his 40s, hung half out of a Chevy, his legs inside, his head and shoulders and arms splayed onto the pavement. Paramedics lifted the man out of the brown four-door car. He had been shot at least three times. There was blood on the seat of his car, a bullet hole through the headrest. A bullet was lodged in his spine, but he was lucid. He told paramedics he couldn't move his legs. They put him in the ambulance.

Ferenzi was unmoved. Though he hadn't seen anyone dead of a gunshot wound until he started working as a police officer, by now he had seen more than a few, the first one, when he was a probationary police officer working in the 9th District. It had been autumn then. A man lay dead at the northwest corner of 51st and Wood streets.

His training officer took Ferenzi for a look. There was a heavyset teenager sprawled on the sidewalk, eyes wide open, killed moments before in a gang-related drive-by shooting. There was a hole right in the center of his forehead but there wasn't much blood. The wound didn't even look real. Officers had left folded cards along the street like tiny, white tents to mark where bullet casings had fallen.

Ferenzi stared, speechless. But that had been months ago.

At the Amoco station, Ferenzi and Ceriale helped with crowd control, chatted with other officers on scene and soon left. They headed back to the projects, still looking for the arrest that would make their night.

"You wanna stop at 4101?" Ferenzi asked.

The building at 4101 S. Federal St. is a high-rise in the

CHA's Robert Taylor Homes whose violence the rookies knew well. Less than four months ago, Ferenzi had been shot at there by a sniper after responding to a domestic dispute. But its brazen drug trade made it an opportune place to pull down an arrest. About two months earlier, Ferenzi and Ceriale had arrested a 16-year-old just outside the building for possession of heroin.

Ferenzi punched the car north along State Street toward 4101.

Though some big-city police departments have rigid guidelines for officers working in plain clothes—they work in teams with a supervisor and stay in touch on the radio—Chicago's have a great deal of autonomy. Ferenzi and Ceriale did not use the radio to tell anyone where they were going. They arranged for no backup. In a CD car, they were not required to.

Ferenzi passed Root Street, then leaned into a U-turn so he could park along State Street facing south. He and Ceriale walked southwest away from Loeb Equipment Supply Co. and its boxy, brown facade, talking in hushed tones.

They turned west on Root and walked along the sidewalk past a dark playground. Then they trudged up a shallow incline into a tangled stand of trees and scrubby undergrowth and turned to the north.

It wasn't unusual for cops working the Robert Taylor Homes to use this as a stakeout. Some—including two officers from third watch with whom Ferenzi and Ceriale each had worked on occasion—even used it during the day. With a little luck, a cop might observe a drug deal, sneak across Root Street, sidle along the high-rise and surprise a suspected dealer. A Class X felony just like that.

Crouching less than 10 feet apart in the dark, Ferenzi to Ceriale's left, the two cops peered across Root Street at 4101. They saw some young men near the breezeway. It was about 3:30 a.m. Saturday Aug. 15, 1998.

* * *

For Ferenzi the perils and possibilities of working in the Wentworth District always seemed to come back to this one building, a red Chicago Housing Authority high-rise with a graffiti-tagged breezeway. Sixteen stories high with 10 apartments on each floor; 4101 served as a drug market for the Gangster Disciples.

That night, like almost every night, the Disciples were hawking cocaine and heroin out of the building, according to prosecutors. And they armed themselves with guns, many supplied by Ezra Evans, a 27-year-old South Side man with a pockmarked face.

Evans was an unemployed high school graduate with a spotty work history and three children.

Prosecutors say he had a problem: He owed the Gangster Disciples money for cocaine.

When gang members learned Evans had a Firearm Owner's Identification Card, they suggested he work off the debt by buying them guns. Evans complied, buying 13 guns between August 1997 and July 1998 and turning them over to a gang member called Kojak.

One of the guns, bought Dec. 28, 1997, at Chuck's Gun Shop in Riverdale, was a Smith & Wesson, six-shot, .357 Magnum revolver with a four-inch barrel and a blue-steel finish, prosecutors say. In the industry the gun is known as a "man-stopper" because it can fire a longer-than-usual round with more power and range.

As Ferenzi and Ceriale crouched in the trees conducting surveillance of the building at 4101, prosecutors say, a suspected drug dealer named Rob Brandt stationed inside the building was finishing up his 2 a.m. to 4 a.m. shift.

Brandt allegedly would tell police in a signed statement that his job was to hide the drugs if intruders were spotted, and about 20 minutes before quitting time, lookouts for the Gangster Disciples noticed movement in the trees.

A member of the gang's "outside security" detail alerted gang members inside the building to grab their guns: "On them popsicles!" he called out.

Two armed gang members—one with the .357 Magnum from Chuck's and the other with a 9 mm—emerged from the building's front door, according to Brandt's statement.

"I think they made us," Ceriale said as a gangly young man walked in their direction.

"What do you mean?"

"The guy in the orange jersey He's pointing this way."

"The guy in the No. 5 jersey?"

"Yeah."

The two gunmen walked toward Ferenzi and Ceriale. The one with the .357 raised his gun.

Ferenzi saw a flash.

A bullet fired from a .357 can travel up to 1,350 feet per second—faster than the speed of sound. This one seared at least 60 feet in less than a heartbeat.

With a muffled thup it tore into Ceriale.

The bullet had a copper jacket and a core of lead. It opened a half-inch hole in the lower left abdomen just below the protective vest, flattening as it burrowed down below the pubic bone toward the hip.

Ferenzi looked at Ceriale on the ground, figuring at first that his partner had hit the dirt because Ceriale thought the fireworks were gunshots. He remembered the following exchange:

"Call an ambulance, I'm shot," Ceriale said, curled up writhing.

"What?" Ferenzi said.

"Call an ambulance. They shot me," Ceriale repeated.

The blood rushed hot behind Ferenzi's face. He dropped to a crouch beside his partner and took his radio off his belt.

"293, emergency," he said, referring to their car number.

"I have a police officer shot at 4101 S. Federal St.," Ferenzi said, his voice uneven and squeaky "We need an ambulance immediately."

Had something caught the light? Had one of them moved? Not that Ferenzi could remember. They hadn't learned much at the academy about surveillance, and Ferenzi and Ceriale hadn't had that much time on the streets to pick up the fine points.

The police dispatcher notified the fire dispatcher. The fire dispatcher turned to the computer to notify the firehouse at the corner of 40th and Dearborn Streets.

* * *

Upstairs in the Engine 16 firehouse, 27-year-old paramedic Billy Sotos sat down on the edge of his bed.

Sotos was tired. It had been a busy night. He and his partner, Al Batiz, had just returned from a run to Cook

County Hospital, where they had taken the shooting victim from the Amoco station. Sotos hadn't noticed Ferenzi and Ceriale working crowd control there earlier.

Sotos began to remove his shoes when the firehouse alarm rang. The radio blared: "Gunshot victim at 31 W. Root St."

He rose from the bed, forgetting his exhaustion.

Sotos pulled on his bulletproof vest, went downstairs and climbed into the ambulance alongside Batiz. The engine still was warm. He turned the ignition and began to drive.

Ceriale wondered what was taking the paramedics so long.

"Where the hell are they?" he grumbled as he lay on his back. "Are they taking the ----ing bus?"

The night had grown strangely quiet. The figures at the building had disappeared.

Ceriale was sweating and cursing. He couldn't feel his leg.

Sirens wailed as police cars descended from every direction.

"You're a jinx," Ceriale told his partner.

Hearing police arrive, Ferenzi shone his flashlight so they could find their way.

Ceriale said he thought the wound was in his leg. Ferenzi studied his jeans in the dark and saw no blood. He breathed a sigh of relief. Maybe it's not too bad.

Then he saw the dark spot on Ceriale's T-shirt. With their palms Ferenzi and another officer pressed the shirt against the wound to stanch the flow of blood.

"I can't feel my leg," Ceriale said again.

Some of the arriving officers stood over him. One of them had planned to play basketball with him come Sunday. Ceriale's face was contorted in pain, but he was conscious. He told them about the shooting. Ferenzi retraced their final steps.

When Sotos and Batiz reached Ceriale, about 20 feet back from the sidewalk, the cops surrounding him backed away. One of them had taken Ceriale's gun—standard procedure when a cop goes down.

* * *

Only a week earlier Ceriale had told his father he never had been happier; he was doing what he loved.

Now Sotos was shoving a heavy gauze dressing against his abdomen to stop the bleeding. The gauze soaked through red almost immediately. Cops were helping paramedics lift the 6-foot-2, 195-pound Ceriale onto a backboard.

Though Ceriale was alert, he didn't say anything as the paramedics put him on the stretcher.

Sotos looked at the bloody wound just below Ceriale's vest and thought: That's a one-in-a-million shot.

"What's your name?" Sotos asked as he carried the foot of the stretcher.

"Mike Ceriale."

"When's your birthday?"

"January 21."

To gauge whether Ceriale was conscious and alert, Sotos continued asking questions. Ceriale looked tired. He told the paramedics everything hurt. His back. His stomach.

Lt. Virginia Drozd, the watch commander who had rushed to the scene, caught Ceriale's gaze as paramedics carried the stretcher past and smiled wanly.

"Hi," she said softly, waving.

Across town Lt. Byrne blinked awake in his bed. His blue eyes bore into the dark, wondering what had broken his slumber.

Byrne couldn't sleep.

Restless, he walked to the car to check his pager. It was filled with "911" messages. He called the station and was told Ceriale had been shot. He was seriously wounded. Byrne threw on some clothes and raced to district headquarters.

At the scene of the shooting, Sotos, sweat shining on his forehead, looked down at Ceriale.

"I'm going to start an IV on you, Michael," he said.

He grabbed Ceriale's left arm.

Ceriale grabbed Sotos' left arm.

"Don't let me go," the cop said, his face gray.

"You're not going anywhere," Sotos said.

Right before the ambulance left, Ferenzi climbed inside.

Ceriale turned his head and looked silently at his partner.

"You're gonna be all right," Ferenzi said.

Ferenzi got out and watched anxiously as the ambulance turned the corner and disappeared.

"Is Cook County a good place to take him?" Ferenzi asked Drozd nervously.

"It's a good place," she said.

"They get a lot of gunshot wounds there."

Lessons Learned

BY ROBERT L. KAISER

During a seven-month stretch beginning in August 1998, three police officers were gunned down on the streets of Chicago. It was an alarming run of cop killings, even for a city with a trophy case full of dead men's badges.

Each time only a few feet separated the doomed cop from the one who would go home that night. But the story of the surviving partner never is told. What's it like to watch someone as close as a spouse go down in a confusing moment of chaos and violence?

What does it require to live anonymously in the outsized shadow of a buddy-turned-hero?

How does it feel to walk the beat haunted?

Looking for answers, I tracked down a boyish rookie cop named Joe Ferenzi—the surviving partner of Officer Michael Ceriale, a cop who was gunned down Aug. 15, 1998, on the South Side.

Months later—after winning Ferenzi's trust, insinuating myself into his life, and infiltrating the insular culture of the street cop—I had the story of his partner's life and death.

Now, how to write it?

I decided to start the series in the moment of greatest peril for Ferenzi and Ceriale, bringing them to the edge of disaster before cutting away. I would leave that .357-caliber bullet hanging—and the reader, too, I hoped.

There was just one problem. News accounts of Ceriale's shooting, and his subsequent battle for life in a Chicago trauma ward, had dominated local headlines for a week. His death and funeral—a vast, elaborate pageant at one of the city's most majestic churches—had held the city spellbound. Was it possible now to build suspense—to make the public forget everything and lose itself all over again in my story?

I had my doubts. But the overwhelming public reaction to "Partners in Peril" taught me never to underestimate the power of the written word. The outpouring was immense. In the days and weeks after the series ran, my editors and I were flooded with letters, phone calls, and e-mail. Hundreds of readers posted comments on the newspaper's website for the series. A cemetery worker who said he thought he was steeled to tragedy called to say he never had been so moved.

Many readers simply said they never had looked forward so to getting their paper each morning.

But my favorite response was an e-mail message from a man who recounted how a normally busy diner in the middle of the city had fallen silent during the morning rush hour because everyone there, it seemed, was reading the series.

"I had bought the *Tribune* to catch the second part of your story and was reading intently when I looked up from my paper and saw different customers reading the same article," the reader, John A. Lupo, wrote.

"I tried to follow their eyes as they were reading, and then it dawned on me that there was this total hush in the room."

Why did the series work? It put the reader there and it gave them a fresh perspective. Television is a mirror, but a newspaper is an impressionistic painting, presenting the world in a new and illuminating way. We synthesize what we find, give it color, give it texture, give it perspective. If we don't, we are not journalists and newspapers are not indispensable and no one will let their coffee go cold because they can't stop reading.

For all we do to give our stories sweep and import, it's often the little things that give them resonance. My favorite scene in the series is that in which the police chief approaches Ferenzi in a hospital waiting room as Ceriale fights for his life in the trauma ward. Struggling for the right words, the chief asks Ferenzi if his boots are heavy.

It's a moment bursting with symbolism and pathos, an exchange that speaks volumes in just a few words. I could have left it at that. But I called Ferenzi back.

I had to know:

What size were the boots?

THE BLADE

Jenni Laidman

Finalist, Non-Deadline Writing

Jenni Laidman came to the Toledo *Blade* as science writer in May 1998. She began writing about science at *The Bay City Times* in Michigan, where she started in 1986 as an assistant metropolitan editor. She was also an assistant features editor for the *Times*. Until 1985 she worked at *The Medina County Gazette* in northeast Ohio, where she covered a variety of beats before becoming city editor. She was also city editor for the *Gwinnett Daily News* in suburban Atlanta. She's been the recipient of numerous state journalism awards for news writing, feature writing, editorial writing, and editing. Laidman graduated from Kent State University in 1977 with a journalism degree.

With passion and compassion, Laidman depicts the life-and-death struggle of a baby gorilla at the Toledo Zoo. Through meticulous reporting, she raises difficult ethical issues about society's strained relationship with animals and the environment.

Small life slips away

NOVEMBER 16, 1999

The gorilla baby is sleeping.

Maybe she doesn't feel well, Lisa French thinks as she rocks the infant. Maybe she had a bad night.

It's Aug. 5, around 10:30 a.m. In eight days, Sindiswa marks her first birthday. The Toledo Zoo ape house is quiet, and Ms. French, one of the volunteers who works with the baby, is alone. Both gorilla troops are outdoors.

It's been a miserable, hot, summer, which in the ape house is accented by a stronger dose of gorilla body odor.

The infant jerks as her sleep grows deeper.

She jerks again. A few more sharp movements follow.

Suddenly, the baby's body curls into a ball of rigid muscle in Ms. French's arms. Arms and legs fold inward. Her head tucks down. Even her fingers and toes curl tightly.

"Sinda! Sinda!" Ms. French cries, trying to evoke a response.

She holds the baby out from her, "Sinda!" But the infant's eyes are fixed in a stare. Ms. French pats the baby's back. It's like striking a board.

She puts Sindiswa in her crib and runs for help. The baby's muscles are so contracted, her head doesn't even touch the mattress.

* * *

It's the beginning of the end.

In September 1998, the month-old Sindiswa contracted a bacterial infection that nearly killed her. Although physicians and veterinarians saved her life, the baby was severely brain damaged. Over the last 11 months, dozens of volunteers have joined a medical team and the zoo's gorilla keepers attempting to rehabilitate the baby who neither can sit, crawl, nor feed herself.

Until this moment in August, they thought they were winning.

Teresa Hatcher is working in the gorilla department when the baby has her first seizure. The regular keepers are off.

When Ms. Hatcher reaches Sindiswa, the seizure is ending, but her eyes remain unfocused. The baby is lethargic, dopey.

A zoo veterinarian is summoned and gives the infant Valium. The baby looks frightened. While keepers wait for the medication to take effect, Sindiswa has another seizure.

Suzanne Husband, the keeper for chimpanzees and orangutans, comes into the gorilla area to help. As the second seizure ends, the infant starts squirming. Ms. Husband takes the baby on her lap.

Sindiswa begins biting furiously, snapping at her own arms and hands. Ms. Husband struggles with the flailing baby, finally pulling its arms out of harm's way. At that moment, Sindiswa arches her back and bites Ms. Husband.

"In 13 years, that's my first serious bite," Ms. Husband says. Because it drew blood, she has to go to the Medical College of Ohio Hospital for an examination. There are no complications.

The keepers are sure the bite wasn't intentional. It was somehow tied to the seizures. Still, it's the first warning that the people caring for the infant may soon face more than they can handle.

* * *

For Char Petiniot, the chief gorilla keeper, the summer runs on a continual video loop in her mind. She looks for clues in her memory that might have warned her.

She feels guilty that she wasn't at work when Sindiswa needed her. Now she's picking apart the days she was.

Was it the heat that made the infant sluggish through July? Or was the baby having seizures when everyone went home for the night?

"Maybe she was having these all along," the keeper says. "What's a little twitch when you can hardly move your arms, and your eyes go in different directions?"

Ms. Petiniot recalls an especially frustrating morning. The infant was truculent and lazy, she says. Now the keeper wonders if she had witnessed the end of an early morning seizure.

Had she been too harsh when she should have been softer? Had she failed to see signs that should have been clear?

She sounds like a mother.

While some may talk about maintaining a professional distance from animals, there seems no reasonable way that a keeper can have a long-term relationship with higher primates and remain detached. That's especially true as keepers have moved from the old-fashioned rule-by-intimidation care for the animals.

That era ended for Toledo's gorillas in 1989 when the zoo brought in animal behaviorist Tim Desmond to train gorilla keepers.

It was a difficult time for Ms. Petiniot, humbling from the very first lesson. The behaviorist asked her to get the animals together to eat.

"I did what I had been taught to do," she says.

She dumped their food and called them to the back feeding cage. Sometimes they heeded the call.

"If they didn't, you went to the keeper door and you pointed the hose at them. Then you hosed them. Then you'd run upstairs and hose them. So I did all this stuff. I thought I was doing real good. This is what I was taught. This is the way a keeper does it. And I got all done and he said, 'Oh, that was terrible.'"

She learned a new way of thinking about her job.

"The basic theory is that keeper attention is probably the best reward you can give an animal, so you have to be very careful what you're doing with it," Ms. Petiniot explains.

"If an animal won't move, and you're standing there screaming and yelling and hosing him and chasing him around, you're reinforcing him not moving, because you're giving him lots of attention. You have to be very careful how you use your attention," she said.

She took time to convince. But gradually she saw the need to adopt this approach in her daily interactions with the animals. Ultimately, it gave her new insight into the gorillas.

"In a way, it gave an indication—you got to learn how their mind works," she said.

Without question, today she's the Toledo gorillas' greatest champion, stubborn in their defense and protective almost to a fault. Her conversation about them is a mixture of insight, anthropomorphism, and, well, the gripes of a mother.

Sometimes it creeps into the daily logs she keeps on the animals.

"Kwisha was such a pest today. He tried to play with both girls and steal the baby," she writes.

"Kelele screamed as if her limbs were being torn off. In sympathy with her, everyone had diarrhea. Some smeared it on the walls, the bars, buckets, tires, etc."

"Kwisha screwed up the whole day by not going outside and he was very proud of himself for being a brat."

She's a close observer of their likes and dislikes, how they learn, and why they learn.

She talks about teaching the silverback, Max, who died in 1991.

"I was trying to teach him to put his feet up, (for inspection) and he just could not get it. I worked and worked and worked on it. I was using a dowel rod, and I would touch his foot and say 'foot.' Then I'd move the dowel rod a little bit and say 'foot.'"

If he even accidentally moved his foot, she'd give him a treat.

It didn't matter. He couldn't get it.

"Then all of a sudden, one day I sat down and said, 'OK, Max, foot.' I touched his foot. And I said, 'OK, foot,' and moved the rod, and he stuck his foot under the bars. It was like he just had it all of a sudden. It was pretty amazing," she said.

"Gorillas are like that. Gorillas don't like to appear like they don't know something. They always want to appear very much in control: 'It's OK. I'm cool with this. I know what's going on.'

"So if they don't know, they will feign disinterest or whatever: 'I'm just not going to do this.' But I think they do think about it. Because I've seen them many times, where you've asked them to do something and it's like, 'Nope. Nope. I don't want to do it,' and then the next day, two weeks later, whatever, if you ask them to do it, they know how to do it. So they've actually gone, thought about it, observed other animals maybe doing it, or something like that," she says.

She would have liked to study psychology, she says. Certainly she has learned a great deal about the psychology of her charges.

Now, the youngest of her gorilla clan seems fated to die. Dr. Tim Reichard, the zoo's chief veterinarian, is worried the seizures are doing further damage to Sindiswa's brain. He's concerned that she'll follow the pattern of the baby gorilla that the Columbus Zoo had to put to death. That animal's seizures increased steadily over the course of a year. He expects Sindiswa soon will be euthanized.

That knowledge permeates the atmosphere in the ape house.

"The hard part is now, knowing that it's probably hopeless, but working with her anyway," Ms. Petiniot says.

"Poor little thing. How frustrated she is. What would it be like to not be able to do what you wanted to do?

"I don't want to give up on her. I know the volunteers don't want to give up on her. But at the same time, look how difficult things are for her," she says.

It's hard to find comfort in the situation.

"The North American Indians believe the spirits of animals go on. Our western religion doesn't give you much hope. I don't know how to think or what to think," she says.

"She's such a sweetheart. She has a great nature. I'd like to think that if there's such a thing that her spirit goes on to something else—I'd like to see her go on to lead a more fulfilling life than she can in this body. I don't think she'll be going very far in this body."

* * *

It's almost surreal listening to Dr. Donald Cameron as the pediatric neurologist examines Sindiswa on Aug. 21.

For 2 1/2 weeks, zoo staffers have steeled themselves for the worst. Euthanasia seems inevitable. People started to feel if not comfortable, then at least resigned to the fact that there wasn't much more to be done.

Dr. Cameron and gorilla keeper Andrea Walters sit on the floor of the small cage where volunteers have worked with Sindiswa since November. Ms. Walters holds the gorilla.

"I'm always amazed how different this young lady looks every time I come," the doctor says.

He checks her muscle tone and her reflexes. He moves a striped piece of plastic in front of her eyes. She follows the motion, tumbling over as the end of it clears her face.

He sees her roll over—even when she's trying to move forward. He holds up a vibrating tuning fork. She reaches for it and pulls it to her mouth.

"So much better," Dr. Cameron says as Sindiswa mouths the tuning fork.

While he notes the areas where she's lagging—she doesn't use her legs, her arm movements continue to be snaky and misdirected, and she shows little sense of balance—he's generally upbeat.

"The regression is upsetting, but not serious," he says. The seizures themselves are a positive sign.

"As cells recover partially, those with the capacity to generate electrical activity cause seizures. Dead cells don't seize. Seizure starts when recovery is well under way," he says. But he adds: "Chances are she will continue to have seizures for three, four years."

If the seizures increase in frequency, it will retard her recovery, he says, but the seizures themselves shouldn't cause significant damage.

Anti-seizure medications often put an end to the problem. In more than half of patients with cerebral palsy—which is what he calls Sindiswa's injury—seizure-control drugs work.

As he and Dr. Reichard walk out of the ape house, he makes a joke about Sindiswa in a wheelchair, going about her life as the first gorilla eligible for protection under the Americans with Disabilities Act.

He leaves behind a small group stunned by his optimism.

Someone wonders aloud: Has he forgotten this is a gorilla?

* * *

But Dr. Cameron's assessment has provided a reason for hope. Two days later, the keepers, vets, and zoo managers decide to give Sindiswa one last try.

She will be given the seizure-control medication, Dilantin. But there's a significant caveat: If she's not sitting up by Sept. 14, she will be euthanized.

That gives her 21 days—three weeks to accomplish what she hasn't been able to do in 52.

At this point, zoo staff members are not unlike a family emotionally punch-drunk by the long illness of a loved one. Few people are prepared for the life-and-death decisions that come with modern illness: The ability to keep an individual alive with no guarantee that the trickle of life will be meaningful.

The details of the discussion are intensely private.

Dr. Reichard acknowledges he lobbied to try seizure-control medication. He cites a scientific justification: "Very little has been done on seizuring in gorillas."

But there's a more basic motivation: "At least we gave it that last shot. We feel we really have to really give it this last shot."

But doesn't it just prolong the agony of the staff?

"People brought that up," he said. But after this much investment of time, why not a little more, he says.

"She's a pretty content little animal. The other apes are more stressed out then she is. She's not in some terrible condition," he says.

For others at the meeting, Sindiswa's future may not be in alignment with the zoo's overall mission of recreation, education, research, and conservation. But zoo mission statements are ultimately designed for the protection of animal populations. While such philosophies make secondary the fate of the individual animal, in this instance, it's the argument for the individual that succeeds.

Ms. Petiniot too argued to give Sindiswa one last try.

"I just decided somebody had to be on her side," she says.

Now Sindiswa has 21 days to learn to sit.

"It's important to emphasize [the deadline] is not based on my or Dr. Cameron's professional medical opinions," Dr. Reichard said. "It would almost be like a miracle if it occurred."

No one really expects a miracle.

* * *

The side-effects of hand-raising haunt the thoughts of those deciding Sindiswa's fate. The next three weeks are full of agonizing: What are we really doing for this animal?

It took Sindiswa six months to learn to roll over and 10 months to sit after someone else puts her in the sitting position. How long will it take her to feed herself? How long will it take her to walk?

Put a toy in front of a three-month-old human infant and the baby will grasp the toy in both hands and put it in his mouth effortlessly. Gorilla babies are remarkably precocious by comparison.

Sindiswa hasn't even the competence of a roly-poly human child.

What happens if the zoo continues its rehabilitation efforts until Sindiswa can walk? According to Dr. Cameron's predictions, she may be 4 or 5 years old by then.

If her rehabilitation succeeds, by the time it is complete, she will be not quite human and not quite gorilla. Humans will cut her off from themselves and she never will feel at ease with her own kind.

It is the worst possible outcome.

Three weeks pass. The anti-seizure drugs work. The seizures stop. Sindiswa still can't sit up.

Zoo staffers gather, and in a private, tearful meeting, they decide to give Sindiswa up.

* * *

"She's a gorilla," a zoo board member says as board members discuss Zoo Director Bill Dennler's formal decision to put Sindiswa to sleep.

That line, "she's a gorilla," sometimes with the companion phrase, "she's just an animal," occasionally creeps into conversations about the zoo's extreme efforts on behalf of the baby Sindiswa.

But to sum up the decision to euthanize Sindiswa by simply drawing a line between them and us is to miss what was at the heart of the entire hard-fought and hope-filled year.

It was a commitment to do the most that could be done. It was the ethic of their professions. For the veterinarians, it was the same thing that motivated Dr. Reichard in the past to seek a brain scan for a polar bear and to take a guinea pig recovering from surgery with him on a trip rather than leave the animal alone for the weekend.

For the keepers, it was a commitment to the creatures

they care for, the kind of thing that brings them in on holidays and weekends when something goes wrong.

For many, it was that feeling of connection with another creature, the understanding of what we have in common, the look into the eyes of another species, and seeing that stranger look back.

For all, it was a long walk down a dark hallway. It was a gamble where everyone knew at the outset that the odds were poor, but one in which the prize was thought to be of such value; the odds were worth playing.

The board unanimously endorses Mr. Dennler's decision to euthanize Sindiswa. Board members stand up from the table and form small, boisterous groups, chatting, saying goodbye.

Ms. Petiniot and Ms. Walters remain seated.

The keepers look down blankly. Their faces are pale. Finally, they rise and go back to work.

* * *

The following morning, the zoo is quiet. Two hours will pass before the first visitor arrives, but already both gorilla troops are outside. Four-year-old Kelele runs back and forth in front of the window, prompting a quick game of hide-and-seek with one of the few people who pass.

In the meadow enclosure, Sindiswa's family eats their morning meal. Johari, Sindiswa's mother, is at the glass when Ms. Walters steps out the door. Ms. Walters glances at Johari beside her. The keeper's eyes are rimmed in red.

Ms. Petiniot follows.

She carries the towel-wrapped body of Sindiswa. Her eyes, too, are red.

Ms. Petiniot said she spent the weekend working in her garden and thinking about Sindiswa.

"What do I think? What is life and death? More time for Sinda? To what end?" she says.

She fears some of the volunteers think she's a traitor; that she's given up on the infant.

"It's not an easy decision for me to make," she told the zoo board the day before. "I'm very torn. I'm very attached to her."

The two keepers cradled Sindiswa this morning

when she died.

Dr. Reichard injected a sedative. As she fell into a deep sleep, he injected the second, lethal drug.

With a single deep exhale, she was gone.

* * *

So what does it mean?

We still don't know much about our place in the world. We cannot decide if we're the Fourth Great Ape or if there's some impenetrable divide between animals and us.

We don't know if they're one of us, or we're just like them. We're conflicted about whether zoos should exist, whether it's educational or obscene to put animals on display. We can't decide whether we should hunt animals, nor can we figure out our responsibilities if we decide we shouldn't.

We can't be sure what they feel or what they think. We fear projecting our feelings onto them, and we risk treating them mechanically if we fail to do so.

But for one year, people in Toledo put the intellectual questions aside and responded first with their hearts, and then with their heads.

Were their efforts misguided? Was their ultimate decision too hasty?

There seems little to gain in second-guessing. Because certainly, as our views evolve about what we owe other creatures, there will be other Sindiswas, other animals that put us face to face with the fact that this is a planet we share.

Lessons Learned

BY JENNI LAIDMAN

Lesson one: People who most resist being interviewed often are those with the most to say and deserve my patience and respect.

The chief gorilla keeper, Char Petiniot, did not want me hanging around when I finally got through the zoo red tape and descended the stairs into the gorilla keeper's area. She had the most to lose, as the person closest to the animals I was writing about, and she was fiercely protective of the gorillas.

After weeks of my regular Tuesday visits, she opened up. Although this was not a part of my original plan, each Tuesday I'd come into the gorilla house around 8 a.m., pull on rubber boots, and get to work with the keepers, scooping gorilla poop, chopping food, hosing down cages.

As Char and I got to know each other, she returned my efforts richly. Although she doesn't really emerge as a character until the third part of the series, it is her voice, in many ways, that guided me through the story.

Lesson two: Work for the right editor.

Zoo administrators were reluctant to allow the kind of access I wanted to report this story. Since my requirements far exceeded what any reading of open-records laws for quasi-public institutions would allow, there was little percentage in stamping my foot and pleading the public's right to know. Instead, I took time creating relationships that slowly resulted in unprecedented access to the zoo and its records. Going through those records required another huge time commitment, as did collecting and reading more than a decade's worth of academic publications on gorillas. My editor, *Blade* science editor Michael Woods, supported me in this approach, which included my unplanned weekly duties as a cage cleaner. I was lucky to have an editor who understood that the No. 1 primate of concern in this story was the human one. And humans take even more time than gorillas to get to know.

Lesson three: Hang on, you're going for a ride.

Projects have a life cycle all their own. Enthusiasm buoys me through most of the reporting stage, but self-doubt and a sense of feeling overwhelmed generally plague me when I start to write. The importance of planning stories—spending time thinking about plot and organization—is crucial here. Having a plan drowns out that second-guessing internal editor. While a second wind of enthusiasm usually kicks in during the writing, by the time I finish the last story and work through the painstaking cleanup of rewriting, fact checking, more rewriting, and more fact checking, I hate the whole thing. Then, the only answer is to keep working.

This emotional roller coaster has been part of each project I've worked on, and I've watched other writers go through almost the same steps. It's just part of the process.

Leonora Bohen LaPeter

Deadline News Reporting

Her award-winning stories often focus on small towns, but Leonora LaPeter's world spans the globe. She was born in Long Island, N.Y., and spent much of her youth in Athens, Greece. Her mother, an anthropologist, was a Fulbright Scholar there and her father taught English. LaPeter also lived in Westport, Conn., and Douglaston, N.Y.

LaPeter attended the University of Illinois at Champaign where, in her junior year, she decided to become a journalist. With little writing experience and no internships by graduation, she spent her first two years after college as a waitress, working in the circulation department of *The Seattle Daily Journal of Commerce*, and managing to get a few stories printed in a weekly newspaper. Those clips helped her land a job with *The Okeechobee* (Fla.) *News*.

LaPeter covered the police, courts, and city government beats. Then in 1992, she moved to *The Island Packet* at Hilton Head, S.C. After writing about the environment and health, she was named city editor. She returned to reporting at the *Tallahassee Democrat* and in 1998 moved to the *Savannah Morning News* as a court reporter.

Over the years, LaPeter has won more than a dozen state and regional journalism awards. Her deadline reporting award came from trial coverage of a case in which four family members were murdered in their home. LaPeter overcame problems of distance and long court sessions to put readers in the courtroom each day.

She is married to Brian LaPeter, a photojournalist, and they have a 2-year old daughter. LaPeter's favorite pastime is international travel.

—Karen Brown Dunlap

Testimony begins in Santa Claus slayings

AUGUST 31, 1999

MONROE—Tap. Tap. Tap. Tap. Pause. Tap. Tap. Tap.

Ashley Lewis hit the counter of the oak witness box with his index finger, mimicking what he heard through a crack in the bathroom window the night of Dec. 4, 1997, as he got ready for bed.

It sounded like a typewriter. But Lewis, testifying on the first day in the death penalty trial of Jerry Scott Heidler for the murder of a family in Santa Claus a year-and-a-half ago, found it hard to believe his mother, a secretary, would break out her typewriter at almost 2 a.m. Just a half hour before, she had told him to turn the television off and go to bed.

Lewis walked to his mother's room and turned on the light. She was asleep in bed. He walked through the house, turning on other lights. Nothing.

"I got this real eerie feeling," Lewis said.

Lewis did not know it yet, but a half-mile away, four of his neighbors lay dead.

* * *

Three hours later, Toombs County Sheriff's Department Deputy Mike Harlin arrived at the doorstep of the Daniels

The Trial

- Jerry Scott Heidler, 22, is charged with murder, kidnapping, aggravated sodomy, aggravated child molestation and child molestation.

- Heidler faces the death penalty in the case, which is expected to last the week and possibly into next week.

- On Monday, the jury was selected, lawyers offered opening statements and about a half dozen witnesses testified for the state.

- Today, District Attorney Richard Malone is expected to call about 15 witnesses.

- Overall, Malone said he would call between 25 and 40 witnesses. Defense lawyers Michael Garrett and Kathy Palmer said they plan to call eight to 10 witnesses. Palmer said she did not plan to call Heidler to the stand at this point.

family on Dasher Lane in Santa Claus. Just about every light in the one-story brick house was on. He thought that was odd for 5:10 a.m.

He knocked on the front door, which was slightly ajar. No answer. Through a window to the left, he noticed the arm of a small child in a bunk bed by the window.

He walked in and announced he was there. He heard a baby crying and a radio playing music. He walked toward the room with the child in it. On the top bunk, he found what was left of 8-year-old Bryant Daniels, who had been shot through the eye.

"I have a small boy myself," Harlin said, swallowing hard as he recalled the image on the witness stand Monday afternoon. "At that point, it was pretty obvious that words wouldn't help."

Harlin moved through the house, running into 4-year-old Corey Daniels near the dining room table. Harlin knelt down beside the child.

"Mama and Daddy are dead. Brother Guy shot them all," Corey said.

A baby continued to cry. The radio, obviously an alarm for early rising postal worker Danny Daniels, continued to play music.

Harlin opened the door of the master bedroom. The first thing he noticed was the gun cabinet with several empty slots where guns had been. Next he noticed a body up against the door, preventing him from opening it further. Corey showed him another entrance to the room, through a laundry room and a bathroom.

Harlin walked into the sunken bedroom and found 10-month-old Gabriel standing between his baby bed and his parents' king-sized bed, hanging onto the sheets. Beneath the sheet lay Kim Daniels, 33, who had been shot in the head. Danny Daniels, 47, also was dead on the bed. And a third body, that of 16-year-old Jessica Daniels, lay over by the door.

* * *

"What's your worst nightmare?" asked Toombs County District Attorney Richard Malone. "If you're a father, it's someone breaking into your house. If you're a young child, it's being taken away from your home and being molested. If you are an infant, maybe it's being left alone in the house among the dead bodies of your mother and father."

Malone, a portly man with an obvious passion for his case, has the attention of the 16 jurors, 12 of whom will decide the fate of Heidler, 22, and four alternates.

"It's about all these nightmares happening to a good family in a very small town called Santa Claus in south Georgia," he continued.

Kim and Danny Daniels met at an Alcoholics Anonymous meeting in 1992 and married. Between them they had four children. Kim Daniels had been in foster homes as a child, and she wanted to help others in her situation. From 1995 to their deaths, the couple took in seven children, testified Jackie Alexander, foster care supervisor for the Department of Family and Children Services.

One of those children was Jo Anna Moseley, Scott Heidler's then 10-year-old sister.

Moseley stayed with the Danielses for six weeks. Her brother, Heidler, came to visit her. Malone said the Danielses realized Heidler was troubled and took him to their church, the Mount Vernon Pentecostal Church.

But soon Heidler became unwelcome in the Daniels' residence. Danny Daniels told Heidler to go away because he thought the Alma man was having an inappropriate relationship with 16-year-old Jessica. He thought Heidler was too old for his daughter.

Malone gave a detailed account of what happened the night of Dec. 4, 1997, during his opening argument Monday. Heidler drank and played pool and stole his neighbor's van, the prosecutor said. He drove to the Daniels' home, entered through the window and went directly to the gun cabinet he knew was in the Daniels' bedroom.

He took a Remington semiautomatic shotgun, loaded it with buck shot and went to the back door, which he cracked. He then proceeded to smoke a cigarette. He crushed it on the floor. Then he walked into the master bedroom and shot Kim and Danny Daniels as they slept, Malone said.

She died almost immediately. He survived.

Heidler, Malone said, reloaded the weapon and moved to 8-year-old Bryant's room and turned on the light. He shot the boy in the eye socket and blew his head off.

Jessica jumped from her bed and ran toward her parents' room. Heidler followed her, and as she opened the door to her parents' room, he shot her from behind in the back of the head.

Danny Daniels was still alive and Heidler knew it, Malone said. So he shot Danny some more until he was dead. Then he went to the other end of the house and ushered three of the Daniels' girls, ages 8, 9 and 10, into a van. He left behind Corey and Gabriel.

Heidler traveled about 15 miles to the Altamaha River, where he asked one of the girls to step out. He sodomized one of the girls, while a third girl watched. He threw the gun into the Altamaha River, drove back to Alma and dropped the girls off on a dirt road.

* * *

Almost immediately, lawyer Kathy Palmer, defending Heidler with Michael Garrett, got to the heart of her defense with two words.

Mental illness.

She pointed out that Heidler, at his arraignment a year ago, stood mute. He wouldn't plead guilty. He wouldn't plead not guilty. So the clerk of court automatically put him down for not guilty.

She acknowledged that what happened to the Daniels family was a great tragedy, but she urged jurors to listen to what people had to say about Heidler's mental state. "I wanted to raise issues of mental illness and put that out there at the outset," she said after Monday's session.

Already it is clear where defense lawyers are going. They won a battle Monday afternoon to get DFACS to release records on all of Heidler's family members, including his two sisters, two brothers and his mother. DFACS had argued against releasing the information.

His mother, waiting outside the courtroom Monday afternoon presumably to testify, declined to comment.

Malone summed it up for the jurors.

"This was a nightmare from which the Danielses will never awake, but it's not your nightmare," he said. "Your job is to take the evidence and come up with the truth."

Writers' Workshop

Talking Points

1) The writer builds her lead around a sound. How does this bring the reader into the courtroom?

2) Two stories are unfolding in this article: the story of the murder and the story of how the murder is recounted in the courtroom. Analyze how the writer weaves these together.

3) Instead of the traditional hard-news approach, the writer retells the story of the murder in a narrative style. What makes this style effective?

Assignment Desk

1) Think of a news story you wrote on deadline and outline how it could have been written as a narrative story. How can you work with your editor to use this approach in more of your stories?

2) Write a summary lead, also known as a hard-news lead, for this story.

Grisly video shows slaying scene

SEPTEMBER 1, 1999

MONROE—Connie Smith bowed her head and kept it there.

Sitting in the front row of a Monroe courtroom Tuesday—surrounded by family and friends—she couldn't bear to look at the television screen.

It showed the inside of her sister, Kim Daniels', home in Santa Claus the morning of Dec. 4, 1997, about seven hours after Kim, 33, her husband, Danny, 47, and their two children, Jessica, 16, and Bryant, 8, died from shotgun blasts as they slept in their beds.

"They're in Bryant's room now," whispered Amy Tomberlin, a best friend from church, into Smith's ear.

The video camera panned through young Bryant's room, showing the bunk beds where he and brother, Corey, 4, slept. A toy truck on the floor near a shotgun shell and a boy's jacket. A closet with boys' clothes and a bowling pin on the floor.

> **The Trial**
>
> ● Jerry Scott Heidler, 22, is charged with murder, kidnapping, aggravated sodomy, aggravated child molestation, child molestation and burglary. Heidler faces the death penalty.
>
> ● Tuesday, about a dozen witnesses testified. The jury saw a videotape of the Daniels' home and another videotape of one of the Daniels' girls testifying to sexual abuse by Heidler.
>
> ● District Attorney Richard Malone said he might finish his case today. Videotapes of the other two girls, who Heidler is accused of kidnapping, are expected to lead off testimony this morning.

And blood. Splattered on the walls next to the bed, near a framed photo of Bryant in a red baseball cap holding a bat. The boy's arm poked out from beneath a sheet on the top bunk bed.

Smith, 33, grasped a tissue and wiped her eyes, still keeping her head down.

Across the courtroom, the man accused of killing the Daniels' family also kept his head down, staring at a spot on the gray-blue rug in front of him for hours on end.

Jerry Scott Heidler, 22, sat solitary at the defense table as his lawyers, the prosecutors and observers moved over to the other side of the room and gathered around a single television that showed the carnage he is accused of causing.

Though offered the opportunity, he declined to view the gruesome video.

Kim and Danny Daniels lying in their bed, shot dead, beneath a white comforter with light blue flowers. Jessica, face-down in her nightgown on the steps leading down to the bedroom between a desk with a calculator and a dresser with socks and diapers and other clutter on top.

Shotgun shells strewn throughout the house, two near Jessica, one in the bathroom leading into the master bedroom where the family's bodies were found; one in a small garden tub in the master bedroom, one in the laundry room, another in Bryant's room, still another on the couch in the living room beneath a plastic pitcher. A Marlboro cigarette mashed into the floor near the back door with saliva on it that matches Heidler's DNA.

Kim was shot two times, once in the stomach, another time in the arm, medical experts testified. Danny may have been shot four times. A bullet to the head finally killed him. Jessica was shot once in the back of the head. Bryant was shot once in the head. Death for the two children was instantaneous, medical experts said. Kim and Danny may have lived for a matter of minutes.

The video moved to an aerial view of the brick house with the cornflower blue shutters located between a pond and larger lagoon lined by trees.

Finally, Smith looked up at the television.

The home where the Daniels lived with seven children, many of them foster children, is in a pastoral setting at the end of a dirt road in the tiny town of Santa Claus in Toombs County.

But Smith could not shield herself from the little girl on the video who told of being abducted from her home and sodomized by Heidler in a van at the Altamaha River that same night. The girl said Heidler, known to her as Scott Taylor, woke her up that morning, holding a shotgun.

He said a burglar had broken into the house and Kim Daniels had told him to take her away. Heidler then got two of the other Daniels' girls to come with him. He took the trio, ages 8, 9 and 10, in a van for a drive that ended beneath a bridge at the Altamaha River.

In a little girl's voice, the child described how Heidler got out for a while and then returned. He drove to the top of the bridge and threw the shotgun into the water, she said. Then he drove some more and dropped the girls on a dirt road on the outskirts of Alma, Heidler's hometown.

Asked if any of the girls had been harmed by Heidler, the girl paused. Then she started crying and buried her head in her arms.

She was only willing to confide her story to a woman from the Department of Children and Family Services. A male Georgia Bureau of Investigation agent left the room. Then the girl, with little emotion and obvious discomfort, told her story.

Smith, friends and other family members of the Daniels and even a few jury members shed tears to varying degrees as the child described Heidler's actions that night.

Prosecutors offered some insight on Tuesday into a possible motive for the slayings. Guy Aaron, Danny Daniels' best friend, said Daniels was concerned that a relationship had sprung up between his daughter and Heidler. Heidler's sister, Jo Anna Mosley, was a foster child in the Daniels' home for six weeks, and the family tried to help her troubled brother also, Aaron said.

"At times, Kim and Danny felt sorry for him," Aaron said. "They were out to help people. Scott (Heidler) happened to be one of those people."

Guy said even he had seen Jessica and Heidler together on the steps of the house.

"You could tell something was beginning to take place, how people get close to one another," Aaron said.

Daniels told Aaron he was concerned because of the age difference between Heidler and Jessica. Several months before the murders took place, Danny Daniels told Heidler to stay away from the home.

"After that I didn't see him no more," said Aaron, who went hunting with Daniels and saw or talked to him almost every day.

After Tuesday's testimony ended, District Attorney Richard Malone said he might be able to squeeze the rest of his case into today. The other two girls, who were not sexually abused, are also expected to offer video-taped testimony. The defense has the opportunity to cross-examine them, but lawyers have not said whether they plan to do so. Still, prosecutors have stowed the girls at an Athens hotel should the need arise.

Family members appeared drained by Tuesday's testimony. Many were unwilling to talk about it. Smith, afraid she might cry, said simply: "It's hell."

Writers' Workshop

Talking Points

1) The writer focuses her lead not on a lawyer or a witness, but on a family member who has come to watch the trial. Why is this approach effective? When would this technique not be effective?

2) Count the number of quotes in the story. Which were from official testimony and which were informal remarks made on the sidelines? How does this compare with other trial stories you have read?

3) Study the sentence structure in the two paragraphs describing the video. How does this affect the pacing of the story?

4) Notice the use of description in the story: "A toy truck on the floor near a shotgun shell and a boy's jacket." How does the use of detail create an emotional response?

Assignment Desk

1) Telling details, such as "a Marlboro cigarette mashed into the floor," "a dresser with socks and diapers," make for compelling trial coverage. Look for ways to incorporate such details in your stories.

2) The writer describes two scenes in this story: the site of the killings and the courtroom. What tools can you use to create vivid scenes in your stories?

3) Rewrite this story using only official sources. How does this change the tone of the story?

Jury sends Santa Claus killer to electric chair

SEPTEMBER 4, 1999

MONROE—The jury had left.

The sentence had been read.

Jerry Scott Heidler's face was still as stone.

Only when Superior Court Judge Walter C. McMillan Jr. actually sentenced Heidler to death for the murder of the Daniels family did Heidler break down for the first time and cry.

Sitting at the defense table surrounded by six guards, his hands and legs shackled, Heidler shook with the force of his tears. He didn't say anything but wiped his nose on his blue and green polo shirt and folded his hands on his lap.

Four death sentences, one each for Danny, 47, Kim, 33, Jessica, 16, and Bryant, 8, whom Heidler shot dead in their beds in Santa Claus on Dec. 4, 1997. Two additional life sentences for kidnapping one of the Daniels' daughters and sodomizing her by the Altamaha River. Another 110 years for kidnapping two other Daniels' daughters and subjecting one of them to witness the molestation of her sister.

McMillan gave Heidler the maximum sentence on all charges, saying the 22-year-old Alma man did not deserve mercy when he showed no mercy on the Daniels family. He set Heidler's execution date for between Oct. 1 and Oct. 8, although the sentence will be automatically appealed to the Supreme Court of Georgia within 30 days.

And McMillan expressed sorrow for the tiny town of Santa Claus, which must celebrate Christmas and remember Heidler in the same month for years to come.

Jurors seemed to take Friday's decision much harder than the guilty verdict they rendered on Thursday. They sent a note to the judge about an hour into their deliberations, saying they had prayed for everyone and wanted to read a statement when they gave their verdict.

About 45 minutes later, they emerged from the jury room, many of them overwrought with tears as jury foreman James Burrows read the death sentence.

"We have shared in this with you and like you, it has changed our lives forever," Burrows read from a sheet of paper. "Yesterday and today, we held hands and prayed for courage and guidance to do the right thing."

Asked after the trial about his decision, Burrows said he just couldn't talk about it.

"It's too soon," he said. "I'm just not ready. I don't even want to talk to my wife about it. It was very hard."

Friends and family of the Danielses said Friday's verdict finally gives them the closure they need, although they felt sorry for Heidler's family.

"It was the right thing, but I do feel sorry for his sister, because she's going through the same thing we are," said Connie Smith, Kim Daniels' sister. "It's hard to lose someone. But he did what he did for no reason, and I feel he needs to pay for it."

Brandy Claxton, Kim Daniels' 17-year-old daughter, worries about her sisters and brothers. Corey and one of the girls are with Kim Daniels' former foster parents. Two other girls are with Danny Daniels' sister. Gabriel, who was 10 months old when the Danielses were killed, has been adopted out of state.

"The only thing that keeps me sane is that the day before (she was murdered) I saw her and said, 'I love you,'" Claxton said. "That's what keeps me sane."

Defense lawyers had tried all morning to raise sympathy and compassion for Heidler, whom they characterized as a mentally ill man with a troubled childhood who needed help rather than a death sentence.

But the testimony of Heidler's mother, sister, junior high school teacher, foster mother, a psychologist and several social workers did not overcome the gruesome crime.

Heidler's sister, Lisa Heidler Aguilar, was the last witness to testify for the jury.

"I don't want them to kill my brother," said the 24-year-old mother of three, breaking into tears on the stand.

Aguilar, who works with her husband as a migrant worker, testified that both her father and her stepfather had been alcoholics over the years, but neither had ever abused Heidler. She denied that black magic or voodoo had ever been practiced in her mother's household, as other witnesses have testified.

A worker from the Department of Family and Children Services testified that Heidler's mother, Mary Moseley, had threatened to cast spells on the child protective services workers who visited her home and checked up on her children. One spoke of Moseley leaving a voodoo doll with a pin in it in her office a decade ago.

Heidler, who had open-heart surgery when he was 4 years old, was placed in two foster homes because of poor supervision by his mother, the DFACS workers said.

He had imaginary friends, a mouse that he carried around in his hand, said Sylvia Boatright, Heidler's foster mother when he was 11. He called her Boatright Grandma. She learned to love him, she said.

"All he'd ever say is 'come on lil' mouse, come on lil' mouse,' " said Boatright, who lives in Alma. "Scotty was also afraid of the dark. He was afraid a knife would come through the ceiling and cut him."

Later, when he returned to his mother, he attended a school in Baxley for children with learning disabilities. He mutilated himself by picking at his skin until he bled, testified Marilyn Dryden, his teacher at the time.

One time, Heidler didn't come to school.

"So I rode over with my supervisor and we stood outside his door and sang, 'You Are my Sunshine,' and that got him up and he came out," Dryden said. "He came to school. He had a big smile on his face."

DFACS workers said by this time Heidler was a troubled young man in need of some help. He tried to commit suicide a number of times, mutilated himself and landed at Georgia Regional Hospital twice for mental problems—once when he was 11 and another time when he was 13.

James Maish, a forensic psychologist from Augusta, testified Friday that Heidler suffered from a severe case of borderline personality disorder. He said Heidler had eight of the nine symptoms, including suicide attempts, outbursts of uncontrolled anger and "frantic efforts to avoid real or imagined abandonment."

About 2 percent of the population suffers from the

disorder and 10 percent of those kill themselves.

His diagnosis was not different from the other three court-appointed mental health experts who examined Heidler. But he took it a step further, saying Heidler had no control over his actions because of his genetic disposition.

"Originally, we thought that every personality disorder was from a bad environment growing up," Maish said. "In other words, whatever was going to happen, you'd lose the battle by age 6."

"In either case, nurture or nature, did Scotty Heidler have any control over this?" asked defense lawyer Michael Garrett.

"No, he can't control that," Maish said. "It's something you're born with."

Moseley, Heidler's mother, acknowledged her son was troubled. But she continued to pledge his innocence on the stand Friday.

"I raised Scotty," she said. "Scotty did not do that murder."

"Even though a jury found him guilty of it?" asked District Attorney Richard Malone.

Moseley shook her head.

"He loved that family. He cared for that family. My family cared for that family," she said. "He's not that kind of person. You've got to know him to know if he's capable of that."

The evidence against Heidler—a confession, fingerprints at the scene, DNA evidence and witnesses—was so strong that defense lawyers Michael Garrett and Kathy Palmer did not try to put up a defense.

They did try to save his life, though.

"About 350 years ago, our ancestors would know what to do about Scotty Heidler, they'd say 'He's possessed by the devil, let's burn him,'" Garrett said. "It's the supreme irony that here we are in 1999 at the end of the third millennium, and we have the same mentally ill person and you are asking to burn him, literally. Have we not progressed as a civilization any farther than that?"

Malone, however, pointed out that Heidler knew right from wrong and was responsible for his own actions.

"What happened in that house is consummate evil," Malone said. "Jerry Scott Heidler had a terrible child-hood, yes, but when are we going to expect him to take responsibility for his actions?"

Writers' Workshop

Talking Points

1) Study the first three paragraphs and count the number of words in each. How does this draw in the reader? How does it affect the pacing of the story?

2) The story ends with a question: "But when are we going to expect him to take responsibility for his actions?" Does this summarize the story? What impact did it have on you as a reader? Is it an effective conclusion?

3) How does the tone of the story reflect the life-and-death decision rendered by the jury? Is it appropriate?

Assignment Desk

1) The story raises the issue of appropriate treatment for those with personality disorders. Research and write a story explaining personality disorders and find others who have been diagnosed with this kind of illness. How are they treated in your community?

2) Do you consider the lead for this story a hard-news lead? Rewrite the lead taking a different approach.

A conversation with
Leonora LaPeter

KAREN BROWN DUNLAP: The deadline writing award is special because some say good deadline writing is a lost skill. How do you write compelling reports when the clock is ticking?

LEONORA LaPETER: A big part of deadline writing is gathering as many details and as much information as possible. The more information you have, the more well-versed you are and the easier it is to write. When you don't know the answers to questions, your writing gets bogged down.

I hate to admit this, but I don't think I was known for deadline writing. I'm known for doing in-depth reporting or in-depth stories, but somewhere along the line, I guess I developed the ability to put it all together fast. The key is knowing your information, knowing where you're going, knowing your focus, asking "What's the point? What do I want to say?" I think that helps.

Tell me how you came to do this story.

Well, I had the court beat. Prior to the trial, this story had been covered by some regional reporters at my paper who had done a really good job. Several trials were going on at the time, so we talked about which one I should cover and we decided this was pretty much the biggest trial.

How did you prepare for the trial?

I looked at all the stories on it in the clip file. I then called everybody who we had talked to before, or as many people as I could reach, while also doing an advance story.

When you called them, what did you say?

I would just try to chat with them. I'd ask, "Are you going to the trial?" I would try to get to know them. Then I'd ask, "How've things been going? What's been happening?" I also talked to lawyers for both sides.

What were your plans for covering the trial and getting the story in on deadline?

The second I walked into the courtroom I started to think about how I was going to write it. I was thinking, "Where's my lead? How am I going to use that? Who am I going to talk to during the breaks?" I tried to talk to as many people as I could during the breaks because there were a lot of different people in the courtroom from the families. There were probably two dozen people who came and went, some of them just for a day, others for the whole trial. I wanted to get to know all of them, not that I was going to use all that information, but you never know what you're going to find. I've gotten information from the weirdest places during my career, and so I think it's important to talk to everybody.

At the same time I didn't want to appear to be a bulldog running at them. I would try to be casual at first, and then once we developed a relationship, once we talked a little bit, I was able to start quoting them.

Were there competitors in the courtroom?

Yes. The *Atlanta Journal-Constitution*, the *Macon Telegraph*, two TV stations, and a couple of smaller papers from the region.

How did the competition affect your work?

Maybe it made me better. In fact, I'm sure it did. It made me want my coverage to be the best. I don't like running where all the other reporters are running. I like to find somebody who's not being interviewed by everybody else.

While you were doing a separate interview, how did you avoid missing something the pack covered?

I was concerned about that, so I always had my eye on

them. I remember that I saw one reporter disappear out a door and I knew that the mother of the accused was out there. I had already talked to her, so I wasn't as concerned; but I was watching what was going on.

Earlier you said that when you walked into the courtroom, you started thinking about how to report the story. What were you looking for and what were you thinking throughout the trial?

I was looking for that moment that's different, for something that starts my story. I was looking for details, for things that people were doing that might be a detail in the story. Obviously, my lead changed several times throughout the day. And the reverse happened. Sometimes nothing was coming. The lead was not there. And then something struck me. I remember several times when that happened. I would go to the back of the courtroom with the computer and get it down, all the while keeping my eyes on the courtroom.

How do you know when you have the right angle?

A scene would take place or something would be said and I would know that was what I needed. Like the "tap, tap, tap" in the first day's story. That guy got up on the stand and I thought, "There it is." And then in the second story when that woman bowed her head and her friend whispered to her in the courtroom. I was sitting right behind them and could hear everything. I thought, "There it is. There's my scene."

How did you develop that sense as a writer?

It's developed over years. I used to struggle with leads, with how to get into the story. I really did. The lead is the part that attracts people, that keeps them, that moves them. Obviously, the writing of the whole story is important, too, but the lead is so important to me.

Trace the course of a day of covering the trial. What time did you start? What time was your deadline?

The trial would start around 8:30 every day. The paper wanted the story in by 8 in the evening, but I could go until 9 if the events were really late.

How did you pace yourself to finish the story on deadline?

The days were very hectic. I was racing. I sat there trying to get all these details and take notes and watch everybody. Then during the breaks I had all my time devoted to trying to get people to talk with me, especially toward the end of the day. So I would be thinking of which people I needed to talk with during the break. If ideas came to me, I would try to maybe write a few sentences in the computer, trying to formulate my lead. On two days, I started trying to write the story in the back of the courtroom.

Then I would race back to my hotel room. My husband, Brian LaPeter, is a photographer at the paper and he was with me covering the trial. We had two computers but mine was the only one that could send material back to the newspaper. So he would start doing what he had to do, and I would write until he needed to transmit photos. Then we would transfer the story to his computer. Later, we'd move the story back to my computer to send it.

How did you write the story? Did you draft the story during the trial most days and polish it in the hotel room?

On the first day, I had written the first couple of paragraphs in the courtroom. The rest was written back in the hotel.

I wanted to write in a conversational tone. I was trying to give it the drama of the trial. Obviously, the material was incredible. And obviously I was moved by it all. It was an intense experience and I guess that came out in my writing. I knew I had this fast deadline. I knew I had to deal with things like the two computers. And I wanted to phone my daughter before she went to bed at night, so I was trying to beat that clock, too.

It was very chaotic in the hotel room.

How did you map the stories?

Well, it depended on the day. On the first day, I knew there would be opening statements and then maybe two or three witnesses. So I immediately thought I had to have something from the opening—something from the prosecution and something from the defense—and then the witnesses. Once I decided to lead with the man describing the tap, the natural next part was to go to the cop. He had this really powerful story. It's very rare that you have a cop who gets up on the stand and doesn't say stuff like, "Officers responded to the scene." He was a really good witness, and I wanted to take advantage of that.

Then the prosecutor's quote was a great way of bringing it home to the reader. And I had to provide the defense's side. That's how I thought of the story.

Did you do much editing of the story?

I think I went over it and worked it a little bit. I don't know how much I did, because this one pretty much came to me. But every time I write a story I try to read over it and make changes because you never know what may have gotten in the draft.

Did you plan to end early enough to edit the story?

I didn't pace myself that way. It flowed this particular night and I was able to have the time to do that. Actually, I did it every single night. I would read over everything.

The stories included a lot of people. How did you decide which ones to write about and which ones to leave out?

I look for the ones who advance the story. If two people said something that was similar, I wouldn't use both those people. I didn't use a lot of the gun experts and other officials. I tried to use the people who gave details and told you what happened and did it well.

Let me try something that I hear from my friends

who teach television and radio reporters. They say the reporter should tell the facts, and let the sources tell about the feelings. Is that what you're saying?

Yes. I would say that I used the people to move the story along and provide the emotional quotient in this story.

I was struck by Connie Smith, the sister of the murdered mother, Kim Daniels. You said that during the breaks you'd walk up to people and try to be casual. What do you say to someone who has lost a loved one, and is now forced to relive the death?

I remember I had tried to reach Connie Smith over the phone and had not been able to reach her. She had friends, a family from church there, and I asked them to point her out. During one of the breaks I went up and introduced myself. That was it that first time. I just introduced myself and chit-chatted about whatever was going on at the time. Then the next time I might have started asking her questions about the case. I just went back up to her and I said, "I was wondering if I could ask you some questions," and she was fine about it.

I was a court reporter for about a year and I had to go up to all sorts of victims' families, and I really didn't like doing it. I just learned to do it in as humane a way as possible, to not be overly aggressive with them. I chit-chat a little bit at the beginning of the trial and then slowly have bigger conversations as the trial goes on, then start interviewing them for quotes.

In this trial, were you ever rebuffed during the breaks when you approached someone?

Oh, yeah.

What did they say?

They would just walk away from me. They would just say, "I don't want to talk." There were several people who did that. And then I would go up to them again. Like the accused man's mother. She wouldn't talk to me at first, then she talked to me, then she wouldn't talk to me. She was going back and forth.

If somebody has walked away from you, when you approach them again, what do you say?

There was another woman that I walked up to the second time, after being turned away. I said, "I was just wondering if there was anything that you wanted to say. I wanted to provide you with an opportunity to have your say. I'm doing a newspaper article about your family member, and I'm trying to provide you with this opportunity."

What was in your notebook?

I write everything, and that's horrible. I'm really bad at that. I write too much and then at the end I've got this big notebook with way too many things. So I've learned to put big stars at certain points and to fold pages over where those big stars are. I'll write out great quotes in quotation marks. It's not a tremendously organized situation.

I'll write details. When Kim Daniels' sister was bowing her head and the other woman was whispering in her ear, I was writing that whole scene, all the little details. Obviously I didn't use all of them. I never use all of them, but I write as many details as I can.

Many writers find that when they get all the details, they're just overwhelmed. They're simply swamped. How do you avoid that?

You know, I've felt swamped and overwhelmed when I've gotten a lot of the details. However, I think it made writing easier because I knew my information. I knew what was going on. I knew what the ramifications were. I wish I could tell you that on every story I planned the whole story while I'm running back to the hotel room and it's all there in my head and it just comes out, but it doesn't. I have to pull writing out of me, too. It doesn't come easily.

Let me ask about fairness. Is it fair to say the prose-

cutors come off far better than the defenders?

You have only three of the five stories of the trial. There's one other day of defense and then one day when he's convicted. The first day is opening statements and then the prosecution begins the case. Second day is all prosecution, and then the final day is the conviction, and in that case they're trying to show you that he deserves the death penalty. They give all the evidence why he does or doesn't deserve the death penalty. I guess the stories selected for the award entry had more of the prosecution in them.

The reader who saw these stories in the newspaper saw bullets that summarized each day, headlines, and photographs. How did you work with others who helped tell the stories? I presume you worked fairly closely with the photographer, your husband. How did others help the story?

I called David Donald, my editor, every day to tell him what was happening, and he would stay at the newspaper every night and get the story that I sent. Then I would call him again in a little while and see if he had questions. As far as the photographer, who happened to be my husband, I guess we work together very well. He was only allowed to stay in one corner of the courtroom to get photos. I provided him with names. We were going back and forth. I was telling him who was who, who he needed to be taking pictures of in the courtroom, who the people were that were in my story. We had a lot of communication going on.

Did he see things that you didn't see or see them in ways that you didn't see?

He would tell me things. He would provide me with details. He got this picture of Heidler in the back of the courtroom smirking. The whole time in the courtroom the guy had this face that wouldn't move in front of the jury. He was like a statue. Then he goes back in this little room where the jury can't see him and he's got this smirk. That was kind of eerie.

Any special thoughts on how to handle the telling of a story that is very familiar to the readers?

I really tried to look for a fresh way to tell the story every single time. I tried to look at the witnesses who had never been heard from before and see what they had to say, see if I could use them to tell the story differently. I tried to get scenes from the courtroom with drama that I could use to tell the story.

Do you plan your endings?

I don't plan my endings. I've heard writers who say they have to have the ending before they have anything else, and I'm just the opposite. I'll get the lead and keep writing along, and near the end of the story, I wonder what to do. That's something I need to change. I need to be thinking about that more.

We often talk about writing as a five-step process. Good writing comes from thinking about the ideas, the reporting, the organizing, drafting, and editing. You told about your reporting, particularly your attention to details, but let's go through these steps. Where do you get good story ideas?

I get good story ideas from all different sources. A good idea comes from talking to people. It comes from looking through documents and getting little things that you then go and call about and ask some more questions about, and it turns into something. It comes from listening to people in the community. A lot of stories are just phone calls. Readers always call you with big huge problems and it sounds like they want you to solve their whole world, but sometimes what they have is a great little story.

Good stories can come from editors. They come from making connections. I did a story recently about churches and money because I picked up about five lawsuits filed by parishioners against people at churches over money. So ideas come from all different places.

The third step in the process is usually organizing.

You've talked about that a little bit. Anything else come to mind about how you organize a story before you write?

Well, it depends on the length of the story, but as a general rule, here's how I've been thinking about my stories. I think in terms of subheads. I divide up the information based on one point or section, then another section, and the next section, and then all related information goes into those sections. Sometimes in a longer story, the final printed version has subheads. I'll have a lead, a middle, and an ending under each subhead.

Do you write the subheads mentally, or do you map the story by writing a plan before writing the story?

I might make notes on the plan, but that's mostly for longer stories. For shorter stories I do think in terms of groups of information. I do follow that rule of trying to keep information together, then transitioning to the next section.

The fourth step is drafting. Some writers get bogged down while they're writing. What do you do to keep moving while you write?

I hate to admit this, but I'm one of those who feels that it's got to be right and then I move on. You know, I'm bad. It's got to be perfect. I'm horrible that way. That's why it's kind of hard for me to believe that I'd won a deadline award.

Different writers have different styles, and yours works well for you. You've already talked about how you finish the story and then edit. If you're meticulous as you write, what are you looking for when you edit?

Usually I want to tighten it. I want to polish it and get rid of some things. Sometimes I'll add a few points that I forgot, or some detail that needs to be in there. Sometimes I have to find a place for things that are required for the story.

What else would you like to add about good writing?

There's one thing that I wanted to tell you that I thought had improved my writing in recent years, and this is very strange. I've been reading books to my child and they're nursery rhymes. They have this rhythm and this pacing, and I actually believe that's improved my writing. I think that my pacing has gotten a lot better in the last couple of years.

Writers grow from reading all types of writing: poems, plays, fiction, non-fiction, and children's books. For one thing, the short sentences in children's books slow you down, while longer sentences speed us up. Learning writing tips from children's books really isn't that strange.
   Tell me about a news story that impressed you as good writing and why.

When I read Thomas French's "South of Heaven" I thought that was incredibly good writing.

"South of Heaven," a series in the *St. Petersburg Times*, **is about a year in a high school.**

Right. I was struck by all the details that French amassed about those kids. I was just riveted. He found out so much about them and was able to weave it together in this extremely compelling narrative. I read it as an out-take. I couldn't put it down until I finished it.

Who are other writers or authors who appeal to you?

I've read all sorts of different things, but in terms of writing style I really like to read Annie Proulx's *The Shipping News*. I also thought *Snow Falling on Cedars* was a wonderfully written book. I read all sorts of different newspaper writers. I try to get my hands on whatever I can.

Why are you a journalist?

When I was in college I had a really hard time figuring out what I wanted to do. I had several languages that I had learned. I was fluent in Greek, and I had studied German and French and Latin in school, and I thought, "What can I do with these languages?" I just couldn't figure it out. I thought maybe I could use them in journalism some day, so at the last minute I decided I wanted to go into journalism. I didn't have any sort of attitude about changing the world.

Now I really enjoy doing this work. I really enjoy writing stories. I enjoy talking to people and finding out about people and finding out other things. I guess I'm doing okay in it. I'm doing decently. I've found my niche and I feel like I'm doing something that I'm meant to be doing.

What did you learn about news writing in your early work?

At *The Okeechobee News*, I learned about everything, I guess. I learned how to get stories. I learned that I was able to write. I remember the first story I did. Compared to today, it's a really bad clip, but at the time they liked it, and I guess I was surprised. I remember I learned all about stories, how to gather news. And I learned to hustle.

Tell me about your development as a writer. Who helped you grow as a writer?

I've had all sorts of different editors, and I've found that editors play an incredibly big role in helping reporters develop. I've found that when an editor did not really pay attention to my copy, or just didn't really do much, I didn't really improve. And then when an editor really worked with me on it and did a lot of things and helped me, my writing was taken to a whole other level. So I have come to value editors a great deal.

In addition to generally paying attention, how have editors helped you?

I've had two different types of editors who have helped

me. The first type would mow through my copy like a Tyrannosaurus rex. That would devastate me. I would think I was horrible because they had to go through and rewrite the first eight paragraphs of my story every time. I hated it at the time, but it would make me rise to the occasion and improve my copy. I would look at my clips from before editing and after and see a difference. Some people would probably say that's a little bit too heavy handed, and I thought that at the time, but I really did improve.

The other kind of editor I've had that's really helped me has been the more subtle kind. That's my current editor. When I first started working with him, I thought he wasn't really doing much to my copy. But I suddenly realized that he was talking to me and making me change my copy, and that has really helped.

You've been an editor. What kind of editor were you?

When I first started, I would send reporters to everything, which I think is a mistake that a lot of beginning editors make. Then, as you develop, you realize you don't have to cover everything. You need to cover certain things really well.

As for the writing, I guess I was the kind who worked on copy a lot. I would change a lot of things on copy but I would always show reporters what I was doing.

How does your experience as an editor affect your reporting and writing?

I guess I learned to get to the point faster. I learned to not weave all over the place. When you look over others' copy you see what needs to be in the story and what doesn't. I learned to get to the point and be a tighter writer.

Before we end, let's return to your winning stories. What worked best about the stories for you?

I guess what worked best was the great material, the way I was able to write it in a conversational tone on deadline. I also was able to keep my eyes open in the courtroom and capture great scenes.

What caused you the biggest problems or what do you wish you had done differently?

I wished that I had gotten a little bit more of the courtroom scene into the first day's story, but it just didn't fit into the framework of what I was doing.

I wish I had not written about the prosecutor, "a portly man with an obvious passion for his case." I wish I had shown that rather than told that. And I wish I'd asked the cop what music was playing on the alarm clock radio. I was trying to do too much and there were so many things going on that I forgot to ask him.

There's one other element we didn't discuss: that's how the story affected you. You covered a trial that tells of a 10-month-old in a room with both parents murdered. You have a 2-year-old. How were your emotions affected by all of this and how did you deal with it?

I was there six days, Sunday through Saturday. I just remember I was exhausted and emotionally drained at the end of every day. Toward the end of the trial it was getting really hard to keep going.

I think I was affected strongly by the little girl who was molested. It was awful to see her describe her experience and then break down when they actually revealed that she had been molested and the other little girl had watched. Ever since I had a child, I have a much harder time dealing with stories that are about kids. Maybe that came out in my writing. It was a really tough trial to deal with. Two children were horribly killed. I guess maybe the way I dealt with it was to write about it.

The Washington Post

David Finkel
Finalist, Deadline Writing

David Finkel has been a staff writer at *The Washington Post* since 1990. He was a staff writer at the *St. Petersburg Times* from 1981 to 1990 and a staff writer at the *Tallahassee Democrat* between 1978 and 1981. Among his journalism awards are a Sigma Delta Chi award for features in 1999 for his coverage of the Kosovo conflict, a Penney-Missouri award for best feature story in 1995, and a distinguished writing award from the American Society of Newspaper Editors in 1986. He has been an ASNE finalist two other times, a Pulitzer Prize finalist three times, and his work has appeared in numerous journalism anthologies. He is a 1977 graduate of the University of Florida's College of Journalism and Communications.

Finkel goes beyond the headlines to reveal an intimate portrait of war's human cost in Kosovo. "Love in Tent 37A" tells a parable for the war: a woman choosing either to wait with her family in a refugee camp until the day they can return to Kosovo, or going to France to be with the man she loves. Under his own deadline pressure, he captures the urgency with which Vjosa Maliqi must make her heartbreaking decision.

Love in tent 37A

JUNE 9, 1999

SKOPJE, Macedonia—She awakens one more time, in a tent on a patch of land that is surrounded by barbed wire and guarded by armed police. Tent 37A, Stenkovic II Refugee Camp. That's her address. To find it, look for the 23-year-old woman with the dark blue dress and the bright blond hair who three weeks ago kissed a man for the first time in her life and now is sadder than even she believed she could ever be.

"I don't know what to do," Vjosa Maliqi is saying.

Because the man she kissed, and then kissed again, and then told she loves, has arranged to get her out of this place by bringing her to his home in France. To marry her.

And her father, whom she also loves, and whom she has never disobeyed, is telling her she cannot go. That her place is with her family. Here.

Vjosa's choice:

"If I decide to go, I'm afraid I'll lose my family," she says.

"If I don't go, I'm afraid I'll never meet him again."

The plane leaves tomorrow.

"Family or him."

In two days there will be news of a peace agreement. Not that Vjosa knows that.

What she knows is she has one day to decide.

* * *

Who would have expected love in such a place? It is hot, without shade, except beneath the brittle leaves of runty bushes or inside tents where the air feels thick. It is lines of people waiting for whatever there is to wait for, which is everything. For news. For water. For food. For doctors. For phones. For toilets that are holes in the ground. For showers that are nothing more than buckets of water heated over scraps of wood, scraps that lately have been coming from the frames of the latrines. The latrines are near the tents. The tents are staked inches apart. The stench is unavoidable. The noise is without pause. There is nowhere to hear silence, nowhere to feel alone, nowhere to find relief. Occasionally there's a bit of cloud cover and a teasing burst of wind, but the wind merely stirs up the dirt, and the dirt, in turn, covers everything, including Vjosa's dress, which is what she was wearing when the Serbs came to her door and told her family they had 10 minutes to leave, and her hair, which is turning from blond back to dark brown, a reminder of how long she has been here.

Two months.

On April 1, she was at home in Pristina, playing cards with her family.

On April 2, she was being forced onto a train so crowded with panicking people that they were pushing their way on board through the windows.

On April 3, she was in a field just inside Macedonia with 60,000 other refugees, all begging for bread and water, and all without shelter from a steady rain that was turning the field into a mixture of thick mud and raw sewage.

And on April 4, she and her family fought their way out of the field and onto a bus that delivered them to Stenkovic II, Tent 37A, where they've been since, and where, every day for two months, her father has been saying the same thing.

"We'll go home soon. And we'll stay here until we go."

And then another day comes to an end and they are still here, only 40 miles from home but living a life that feels borrowed. They live in a donated tent, and they sleep on donated blankets, and they eat donated food, and they sweep out the dirt with a donated broom, and they own nothing except what they were able to pack in 10 minutes into a single suitcase while three Serbs wearing masks and aiming rifles stood in their doorway.

Her passport. Her ID card. A toothbrush. A little bit of money. A few pieces of clothing. That's what Vjosa (VYOH-suh) thought to pack as she scrambled around the only house she ever lived in, crying from fear. And a bottle of perfume. "But it's finished now," she is saying.

She is on a plateau overlooking the camp, in a tent set up by a relief organization where people can come to write letters. This is where Vjosa works, and where she was when she met the man from France. She had been in the camp for two weeks. By then, she had stopped crying. She had gone from depression to the subset of depression that is numbness, had stopped greeting the new buses to see if anyone was from Pristina, was settling into this place, when the man asked her her name.

She, in turn, asked if he wanted some tea.

How do these things happen?

"This just happened," Vjosa says. "It's not my fault."

His name, he said, was Gilles, and he was in Stenkovic with a team of firefighters from France to help build tents. He spoke no Albanian. She spoke no French. But they both spoke some English, and that's how she learned that he was 33 and lived alone and wasn't married and had a dog, and that's how he learned that she was the daughter of a man named Aziz who, 30 years ago, when he was Vjosa's age, lived briefly in Paris.

So Gilles decided to meet Aziz Maliqi and suggest to him that his family resettle in France. Such resettlements, in fact, were what Stenkovic II was set up for, as a transit camp where people would stay only until they could be evacuated as humanitarian cases to countries such as France and England and Germany and the United States.

They shook hands. They talked. And after Gilles was gone, Aziz Maliqi, who expects his daughters to marry Albanian men, turned to Vjosa and said, "He wants you, my daughter."

So many weeks later, Vjosa can still hear him saying that, and what he said next. "He said, 'French men are no good. They are like Serbians.' So I said nothing, and I left the tent, and cried, and walked, and thought, 'Maybe it's better without this man. Too many problems.' But I can't stop. I can't stop myself. When they bring me the phone and I hear his voice, I'm so happy."

The phone. That's what their relationship is now. It went from learning names, to talking tentatively, to talking every day for hours, to a kiss late one night while they sat on the edge of the plateau overlooking the tents. "What are you doing?" she said. Which led to another kiss, which led to using the word love and then using it every time they talked, and then it was time for him to return to France. He has been back now for two weeks, but he calls his French colleagues every day, and they get in their trucks and climb the hill and bring Vjosa a mobile phone.

"My French man," she calls him.

Her family doesn't know this.

No one knows this, except a few friends and the French delegation.

She brushes the dirt off her dress. Gets up. Wanders down the hill, toward the French compound, where everyone is busy. They are packing. They are leaving tonight. Their time in Stenkovic II is done and they are taking everything away, including the phone. So there is that, too. Starting tomorrow, if she doesn't go, she won't be able to talk to Gilles at all.

"Hello, pretty girl," one of the firemen says as she approaches. He reaches in his pocket, takes out a phone, dials, hands it to her.

"Gilles?" she says. "Hello?...Fine, and you?...Are you all right?"

She listens. Whispers something. Realizes he is no longer there.

"Gilles?" she says. "Gilles?"

The line has gone dead. She redials. Dead. She gives the phone back and begins walking toward her tent.

IN THE TENTS

Her father is out front. Doing what he does. Sitting. Waiting. Sitting. Waiting. He is 54. He worked in a university registrar's office. He has a stubbled, sunburned face. He has a quiet voice. He is unfailingly polite. When he saw the three masked Serbs approaching his house, he opened the door as if they were guests. He is fiercely protective of his family. "Just to save my children," he says of why he left his house.

That was the easy decision.

But now what?

How does a man who decides everything for his family decide what they should do next, when they are living in a tent and there is no possible way he could know? How does a man act the way he is used to acting, as if there were a single best decision to make and he will steer his family to it?

So he sits. And thinks. "He thinks, he thinks, he thinks," Vjosa says. And? "Sometimes he goes out of the tent and walks." And? "Sometimes he listens to the news on the radio." And? It is news that peace may be coming closer, sometimes delivered in Albanian but other times in languages he doesn't fully understand. But he listens anyway, as do his neighbors, none of whom understands any better. They pick up what they can, and then, based on such things, they talk about what they've heard. What might happen. Where they should go. How long they should wait.

Refugee calculations.

The conversations occur every night with the neighbors to the left, five men, none of whom knows where his family is, and the neighbor to the right, who is approaching now to say that he wants to go home, but to what he isn't sure.

"Everything is destroyed," he says of the home he left behind.

"Everything is destroyed," Aziz Maliqi repeats, thinking, of course, of a different home.

He doesn't know what happened after he left.

He doesn't know when he'll be able to go back.

He just knows that his father was born in Kosovo, and died there, and that he wants to do the same, and that, "I want to live here, in the tent, just to be able to go," and that, "Every day I think we're going back, soon." And it is that last word, soon, that causes him to begin crying, which causes his wife of 28 years, Miradie, to begin crying as she sits behind him, watching him, waiting to hear what he has to say, waiting to do what he says to do, because that's the way so many Albanian families work. The father says, and that's what the family does.

Even though, in this particular family, there's so much the father doesn't know.

He doesn't know, for instance, that Gilles the French man would drive up to the plateau every morning and say, "Hello, my darling," and Vjosa would wave nonchalantly, just in case her father was watching from down below, and that she and Gilles would then spend hours together in the Post Office tent.

He doesn't know news of a peace settlement is less than two days away.

He doesn't know that Gilles, when he went back

home, began making calls about the humanitarian evacuation flights, and that yesterday someone from the
French embassy came to the camp and told Vjosa that
she and her family would be put on the next plane to
France. Which is the one leaving tomorrow.

THE LIST

"Gilles?"

She is back up on the plateau. The French have
brought her the phone. It is 5:30 p.m.

"…The list is not up…"

"…No. The list is not…"

"…Do you understand me?"

"…Yes, but…"

"…Yes. Yes, my love."

"…Yes, Gilles, I'm here…"

"…Gilles?"

The line is dead.

She waits for the phone to ring.

Oblivious to the sound of stapling a few yards away.

Oblivious to the sight of her younger sister, Arieta,
squeezed in the middle of a suddenly formed crowd,
looking at the bulletin board and now running toward
her, shouting:

"Vjosa! France! Vjosa! France!"

But now her sister is hugging her, and now she
knows the list of tomorrow's evacuees is up, and now
the phone is ringing, and now she is saying, "My name
is on the list…Don't worry…Yes, yes, yes, yes…Yes, I
am sure, don't worry, I will do everything, don't worry,"
and now she is looking at Line 13 on the list, which
says, "Maliqi, Aziz, 37A," and now, scared, truly scared
of the gentle man who has decided everything in her life
so far, she is going down the hill to ask Maliqi, Aziz,
37A, if they can go to France.

NIGHT THOUGHTS

"He said no."

It is later. Dark. After dinner, which was tins of chick-
en and glasses of warm milk, and a family eating in
silence. The light came from two candles, burning low
to the ground in the center of the tent, casting exaggerat-
ed shadows on the white canvas walls. A father on one

wall. A daughter on another. The tent flaps were down. The radio was on. No news. Just soft music. Vjosa excused herself. She ducked through the tent flap, and as she did a sudden wind gust coated her anew with dirt, and then, without warning, every light encircling the camp went out, and from every direction came the eerie response of thousands of unseen people whistling. Into such noises and darkness went a silhouette, walking along a pitted dirt path, not even slowing down. "I know this road," she said. "With my eyes closed, I know this road by now," and she kept walking, and hours later is walking still.

Thinking, thinking, thinking.

"Everybody comes here to go away, and my father doesn't go," she says.

"I'm going to break the heart of my French man. I'm going to be with my father, but it will never be the same as before," she says.

"Why does he not let me go to see what life is?" she says.

"For two months, I've not slept in a bed," she says.

Long after midnight, she winds her way back to the tent. Everyone is asleep. She doesn't want to see them. But she does want to be near them. So she sits outside the tent, just outside the opening, never once looking inside, until sunup, and leaves before they awaken.

She makes her way to the center of the camp where a bus is being loaded for an evacuation flight to Sweden. The bus is full, and it is ringed by people here to say goodbye. Women are crying. Men are crying. This is what happens every day. The buses go to the airport, and the refugees disappear. On the left side of the bus, third seat back, is a friend Vjosa has made here, whom she confides in, who is leaving with her family, and she is crying, too, and so is Vjosa. The bus engine rumbles to life, and Vjosa's friend uses these last moments to draw letters onto the window with her finger, a final message. "Go to France," she writes, and the bus leaves, and it is 9 a.m., and Vjosa has three hours left to decide.

She goes back up to the hill and into the Post Office tent and sits in a chair in a corner.

"It's impossible. If I go, maybe my father will die. I've never been out of my country. I've never been more than two days out of my house."

Refugee calculations.

"If I marry an Albanian boy, maybe he'll be like my father. It's hard to be an Albanian woman. You have to wake up early. To make breakfast. To make coffee. To do everything. And the husband, he does his job and sits down."

Outside the tent is a water truck, and behind the truck is a line of people with plastic jugs, hoping to catch any overflow.

"I'm going to talk to my father now, and I'm going to be angry, and I'm going to be strong, and I'm going to say, 'Take your clothes and come with me,' and he's going to say no, and I'm going to say, 'You are old, and I'm going to do this,' and I'll promise him I'll come back to Kosovo."

Outside the tent are more tents, tents that are coffee bars, tents that are schoolrooms, tents next to tents next to tents.

"Maybe he's going to ask me, 'Are you going to come back to Kosovo with your French man?' 'Yes, father, if you want me to.'

"Maybe he's going to say, 'Okay, my daughter, go alone. Find your future. But if you do something bad, don't come to me.'

"Maybe he's going to say, 'Sit down and shut up your mouth.'"

It's 10 o'clock.

"I think, I think, I think, I think better is to go."

Ten thirty.

"But maybe I change my mind. Maybe I stay here."

Eleven.

"In two months, look what's happened to my life," she says, and down the hill she goes. Past the two-hour-long line for the phones. Past the stinking latrines. Past a tent where bath water is being heated over a fire made from cardboard. Past a tent where two boys have just had their heads shaved because of lice. Past a tent where a woman is sweeping the dirt off her donated blankets. Past a tent where a little boy is rolling a donated toy truck over the bare chest of a man who is looking up at the cloudless blue sky. Past a tent where the three people inside are doing nothing at all, which is next to a tent where the eight people inside are doing nothing at all. Past 50A and 45A and 40A, and on toward 37A, where, earlier in the morning, unknown to Vjosa, a man was sitting out front, alone, in the spot where his daughter had been the night before, with his head in his hands.

LIKE A BIRD

While in France, a man with a dead father, a distant mother, no brothers or sisters and an empty house wonders if a woman will leave a refugee camp for him.

He calls the police station at the airport in Skopje. No, he is told, the plane hasn't left yet.

Noon.

And here comes Vjosa, out of the tent, purse over her shoulder, shoes freshly wiped clean.

Followed by no one.

"I'm going," she says. "Alone."

She walks toward a bus that, like everything else in this place, looks like it's sagging.

"My father said, 'If you want to go, go.' My mother cried. My father said, 'Let go. She's never going to be my daughter again.'"

There are 53 seats on the bus, six of which are for the Maliqi family, five of which will remain empty.

Except here comes Vjosa's mother, and here come her sisters, and here comes her brother, toward the bus.

"Don't go," the brother says.

But she's going.

"Don't go," he says again.

And she is wondering: Where is her father?

In the tent, dreaming of being in Kosovo? Making his way once again in his mind to a house that may or may not even exist any more?

It doesn't matter.

She has decided.

"My heart," she says of how she decided.

She puts her hands over her chest.

"I'm so happy," she says. "I'm like a bird now," and maybe she is, but as she leaves this place where she has been for two months, away from her mother and brother and sisters who remain watching behind the armed guards and barbed wire, she doesn't seem happy at all.

"If you want to go, go."

That's what she is thinking of. Not of the man ahead of her but of the one behind her, and of his last words, and of his anger.

"She's never going to be my daughter again."

Those were his last words, and his voice is never loud, but it is loud now, in her ears, and now she is crying, and now she is at the airport, and now she is walking toward the plane, and now a policeman is looking at her, at her blue dress, at her blond hair.

"Vjosa?" he says.

"Yes?" she says.

He motions her to follow him. He leads her to the police station. To a desk. To a phone. There's a call. For her.

"Hello?" she says.

"Vjosa."

The voice goes right through her.

"I love you," he says.

"Come back," he says.

"No, father," she says, and she hangs up the phone, and gets on the plane, and goes to the other man in France.

FALLOUT

Who is waiting for her, as he said he would be.

Who is crying because he didn't think she would come.

Who sees that she is shivering, and listens as she says that she is frightened, that she has made a mistake, that she wants to go back.

Who hugs her and says he will take care of her.

Who takes her to a temporary refugee center where she will wait for her papers, a place that has a shower and a bed and electricity and a door that closes, allowing her, for the first time in two months, to be alone.

Who gives her a ring.

"For you, my love," he says.

And now she is the one crying.

And meanwhile, at Stenkovic II, Aziz Maliqi, who knows none of this, is the one with his hands over his chest, saying, "My heart."

He is having a heart attack.

He is on a stretcher.

He is being taken to the dirt-coated tent that is the hospital.

AFTERMATH

Four days later.

This past Monday.

"I begged her," Aziz is saying.

He is still in the hospital. His breathing is better. His temperature is better. His heart, according to the doctors, is better, though damaged. So many things collapse in this part of the world. Peace talks. Daily hopes. Human hearts.

"But she left," he says with a sigh.

She left, and he had a heart attack, and now, as far as he's concerned, she is gone for good.

"All the time," he says, of whether he has thought about her since she left. He turns away, begins to cry, covers his eyes.

"Never," he says, of when he will talk to her again.

"She was my first child. I loved her very much," he says, as if she is dead, and in France, his daughter is crying too because of a phone call she received from her sister.

"Violetta!" she said, and there was a pause because Violetta didn't know what to say.

Should she tell Vjosa about what happened to their father after she left?

Should she describe how sick he is? How angry he is? How hurt he is? How sad he is? How, when someone mentions Vjosa's name, the pain in his chest is so sudden and severe that he gasps?

Should she explain that the family has been forbidden from ever speaking to Vjosa again? That she shouldn't even be making this call? That when they go back to Kosovo—and they will go back because Aziz says they will—that Vjosa won't be welcome there?

"He is sick," she finally said. "His heart. He is not doing well."

"Violetta," Vjosa said.

"You did something very bad," Violetta went on.

"Violetta, tell father he must be strong," Vjosa said.

"You are not my sister," Violetta said, hanging up, and in France a woman with a bed and a shower and a ring and hope and an address that is no longer Tent 37A makes another choice, this time of what to believe.

"My sister, she's lying," she says.

"I know my father's okay.

"And I know I'm going to be happy."

Newsday

Hugo Kugiya
Finalist, Deadline Writing

Hugo Kugiya has been a reporter at *Newsday* since 1998, covering transportation as well as general news and features. He writes for the Long Island desk, and occasionally the national and foreign desks. He came to *Newsday* from *The Seattle Times*, where he worked for three departments in almost nine years. He started at the *Times* as a sportswriter, covering the NBA, college football and basketball, and high school sports. After leaving sports, he joined the staff of the *Times*'s Sunday magazine to write about consumer culture, before joining the metro desk as an enterprise reporter. Kugiya began his career as a sportswriter, writing for two newspapers in Florida, the Fort Lauderdale *Sun-Sentinel* and *The Orlando Sentinel*.

Traveling at the last minute from New York to Turkey, Kugiya overcame logistical problems and language barriers to record the physical and emotional devastation of a country shattered by an earthquake that killed 20,000. His writing shows the power of words to bring readers on an unforgettable journey as one man returns to Turkey after his father's death in the earthquake.

Living on memory

AUGUST 30, 1999

DERINCE, Turkey—The son honored his mother's request to save the tea kettles, the steel cooking pots and the silver serving platter, all bent into liquid shapes, twisted beyond usefulness.

"Look at these," said Ali Gunhan, carefully holding some of what he could recover from his father's destroyed apartment building. "You can't use these anymore. But my mother, she wants these things. I don't want to hurt her feelings. Maybe she will keep them for a little while, then she will throw them away."

Almost two weeks after an earthquake destroyed or damaged most of his boyhood village, Gunhan is grateful for even the simplest of profitable assignments.

He also found unbroken some bright orange dishes made of glass, sunglasses, a candle holder and a nearly complete set of china, loading them into a cardboard box. He left behind what clothing he found, belonging to his dead father. Not knowing what to do with them, he burned them.

"No one is going to use them," he said.

Most of Derince's residents are homeless, living without humor, guided by only a vague sense of purpose. The urgent euphoria of having survived has been replaced by boredom, a weariness caused by a loss of sleep, and an agonizing uncertainty at what awaits them in the coming months.

"We will stay in our tents for a few more weeks," Gunhan said. "Then, I don't know. Nobody knows."

Turkey has made a national mission of rebuilding the towns felled by earthquakes. Taxes on cellular phones, cigarettes and fuel have been proposed, as have encampments of temporary bungalows. But confidence in the government is flimsy.

Even the thousands of canvas tents provided by the Red Crescent have been met with objections that they did not stand up well to the rain that fell throughout the week.

Gunhan plans to stay with his family for two, maybe three more weeks, before returning to Dix Hills, where he runs a small business and lives alone in a two-bedroom apartment. His family will need his income.

They had been counting on the apartment Salim Gunhan was building, the one he died in. He had gone to spend the night in the nearly completed five-story structure, which he owned, only four hours before the earthquake struck. He and four other family members were to have moved in last week. Rent from the other apartment units was to provide the family with income. Now it has none. Ali's brothers are construction workers, but they have no work.

"I hope it will be OK, but I don't think so," Ali said. "It's going to be hard. But we will try. I heard the government has started already to inspect the buildings. They will tell us if it is safe to live in our house. I have not heard any promises, but they say they will come."

The Gunhans' home survived the earthquake with barely a crack, but the family cooks, eats and sleeps in three plastic-covered tents across the road from the house. They dare to go inside for only a few minutes at a time, and only in pairs. Alone, they are too afraid to enter. Only Ali is brave enough to do this.

"I wasn't here to feel the earthquake," he said. "So I am not as afraid."

The family, for now, is content to live outside, sleeping 10 to 18 per tent. Gunhan's female relatives cook all meals on a propane burner. They boil potatoes, rice and wheat, and they heat canned vegetables and soup.

"We feel like gypsies with no place to live," said his aunt Nedime Gunhan. "Of course, it's very difficult."

The family is luckier than most, with at least a structure in which to house their possessions. They have a telephone, running water (which they can use only for washing and bathing), a bathroom, and electricity to run a refrigerator and a television.

Those with no proper shelter moved into the Red Crescent tent camp in nearby Korfez. Another camp is being built by a private organization from Singapore in a pasture near Derince's cemetery. It stands mostly empty because tents have not arrived, even as a latrine and an outdoor kitchen stand ready.

"We don't have any idea when we're supposed to get tents or how many we'll have," said Steve Findlay, an American overseeing the camp. "We're hoping to put up about 200 tents."

He hopes they arrive in time for them to be useful.

The town government is similarly overwhelmed. Mustafa Mollaoglu, a member of the local parliament, said the country's interior ministry has ordered inspections of all surviving buildings but does not know when they will be completed. He guessed it may take up to three months, when winter typically begins here. He does not know for sure what the homeless will do when it becomes too cold to sleep outside.

The men of the village no longer spend their days digging for bodies. That stopped when the big machines arrived to clear away the debris. Families have buried all the dead they expect to find. Many were placed in the ground hastily in a cemetery high above the village. Away from the established gravestones is a field of saffron-tinted dirt pocked by mounds of varying lengths and heights.

The freshly buried are marked by simple wooden stakes, their names written in pencil. There was little time to dig a proper grave, so late into last week, the smell rose again. The 60 or 70 bodies are buried nearly side by side, in some cases on top of one another.

Gunhan's father is not among them. The family has a small plot where Salim Gunhan was buried next to his parents, Halim and Agca. When the family will install a gravestone for Salim Gunhan, Ali doesn't know.

For the village down the hill from the cemetery, life goes on, if only in the literal sense of the word.

The commercial center of Derince has been largely swept clear of debris from fallen buildings. Smashed cars have been taken away. Most of the streets are passable. In a barbershop across from the former town hall (it has been condemned and will be destroyed), the two chairs are occupied. It is one of the few businesses that are open. Nearby, the supermarket is doing a steady trickle of business. It was once a restaurant owned by Ali Gunhan. He cooked and sang during dinner, a talent that made him a friend to the mayor and other city officials who often ate there. The restaurant was a success, but his dream, he said, was always to live in America. He received a visa 10 years ago, moving to Brooklyn, where he was a cook in a kosher restaurant.

Now his livelihood in America is the key to his family's recovery.

Unsmiling, Gunhan watched cartoons late into Friday morning. He took them in like medicine, grateful for it if not enjoying it.

"All the television stations show nothing but earthquake, earthquake, earthquake," Gunhan said. "And the stations, they show the same thing over and over."

His appetite returned later that day for the first time in a week. He craved lahmajun, a sort of Turkish pizza, but could not find an open restaurant. More than 320 businesses were destroyed by the earthquake, and many remain closed.

Friday was the last day Gunhan spent at the wreckage of his father's apartment. He had excavated all that he was willing to risk his safety for. He tried for an album containing photos of his daughter, but he could not free it from under a broken desk.

"I'm scared to dig more," he said.

Over three days, he turned a hole the size of his foot into a small pit large enough to crawl into. He dug with only the head of a broken shovel, stopping occasionally to pray across the street where men had convened a temporary mosque.

For hours at a time, Ali foraged around the very spot of his father's death. The bloodstained bricks were proof of that.

From the wreckage, Ali recreated his father's failed escape. Salim fled through the bedroom door and became pinned in the hallway, just a few feet from his bed and the chair he had placed his trousers on. Had he gone for the window instead, he might have survived, Ali said, pointing to a large air pocket nearby.

Ali found legal papers indicating Salim Gunhan as the owner of the property. He also found a list of materials used in the construction and blueprints.

His father's telephone was undamaged, still connected to its cord. He remembered trying to call his father from New York before he knew what had become of him.

"It was ringing," Ali said. "It just kept ringing."

Near the phone, Ali found a calendar, each page corresponding to a day. His meticulous father had tended to the calendar every day. It was not so much as torn. The last day showing was the day Ali expected to see: Aug. 17, 1999.

Lessons Learned

BY HUGO KUGIYA

The best stories are often one of two types: the small, personal story within the big story, or the universal story extrapolated from the small story. In other words, the best stories either zoom in or zoom out. This seems to hold true when covering any type of news. With that in mind, I prepared to travel to Turkey for what amounted to my first foreign assignment: the 1999 earthquake that killed more than 20,000.

I was told that another reporter, through contacts at a local mosque, came upon a Long Island man who grew up in one of the villages ravaged by the quake. He was on his way back to Turkey to search for his family. I was to find him at the airport and get on his flight, scheduled to leave Kennedy Airport at 6 p.m. I was to tell his story, with the hope that it would lead to other stories. I got to the gate 20 minutes before the flight. I left New York on a few hours' notice, knowing only the basic details of the earthquake and almost nothing about Turkey.

STARTING FROM SCRATCH

I had plenty working against me. I was going to a foreign country I knew little about; I did not speak the language; I had never covered a disaster of such magnitude; I had no time to prepare; and I would have to solve logistical problems (how I would get around, where I would work) as I encountered them. The challenge, or lesson, was to remember that news is news, and reporting is reporting, and not to become overwhelmed by an unfamiliar and chaotic environment. In other words, do what you always do, follow your curiosities, ask questions any way you can, and notice everything. And although this may sound counterintuitive—relax. Take time to think.

REPORTING, WRITING, AND THINKING

Thinking a story may be the most underrated, and overlooked, aspect of good writing. Don't be so determined to write down everything in your notebook that you're not listening to what people are saying. Take time to listen, so you can respond with a thoughtful question. And before you start to write, ask yourself what the story is really about, what makes it unique and powerful. The newspaper business is about reporting facts. But it's also about constructing and conveying the truth. A good story is not simply emptying your notebook. It's presenting the most compelling facts in a way that reveals some kind of reductive truth. That doesn't always happen, of course. Sometimes the story is just about a tree that fell on a car. But if you get into the habit of thinking that way, you'll write better stories.

So remember to relax. Take time to let the facts reveal themselves, and to notice them. Take time to focus on small details. You may be writing about an entire country, but you have to do it one block at a time. In that sense, it's no different from covering local news. Not speaking the language was sometimes a benefit. Because I could not always rely on words, I noticed visual details, colors, contours, smells, facial expressions, gestures, the length of stubble on a man's chin, the stains on his pants.

THE ELEMENT OF SURPRISE

There is a rule of thumb that has often appeared in this book and one that you've no doubt often heard from colleagues: "Show, don't tell." This is a great rule but somewhat incomplete, I've sometimes thought. I've always taken the rule to mean "tell me by showing me," in other words, carefully choose what you decide to show me and do it with purpose and clarity so that when you're done showing me everything, I feel as if I've been instructed and enlightened. Help me connect the dots.

If the story is about suffering and pain, I don't need 100 images of suffering and pain to understand that it hurts. I assume it does. I might learn more from contrary images mixed in. Tell me about the smell of decaying bodies, but also tell me that when the wind shifts, the scent of pine from the hills dominates, that the pines were planted there by villagers, that they retreat there to camp and recreate during hot summer nights, and that when the quake hit, the hills were the only safe ground to sleep on. In other words, surprise me and challenge me. If I'm supposed to hate someone in a story, show me how I might like the person; and if I'm supposed to love that person, show me how I might hate them. Show me bad people doing good things, and vice versa.

BECOMING AN 'INSTANT' EXPERT

Initially I felt overwhelmed and outmanned. Some newspapers had three or four reporters covering the quake, from the capital, from Istanbul, and from the quake zone itself. *The New York Times* had a bureau in Istanbul and presumably a reporter intimately familiar with the region. To compensate for my lack of experiential or scholarly background, I became sort of a folk anthropologist. I found no shortage of people who had an opinion of what was wrong with the country, based on their own experiences, and who were more than willing to expound on them. I met a carpenter, a gas station attendant, someone who owned an Internet café, a photographer, a college student, a truck driver. Now none of these people may be experts, but they all owned their views. Similar emotions and observations emerged. They were backed up by the things I was seeing on local television and the things I learned from Ali Gunham's family.

I was helped by the fact that English is spoken by a large number of Turks. I hired translators, which is to say, anybody who spoke English and Turkish. I kindly asked an English-speaking hotel concierge to read and translate stories that ran in the Turkish papers. I met American doctors, paramedics, and military officers who were in Turkey to help quake victims. They were useful in getting some information, and there was a temptation to stick with them because they spoke English. But the real story belonged to the Turks.

REPORTING WITH CONTEXT,
WRITING WITH AUTHORITY

I took whatever information I could get, and before too long I noticed an understanding was starting to emerge. I could now put the earthquake into context of the larger issues that consumed Turkey prior to the quake: the Kurdish rebellion and the intense ethnic tension between Turks and the Kurds; the clash between traditional Muslim values and those of the emerging secular society; the desire of many to catch up with the rest of the Western world by creating a civil infrastructure able to, for instance, respond to a major earthquake; resentment of the military-run government; the desire of Turkey to join the European Union, amid rampant inflation; and an exodus from Turkey's heartland into its city, a journey undertaken by rural Turks in search of a more reliable way to make a living.

All of these things came to be relevant in the earthquake's aftermath and I could write about them as I surveyed the damage. The eastern flight created overnight suburbs, much of which was hastily built on shifting earth, for reasons of profit and necessity. To describe the damage, the rows of fallen buildings and the piles of crushed bodies, it made more sense if you understood there was a pressure to build high, and to build fast and cheap to house the migrating Turks. Many of these people bought their apartments because real estate was one of the few safe investments in a country whose inflation was out of control. It wasn't until I understood the country's larger problems that I could fully appreciate the impact of the quake.

FINDING OTHER STORIES

After the quake, nationalistic hatred between Turkey and Greece was set aside as Greek doctors helped quake victims. Even the Kurdish issue seemed small by comparison. Once Ali accounted for his immediate family, he began to learn of what had happened to distant relatives. One distant cousin, it turned out, died with her entire family on the eve of her wedding to a Kurdish boy. The girl's Muslim family was once highly opposed to the union. Only after she ran away and threatened to kill herself did they relent. Within the story of the earthquake was a modern tale of another Romeo and Juliet.

Their story led me to the seacoast town of Golcuk, where the couple lived. Part of the town was still submerged in water, the result of a giant wave that followed the quake and never receded. So I got yet another story, one that was largely missed by initial coverage of the quake. The lesson here is to chase every rumor and, while doing interviews, keep your ears and eyes open for other stories. If you hear old men whispering under a tree, if you see soldiers sitting on a corner, ask what they're talking about. It may be nothing, or it may be your next story.

THE FINAL STORY

"Living on Memory" was in some ways the epilogue to the story of Ali's family, and in some ways the digested conclusion of more than a week spent covering the earthquake. Up until then, all the stories had been about coping with death. "Living on Memory" was about dealing with the consequences of surviving. It might not have been the story with the most detail or the most context, but it was compelling because it was about the ordinary things: about craving your favorite food, about watching TV late at night, about getting a haircut, all while the thin piece of plastic served as the roof over your head. I chose to lead and end with Ali's task of salvaging personal belongings because it seemed a pointless task and yet the only thing he could think of doing. It was quite an image: Ali digging through his father's fallen apartment building, standing where his father had died, risking his own safety for belongings that are of little use or value when you have no home. Already he and many others were worried about the winter. And it was still August.

These *St. Petersburg Times* team members are David Karp, Leanora Minai, Linda Gibson, Kathryn Wexler, and Steve Huettel. Also contributing were *Times* staff writers Wes Allison, Graham Brink, Jean Heller, Amy Herdy, Sharon Ginn, Joe Newman, Alicia Olazabal, David Pedreira, Scott Purks, Adam C. Smith, Pete Young, Times artist Don Morris, and Times researchers Caryn Baird, Kitty Bennett, John Martin, and Cathy Wos.

(*St. Petersburg Times* photo by Tony Lopez)

St. Petersburg Times
Team Deadline News Reporting

December 30, 1999, was one of those news days familiar to any newsroom on the eve of a holiday. At the *St. Petersburg Times* that afternoon, reporters and editors not on vacation were busy with New Year's Eve and Y2K stories—until word filtered in about shots fired in the lobby of a hotel in Tampa. Minutes later, police scanners started squawking about another shooting elsewhere in the city, this one during a carjacking. It was shortly after 3 p.m. Over the next hours, reporters, editors, photographers, and news researchers in the paper's Tampa bureau, aided by colleagues in the main newsroom in St. Petersburg, had to overcome a series of daunting hurdles to get the story. The isolated hotel could be reached by only one road and police quickly sealed it off. Dispatchers initially discounted the shooting report. It was 11 p.m. before officials would confirm the names of the suspect and his victims. Aggressive street reporting, creative database searching, and constant communication between reporters and editors, along with a newsroom culture committed to local reporting and narrative writing, enabled the paper to beat these odds.

The result: a dramatic, detail-rich package of stories about the moments of horror that left five people dead, as well as a profile of the accused shooter—and the Jesse Laventhol Prize for deadline reporting by a team.

—Christopher Scanlan

Gunman kills 5; worker's rampage spills from hotel

DECEMBER 31, 1999

TAMPA—Beside the pool, a man lay shot to death, draped over a blue lounge chair. At the rear of the hotel, near the employees' entrance, lay two more bodies, sprawled in front of a minivan. In the hotel's lobby, near the registration desk, was another body. Elsewhere in the hotel were three more people, shot but still alive.

The stunning scene unfolded in the space of just a few minutes Thursday afternoon at the Radisson Bay Harbor Hotel on Courtney Campbell Parkway.

The dead and the injured were all hotel workers— and so was the gunman, Tampa police said. They identified him as Silvio Izquierdo-Leyva, a 36-year-old refugee from Cuba who had worked at the hotel for only a couple of months.

A fifth person would die before one of Tampa's most tragic days was over.

After the gunman fled the hotel in a stolen car, he abandoned it near West Tampa's famous La Teresita restaurant. He shot and killed a motorist who refused to give up her car, police said. Then he stole another car— after thanking the driver for getting out promptly—and sped off.

Minutes later, cornered by police on a city street, the suspect gave up quietly.

Two of the wounded Radisson employees remained hospitalized late Thursday, one in critical condition; the other, serious.

Izquierdo has been charged with five counts of first-degree murder.

What had set off the killings? There was no clear answer to that question late Thursday.

Tampa police Chief Bennie Holder said at an 11 p.m. news conference that Izquierdo had refused to talk to police and was maintaining a casual demeanor.

"At this time we don't have a motive for the shooting," Holder said. "Apparently he's not concerned about what happened. He's upstairs sleeping."

Some relatives of Izquierdo's told the *Times* that during the rampage, he went after his sister-in-law, Angela Vazquez, who supervises housekeeping at the Radisson.

Vazquez and one of her daughters were in the lobby collecting their paychecks when the gunman stormed in. He fired at them but both escaped without injury.

"My uncle came in just shooting," Izquierdo's niece, Liza Izquierdo, said later. "He was chasing Mommy through the halls."

Silvio Izquierdo came to the United States from Cuba in 1995, and has no criminal record in Florida or Alabama, where he lived before coming to Tampa. Relatives said he has a daughter in Cuba and visited there a month ago, returning intent upon becoming a priest in the Santeria religion.

It appeared that only hotel workers were the gunman's targets.

Wendy Sobaski, a member of a Missouri women's college basketball team staying at the hotel, told her father that one of her teammates, Robyn Gerber, came face to face with the gunman as she tried to flee.

"He told Robyn he wasn't interested in [shooting] anyone else, the team was okay," Kenny Sobaski said.

'I THOUGHT THEY WERE PLAYING SOME GAME'

Thursday's mayhem started about 3 p.m. amid Christmas lights spread throughout the waterfront Radisson Bay Harbor Hotel. Employees were milling around the lobby preparing for the night shift to come in.

Waitress Kathy Pruniski heard sounds—Pop! Pop! Pop!—and assumed they were part of the holiday celebrations at the hotel.

"Isn't that funny, they're getting a jump on New Year's," she said to some guests.

Rafael Barrios, a bellman at the hotel, had arrived to get his paycheck when he saw men and women running out of the lobby and hiding behind cars.

"I thought they were playing some game," he said.

Diana Izquierdo, the suspect's niece, was just about to leave with her mother when the shots started.

"I thought it was firecrackers. My mom was screaming, 'Diana, come on! Come on!' " she recounted, crying and clutching her baby daughter's teddy bear.

Silvio Izquierdo saw them and began firing, said Liza Izquierdo, who spoke to her mother by telephone afterward. Police identified the weapons as a 9mm semi-automatic handgun and .38-caliber revolver.

Diana Izquierdo said she could not fathom a motive. "My uncle snapped," she said.

Rafael Barrios, 20, the bellman, pulled up in his white Honda Accord. He saw the men and women running out of the lobby and hiding behind cars. Suddenly, a man calmly stepped from the bushes, stood in front of his car and lifted a pistol.

"He pointed it at me right through the window," Barrios said.

The man didn't say a word, but his expression said everything.

"Evil—just evil in his face," Barrios said.

Barrios watched in horror as the man reloaded a clip. "My life was in his hands," Barrios said. Barrios jumped from the car and ran before the man could reload.

The man, whom Barrios recognized from housekeeping, walked back into the hotel. A few seconds later, Barrios heard more shots.

When Barrios finally went into the hotel, he saw people he worked with lying on the floor, shot.

"It's tragic. There's so many things going through my mind right now," he said.

The hotel was bustling with fans preparing for the New Year's Day Outback Bowl between Purdue University and the University of Georgia.

Carson Woods of Dayton, Ohio, said he was leaving the lobby to retrieve a bag from his car when he heard shots.

"I heard two pops and saw people running out of the hotel," said Woods, who was wearing a Purdue shirt. "I knew I had to get out of there."

Members of the women's basketball team from Missouri's Truman State University, in town for a game against Eckerd College, encountered a body as they fled a pregame meal. None of the players was injured.

Wendi Sobaski, a junior guard for the Bulldogs, told her father that as they were finishing their meal, "employees from the hotel came in and said, 'Get out! Get out!' " said Kenny Sobaski, who talked to his daughter by phone Thursday evening.

As the team heeded the warning, some members encountered a body and "took off running," Sobaski said.

'I KNEW TO GIVE HIM THE CAR'

The gunman sped away from the hotel in the Honda owned by Barrios, the bellman.

Inside a food concession stand in the parking lot next to La Teresita, restaurant owner Confesor Rodriguez saw what happened next:

The assailant, who had abandoned the Honda, aimed a nickel-plated handgun at a woman in her four-door burgundy Mercury.

"Lady, give me the car," he told her, said Rodriguez.

When the woman didn't comply, the gunman shot her through the driver's side window, Rodriguez said.

After she was shot, she put the car in reverse and began to back up.

The gunman moved on to the next car. He shot at a Jeep traveling south on Lincoln Avenue. The vehicle was hit, but the driver sped away, Rodriguez said.

"He was acting real crazy," Rodriguez said.

Next, the gunman turned to the owner of a sports utility vehicle parking in the lot. He wanted the car, but before he took it, he asked whether it was a standard or automatic transmission, Rodriguez said.

It was the owner's lucky day. The car had a stick-shift, and the gunman wasn't interested.

Just then, he saw a white Chevrolet Celebrity station wagon heading toward him on Lincoln Avenue. Inside, Angel Marteliz was heading home, listening to an afternoon radio talk show.

The gunman stepped from the curb as Marteliz came to a stop. He pointed his nickel-barreled gun at Marteliz.

"Take the car," Marteliz told the man, as he stepped out.

"Thank you," he replied.

"I knew to give him the car," Marteliz said later. "I didn't argue."

Soon after—about 3:40 p.m.—Izquierdo barged into the home of Angela Vazquez, his sister-in-law, at 3023

Green St. The house, which faces Interstate 275, was a place he had stayed off and on over the last year.

Nely Rodriguez, 16, a longtime friend of the Izquierdo family, said she was the only one at the house when Izquierdo barged through the front door.

He was dressed entirely in white, as was his custom, and had an urgency Rodriguez found unsettling. She hadn't heard a word about the shootings.

"Where everybody at?" he demanded, as Rodriguez sat on the couch, watching TV. She said she didn't know.

"He looked weird. He looked paranoid," she said.

"They in back?" he called to her, as he darted into a bedroom where he sometimes slept, now used by Angela's daughters.

When he didn't find anyone, he went to the kitchen sink and splashed water on his face.

He ran outside, then. The faucet was still running. He left the door wide open.

Rodriguez said she stood in the door frame, watching Izquierdo go toward a white station wagon. She dialed a number on the family's portable phone.

Izquierdo suddenly wheeled around.

"He looked at me. Like paranoid," Rodriguez said. "Maybe he thought I was calling the police."

But he turned around, jumped into the car and drove off. Police cruisers stopped the car a few blocks away near Spruce Street and N. MacDill Avenue. The block is next to the city's MacFarlane Park and around the corner from St. Joseph's Catholic School.

Police Chief Holder said Izquiedro was calm immediately after his arrest: "It was just like someone had been stopped for a traffic violation."

It was one of the deadliest days in Tampa's history.

In July 1983, Billy Ferry Jr. firebombed a Clair Mel Winn-Dixie grocery store, killing five people and injuring 13.

Newton Slawson murdered a family of two adults, two children and an unborn baby in Tampa in 1989.

Thursday's rampage at the Radisson brought back sharp memories of Jan. 27, 1993, when a man fired eight months earlier from the Fireman's Fund Insurance Co. office at Rocky Point walked into a cafeteria at lunch time and shot five company supervisors, killing three of them.

Paul L. Calden, 33, fled the scene and took his own life later that day with a revolver at Cliff Stephens Park in Clearwater where he often played Frisbee golf.

'OH, MY GOD, THIS IS JUST AWFUL'

Soon after Thursday's shootings at the Radisson, staffers, such as Dana Hagerman, streamed in for work. She had no idea about the shootings until she saw the mob of reporters and emergency workers.

"So that means George was in there? And Sam? Did any of the managers get hurt?" she asked, breaking into tears. "Oh, my God, this is just awful."

Guests, many barefoot and in T-shirts, wandered teary-eyed and visibly shaken. They were told it would be two hours before they could get to their rooms.

Hotel employees, paramedics and guests received counseling from the Critical Incident Stress Management Team, a group of volunteer paramedics, police and mental health counselors. They plan to meet again next week after the shock of Thursday's events have sunk in.

"A lot of guests were stepping over bodies," said Diane Fojt, director of the counseling team.

Thursday evening, relatives and family members of the victims walked out of the hotel crying and holding on to one another.

One woman wailed over and over, "Why Lord, why?"

Written by Times staff writers Steve Huettel, Linda Gibson, Kathryn Wexler, Leanora Minai, and David Karp. Also contributing were Times staff writers Wes Allison, Graham Brink, Jean Heller, Amy Herdy, Sharon Ginn, Joe Newman, Alicia Olazabal, David Pedreira, Scott Purks, Adam C. Smith, Pete Young, Times artist Don Morris, and Times researchers Caryn Baird, Kitty Bennett, John Martin, and Cathy Wos.

Writers' Workshop

Talking Points

1) This story begins with a vivid description that engages the reader, then provides key information in a chronological retelling of the events. What makes this structure effective?

2) Quotes are used for the subhead breaks in the story. Study the placement of the subheads. Are they necessary? Discuss why quotations are used for the subheads rather than headlines written by reporters or editors. Which would be more effective?

3) The difference between telling readers what happened and giving them a compelling narrative is in the use of details. Note the number of details in the story: "amid Christmas lights," "wearing a Purdue shirt," "nickel-plated handgun." Isolate as many as you can. What were their sources?

Assignment Desk

1) Rewrite the story's opening as a summary lead. List your reasons in support of each approach.

2) Count the number of official sources cited in the story and the number of witness accounts. Look for ways to incorporate more voices in your stories.

Suspect devoted to Santeria

DECEMBER 31, 1999

TAMPA—When Silvio Izquierdo-Leyva returned from a visit last month to his native Cuba, he was a changed man.

He had always been drawn to Santeria, a religion rooted in Africa with gods, spirits and sacrifices. But now, Izquierdo had embarked on a year's worth of studies to become a *Santero*, a priest of the faith.

And as such, jeans and T-shirts would no longer do, his family said.

"He must wear white," said his niece Liza Izquierdo, 16. That included even his shoes.

When, according to police, Izquierdo sprayed the Radisson Bay Harbor Hotel and the streets of Tampa with bullets Thursday, he was dressed entirely in the color of purity in Santeria lore.

The rampage left Izquierdo's family dumbfounded. Never had they seen a sign of violence, his nieces and nephews said.

And he seemed stable.

"He must have been crazy but he sure didn't seem like it," said another niece, Sheena Vazquez, 14.

Even at the West Tampa house where Izquierdo lived periodically over the last year, family members said nothing seemed to bother the man who was well over 6 feet tall and had a belly that revealed his hefty appetite.

"He was the quiet type," Liza Izquierdo said about the uncle whom they affectionately called "Kaki."

And maybe, they said Thursday night, as police tallied five dead and three wounded, the silence was the problem.

"I guess he's the type of person to hold it all in," she said quietly against the noise of cars rushing down Interstate 275, just beyond the front yard.

When he came to the U.S. several years ago, Izquierdo left behind sisters, brothers and a young daughter in Cuba. He lived for a while in Alabama, according to officials, and in Mississippi with a woman, either a girlfriend or wife, said Liza and Sheena.

Maria Col, a Catholic Social Services worker in Mobile, said Izquierdo arrived in Mobile in 1995 with a group of Cuban refugees who had been detained at the U.S. naval base at Guantanamo Bay, Cuba.

He left several months ago, said Col, who described him as a hard worker who didn't drink.

Izquierdo had a few traffic citations but no criminal record in Mobile, said officials with the Mobile Police Department. Police in Hillsborough said they couldn't find a criminal record under Izquierdo's name, either.

Liza and Sheena's father, George, who was Izquierdo's brother, died years ago. But when Izquierdo moved to Tampa, he came to live with them, their three siblings and their mother Angela Vazquez, 40.

"He always liked my mom," Liza said. "When my dad and mom got together, she said (Izquierdo) had a little crush on her."

And yet, it appears Izquierdo might have been targeting the family Thursday. Liza got a near-hysterical call from her mother Thursday afternoon that Izquierdo tried to shoot her at the Radisson hotel when she stopped by to pick up a paycheck.

He then went to their house, at 3023 Green St., looking for family members but found none home.

When Angela Izquierdo asked him to move out seven months ago, he moved into a West Tampa home with a woman he was dating. The woman, Adrianna, who was reached by phone Thursday and would not give her last name, said there weren't any problems between them, and that he never bad-mouthed the family.

Six months ago, though, he bought a gun. Adrianna said she didn't know why he got one or how, or even what kind.

When Izquierdo was handcuffed Thursday, he was carrying two firearms. One was a 9mm pistol he bought from the Floriland Mall flea market on Jan. 2, said police Chief Bennie Holder. The other, a .38-caliber revolver, was purchased from Nationwide Sports by an unknown person, he said.

But Adrianna said that Thursday morning was like any other. Izquierdo left for work at 8:30, and when she called him an hour later, everything seemed normal.

"Get the clothes ready because when I come home, we're washing them," he told her.

But at least one co-worker thought Izquierdo seemed troubled Thursday. Hotel employee Dolly Guzman, 35, said that since Izquierdo started work there two months ago, he usually was nice, if taciturn.

"He seemed weird today," said Guzman, a maid at the hotel for 13 years. "I talked to him and he didn't answer very nicely."

Guzman also said he was known to be involved in witchcraft and once refused to go to a employee party because it was against his religion.

But even to family, he didn't reveal much about his faith. Santeria is a secretive religion begun several centuries ago by West Africans enslaved in colonial Cuba. His trip to Cuba lasted 21 days—the longest allowable by visa.

Before he left, he collected numerous photos of Angela and her children and took them with him. Sheena Vazquez said she wasn't sure if they were part of a Santeria ceremony or if he just wanted to show them to family.

And despite his recent voyage and steady employment, money was always tight, family said.

"He was always calling us, asking for money," Liza Izquierdo said.

But the family wasn't bothered when he came around. On weekends, he took his bait and tackle and headed to the Courtney Campbell Parkway to fish. At home, he watched Spanish-language soap operas.

The day before Christmas, he was at Angela's house watching action and horror movies with the group, including *Rage*, *Rush Hour* and *Carrie II* at least twice.

A month earlier, Izquierdo had asked Angela if he could move back in.

She said no. She didn't want her five children to have to give up any of their bedrooms.

Izquierdo didn't bring it up again. And he didn't appear offended.

But family members still grappled with what may have triggered the rampage police say was Izquierdo's doing.

Said Sheena Vazquez, "Something must have happened that he didn't like my mom and us."

Times staff writers Wes Allison, Graham Brink, Jean Heller, Amy Herdy, Steve Huettel, Linda Gibson, Sharon Ginn, David Karp, Leanora Minai, Joe Newman, Alicia Olazabal, David Pedreira, Scott Purks, Adam C. Smith, Kathryn Wexler, Pete Young, Times artist Don Morris, and Times researchers Caryn Baird, Kitty Bennett, John Martin, and Cathy Wos contributed to these stories.

Writers' Workshop

Talking Points

1) The suspect's devotion to Santeria is a key element of the story. What is the tone of the story as it describes the suspect's faith?

2) Note the number of sources in the story. How do all these accounts contribute to the profile of the suspect?

3) This story details the events of the suspect's life, but one element is missing—the motive for the shooting. How is the mystery surrounding the motive reflected in the story?

Assignment Desk

1) Editors and reporters credit the database search as a valuable reporting tool in this story, providing addresses for and background about the suspect. How can you incorporate databases in your reporting?

2) Research Santeria and write a story about the faith and its followers.

3) Interview a news researcher or librarian about the contribution he or she makes to news stories. Write a story based on your conversation.

Motive for targeting co-workers still unknown

DECEMBER 31, 1999

TAMPA—When Silvio Izquierdo-Leyva went on his rampage Thursday, police say he targeted those he worked with every day.

Four of the five people that police said Izquierdo killed were employees of the Radisson Bay Harbor Hotel.

The fifth victim, 56-year-old Dolores Perdomo, simply got in the way of his escape. Izquierdo shot her as he was trying to steal her car, police said.

Those killed at the hotel were Eric Pedroso, 29, of 3907 N Tampa St.; Barbara Carter, 55, of 8718 Fountain Ave.; Jose R. Aguilar, 40, of 101 Newbury Avenue; and George C. Jones, 44, of 1003 E. Poinsetta Ave.

Perdomo, of 7803 Haversham Place, was killed in her car on Columbus Drive. Records show she received her first Florida driver's license two months ago.

The surviving victims are Jorge Cano, 40, who was in critical condition at St. Joseph's Hospital; Charlie Lee White, 43, who was treated for a gunshot wound to the leg and released from St. Joseph's; and Geraldine Dobson, 53, who was in surgery Thursday night for a gunshot wound to the buttocks.

One of the dead workers, Carter, had worked in housekeeping at the hotel for 15 years. Todd Hixon, a friend, told the *Times* late Thursday that Carter was sitting next to fellow employee Cesar Bustamante when Izquierdo approached and fired from point-blank range. Hixon is Bustamante's roommate.

Izquierdo turned toward Bustamante. Only 2 feet separated him from the gun, Hixon said. But the gun didn't fire. Izquierdo calmly walked away.

"There was no warning and no words said," Hixon said Bustamante told him. "There was no reason for it that we know of."

Bustamante had trained Izquierdo a couple of months ago for his job as a housekeeper. He did not seem to be outwardly hostile toward any of the other employees, Hixon said.

Hixon had visited the hotel early in the afternoon. He had brought sandwiches from Schlotzsky's Deli to eat with his friends. The housekeeping staff was in a jovial mood for they had received their paychecks a day early due to the New Year's Eve holiday. Most had just finished their shifts when the shooting started.

"Barbara was in a good mood like usual," Hixon said.

Hixon described his friend as a fun woman who could take a joke. She startled easily so Hixon and Bustamante would often leave plastic spiders lying around to see her reaction.

Carter lived in Tampa most of her life and had little family, Hixon said. Carter enjoyed collecting Elvis records and was a sucker for a good western movie and model cars.

She was planning to move to a new mobile home in the next few weeks, Hixon said.

"It's still shocking that she won't be able to do that," he said. "The whole thing doesn't make much sense."

As police worked to notify next of kin Thursday evening, frightened relatives of hotel workers scrambled for any information they could find. Many arrived at St. Joseph's Hospital, where most of the wounded were taken.

Darron Duval was at work in Bradenton when his sister and cousin frantically called him Thursday afternoon, telling him his mother, Geraldine Dobson, had been shot.

Duval jumped on the highway and drove to St. Joseph's—only to learn his mother was in surgery at Tampa General Hospital for a gunshot wound to the abdomen.

"They told me St. Joseph's," Duval said as he rushed to his car outside the wrong hospital. "I don't know anything yet. I'm going to see what's up."

Late Thursday, officials at TGH said Dobson was in serious condition.

Dobson has been a housekeeper at the Radisson Bay Harbor for a few years and enjoyed working there, Duval said. Other relatives who arrived at St. Joseph's said Dobson was engaged to White—a hotel kitchen worker who also was shot.

Dobson's sister, Vera Ward of Tampa, was frustrated that authorities didn't know Dobson's condition—or even point her to the right hospital.

"We just haven't heard any details," Ward said. "They just told me to get over to the hospital."

Meanwhile, others who had relatives working at the Radisson arrived at St. Joseph's to see if they were among the wounded.

Jessica Aviles arrived at the hospital with several members of her family after hearing her uncle, Jose Aguilar, may have been wounded. Aguilar worked in the kitchen at the hotel, Aviles said.

"The police and the hotel won't tell us anything," she said.

Police later confirmed Aguilar was one of the five people killed.

Writers' Workshop

Talking Points

1) Mark the verbs in the story. How does the word choice of such active verbs as "scrambled" and "rushed" convey the confusion surrounding the story?

2) Study how the story weaves quotes from witnesses, family members, and friends together with the details of the shootings.

3) The lead in this story repeats the information from the main story: five dead, a suspect who was an employee at the hotel. How does this story convey the information in a fresh way? Is the repetition necessary?

Assignment Desk

1) Outline the structure of this story. Rearrange the elements and rewrite it. What makes each structure effective?

2) For this story, reporters had to interview witnesses and relatives who had just discovered that their friends and family members had been shot. Discuss how you would approach such an interview.

Recalling deadline with the
St. Petersburg Times

Linda Gibson, reporter

We started hearing all this hysterical chatter on the scanners about a man down and shots fired at the Radisson Hotel, so I was sent over there. As I was leaving, there was talk on the scanners about another shooting. It was the shooter from the hotel who had hijacked a car and driven it across town. But we didn't know that at the time. We thought we had these two separate incidents. I saw a group of women huddled and crying and clutching each other in a side entrance to the hotel. I made a beeline for them, and yelled, "Do you know anything about what happened in there?" And one of them yelled back, "My uncle went crazy." My reporter's alarms started going off. They turned out to be relatives of the shooter, and they gave me his name. I called up Tampa city editor Tom Scherberger and said, "I have the name of the shooter." But I got it garbled. The correct name was Silvio Izquierdo-Leyva. The name I gave him was Silvio Leyva-Izquierdo. He passed it on to John Martin.

Deadline Tip:

Get there as quickly as you can. Get as close as you can to the scene of the action, and then look for anybody you can find who appears to know what may have gone on. If it's a disaster, they're going to look upset. Then you want to ask the very basics: "Did you see what happened? Did you hear anything?"

Linda Gibson is a reporter in the Tampa bureau of the St. Petersburg Times.

John Martin, news researcher

The day of the shooting we had a scanner alert that shots had been fired and people were down. A license plate number was being repeated by police. I was able to take the number and search in a commercial database called AutoTrack that allows us to synthesize a variety of public records information into a single report about an individual. You can start out with a bit of information, like a license plate. I pulled the name of Pedro Izquierdo-Leyva. We didn't know if Pedro Izquierdo-Leyva was a victim, a perpetrator, or the owner of a car that might have been carjacked. I was playing hunches about who this person might be and was finding very little about Pedro in Tampa other than an address in West Tampa. We sent a reporter there, but there was no one at that address. A few minutes later—and this is where Linda Gibson's role was just absolutely crucial—she found out that the shooter's first name was Silvio. She said Silvio Leyva-Izquierdo, and when I heard that, I knew we had something significant because even with the transposed last names, I was almost certain they were related in some way. I started playing around with the name in AutoTrack. I was able to pull up a home address and we were able to send Kathryn Wexler to the address and she was able to interview some family members.

It affirmed for me the value of being intertwined with the reporting process, listening to what editors are discussing, listening to what reporters are talking about, being proactive in following through on what is newsworthy. Sometimes researchers function just like journalists, having to pound, not the pavement, but at least the phone lines, to get information.

Deadline Tip:

Don't wait for editors to come to you with questions. Offer them suggestions, bearing in mind that they're trying to filter an incredible amount of information in a very short period of time. The more you can help them see clearly what's crucial and what's not, you're going to help the editors get to the heart of the story quicker and you're also going to help researchers not follow dead ends.

John Martin is a news researcher in the Tampa bureau of the St. Petersburg Times.

Kathryn Wexler, reporter

My job initially was to go to La Teresita restaurant, where one of the victims was shot in the head. I spoke to a woman whose husband's car had been carjacked. About 15 minutes later, I got a call from my editor, Tom Scherberger, who said they had an address linked to a tag number that came over the radio. I knocked but they wouldn't answer, but I saw the curtain move. I went next door to the neighbor and persuaded her just to walk me over. I made sure my notepad was put away because sometimes people will get threatened by that. I just tried to be friendly, asked if she was okay, if the family was okay, and after a few minutes I asked if I could come inside. The niece reluctantly let me in and I sat on the couch and talked to her and her friend. After about 45 minutes, I took out my notepad when they were feeling more comfortable. I find if they see me as a person first, it makes them relax enough to give me what they know. As soon as they said that (the suspected shooter) had been there that day, I knew that this was going to be an important part of the story. There are some interviews that you just can't rush. You have to let people take their time and decide to reveal themselves to you, and if that cuts into your deadline, so be it.

The editors decided I had enough compelling information to make it a separate story. I went through my notebook and highlighted quotes, then I put the notebook aside. Bill Claiborne, a veteran reporter at *The Washington Post,* once told me, "Never let your notes dictate your story. At a certain point, you must put the notebook aside and write from what you know." It forces you to analyze what you're trying to say, rather than hooking the story on a couple of good quotes and filling in the spaces. It makes for a better story.

Deadline Tip:

Take in everything you can. Don't rush it. Don't let the hype overtake you. Let people reveal their story slowly.

Kathryn Wexler is a police reporter in the Tampa bureau of the St. Petersburg Times.

Leanora Minai, reporter

By the time I got there, most of the hotel was taped off and there was a pack of journalists waiting. I tried to stake out my own area. I made my way to the back of the hotel. I was trying to get to the pool, but I got chased off. I ended up talking to a couple of waitresses. One was by the pool serving drinks and she heard something like gunshots. She commented to one of the guests that, "Oh, people must be getting started early on the holidays." And when she went inside, the manager of the restaurant was running out toward her saying, "Get the f--- out of here, get the f--- out of here!" and the shooter was behind him and they ended up running out. She basically ran for her life. I don't think I would have gotten that if I was standing with the 20 other people. I didn't have a laptop, so they asked me to file over the telephone. I sat down on the curb and ripped out my notes and then used my notebook as my computer and by hand wrote anecdotes about the waitresses and the guy who had the gun pointed at him through the windshield. When I called back, I wasn't fumbling through my notes. I actually had paragraphs written out.

Deadline Tip:

"Anyone see it happen?" If I go to a fire or a shooting, I just start blurting out that question with my notebook out. It's what a cop would do, but you've got your notebook. Then you have witnesses who can tell the story. Most people who aren't involved are willing to talk.

Leanora Minai is a police reporter for the St. Petersburg Times.

David Karp, reporter

I was at the courthouse looking up lawsuits on a candidate, and I got a page at about 5 o'clock. As I was driving to the office, I got another page with a message saying to go to La Teresita. When I pulled in, there was already a large crowd of people. I went up to the first person I saw that seemed sort of animated, and he said there was somebody inside who saw the shooting. He was very shaken up. I remember thinking that this was going to be my one really strong interview, and I had to make sure to get the picture right because it was already pretty late in the day. I just listened to him, and I remember asking him a lot of very specific questions that were designed both to help me picture the scene but also help him get a firmer grasp on his memory of details. "Were his windows rolled down? Did he have a tape in the cassette player? What did he have in his back seat? Was he wearing a seat belt? Was he wearing the same clothes he had on? What radio station was he listening to? What song was playing? Was he smoking? Did he have anything hanging from the rearview mirror?"

At one point he gave me this look as if to say, "Why are you asking me that question?" I wanted a story, and stories require a little bit more patience. I thought to myself, "I'm showing up late in a way. Since I'm not going to get any sort of exclusive, I might as well write a better story than the other guy."

Deadline Tip:

Be decent to people. Don't be part of the media whore pack. Listen and watch. Things will unfold before you. Be sure to get it all down.

David Karp is a reporter in the Tampa bureau of the St. Petersburg Times.

Steve Huettel, reporter

I ended up being the rewrite person. They told me around 7 that night that I had to have my draft in by 10. At about 8 some editor yelled over, "What do you need? Two hundred or 250 lines?" I remember thinking it takes me two days to write that much. Fortunately, a lot of the feeds came in very clean and very good. I did smooth out the transitions a little bit, but a lot of it was just cut-and-paste type work, then going back to smooth it out. So after a top, which brought readers into the scene, and then a "nut graph," which explained how many had died and the fact that this was one of the biggest mass killings in the city of Tampa, then back to the beginning and going chronologically and taking people through. You had multiple scenes and various witnesses who had seen things at different times. I tried to keep it chronological. I thought it would confuse readers if we went back and forth. As I wrote, I just kept filing it back into the system because Neville Green, the managing editor, was doing the rewrite on my work. He reworked my lead and made some wonderful improvements to the draft.

I have always had the attitude that if an editor could take the story that I wrote and make it better, that's the best of all worlds. There were probably 14 reporters working on this and maybe half a dozen photographers and God knows how many people on the desk. I was a cog in the machine. I don't think there's any way one writer or editor can say, "This is my story. I don't want you to change anything," like you might on a daily story or a project. I admit the next day I said, "Gee that's not the way I wrote it," but after getting past the ego thing, I looked at it and said, "This is better," because a lot of people who were very talented had a hand in it after I let go.

Deadline Tip:

Don't panic. You can do it. Take all the fears and leave them behind you and write. It's just going to get in your way if you spend too much time worrying about it. Don't worry about making it perfect.

Steve Huettel is a reporter in the Tampa bureau of the St. Petersburg Times.

Jennifer Orsi, assistant metro editor

When this story broke, Rob Hooker, our assistant managing editor for metro, realized that the Tampa bureau staffers were going to have a lot of work on their hands. They had a ton of reporters attacking the story, their night city editor was on vacation, Neville Green and

Tom Scherberger were very, very busy, and so Rob thought it might be helpful to have another editor in Tampa. You have all this reporting, all this news breaking, and it's easy to just keep reporting, but we had a deadline closing in on us quite fast and the longer we waited to start writing, the more hurried the writing was going to be and the less polished the finished product was going to be. So at one point I looked over and saw that Steve Huettel was still making phone calls and trying to check on a couple of things, and so I said, "You need to stop reporting and start weaving this story together." I think he may have needed somebody to say, "Okay, your job now is just to write. If you need information, if you need something, we'll get it for you, but you have to be the writer here."

I think that an editor's role is to help the reporter focus on what we have to do right now and then try to help them decide how to approach it and how to tell the story the best way.

Deadline Tip:

Stay calm and try to think about what needs to be done to get the best story in the paper, trying to help a reporter in the field get a feed in, or get a reporter who's struggling focused on how to deal with a particularly tough part of the story. The small things and the big things all make a difference.

Jennifer Orsi is an assistant metro editor for the St. Petersburg Times.

Tom Scherberger, city editor

I was basically the traffic cop for the story. I was directing the coverage, making sure the reporters got where they needed to go, in constant contact with them through deadline, coordinating with news photo, news graphics, the editors in St. Petersburg, trying to keep things flowing, and making sure we had all the bases covered. This was a story that didn't really end until after 11 o'clock, when police finally confirmed the name of the suspect, even though we'd had it for hours. It was the first time they released the names of victims, even though we had a few of the victims' names from relatives at the hospital and from some of the witnesses. We were getting kind of nervous at that point. Are we going to be able to go with this story without official confirmation? We had decided we were going to do that, couching it by saying the officials hadn't confirmed the identities, but witnesses and relatives said this. Fortunately at 11 we were able to rework some of the story to make it official at that point. It was a really good team effort.

A key to this whole thing was that the story didn't just get written and then thrown in the paper. It got a very thorough edit by Neville Green. We also got some extra help in St. Petersburg. The editors over there took our routine daily stories so we didn't have to focus on those. We value good writing here at this paper, but we also know good writing requires close editing, and the reporters don't mind having their stories edited. They checked their egos when they came in and realized that this is not a personal thing; we're just going to do the best we can with what we've got in the time we have.

Deadline Tip:

Trust your reporters' instincts. They're the ones who are out there.

Tom Scherberger is the city editor of the Tampa bureau of the St. Petersburg Times.

Neville Green, managing editor, Tampa

Everybody was feeding to Steve Huettel, and I was looking at the feeds as they came in so I could familiarize myself with the material. I took a copy of the top of the story—a waitress hearing the shots fired and thinking that it was fireworks for New Year's Eve—and started to work on it myself. When we got to our deadline for the first edition, I diplomatically, but bluntly, said to Steve that I had redone the top of the story and that there wasn't time at this point to do too much quibbling about it. We could send in this edition and tinker with it on the later editions. Very much to Steve's credit, he gulped a little and said, "Fine."

Chuck Murphy, one of the night editors over in St. Pete, called saying, "Isn't the lead of the story here?" At that moment I was putting a new lead together that described the scene. I had seen the photos of the bodies lying around, and a couple of photographers had pointed them out to me, knowing that they wouldn't get published. Too graphic. One of the photos was in some ways a great Florida violence photo. It showed one of the hotel employees beside the swimming pool sprawled in this lounge chair. It really wasn't a ghastly photo until you knew the man was dead. I started to think, "Wow, we should just describe where the bodies are, what the scene is." Amy Herdy, a reporter who has superb contacts within the Tampa Police Department, called a cop who was involved in the investigation and said they were trying to determine exactly where all the bodies were. And he, as long as he was not quoted, led us through that. That enabled us to write with authority between our photos and what the cop told us.

I thought that one of the weaknesses of the original draft of the top with the waitress thinking she was hearing firecrackers, was that it softened the fact that five people had been shot dead in our town. Often the reader sees us as enjoying tragic events, and I wanted to make sure that the reader understood that the writers of the story thought it was tragic.

Deadline Tip:

On the budget, put editors' names along with the names of reporters. On a complex story, it's vital. You're not just simply sitting there reacting to what the reporter has placed in the system. You're clued in.

Neville Green is managing editor of the Tampa edition of the St. Petersburg Times.

Chicago Sun-Times

Chicago Sun-Times team members Carlos Sadovi, Bryan Smith, Scott Fornek, and Mark Skertic. The following reporters, photographers, and artists were also involved with the *Sun-Times* coverage of the Amtrak derailment: John Carpenter, Robert A. Davis, Lorraine Forte, Art Golab, Greg Good, Lon Grahnke, Lucio Guerrero, Rich Hein, Dave Hoekstra, Gilbert Jimenez, Bob Kurson, Curtis Lawrence, Dave McKinney, Charles Nicodemus, Al Podgorski, Alex Rodriguez, Jon Sail, Jon Schmid, Lynn Sweet, Ernest tucker, Jim Wambold, and John White.

Finalist, Team Deadline Reporting

When Amtrak's *City of New Orleans* crashed into a truck on the railroad tracks south of Chicago, the staff of the *Sun-Times* assembled a vivid report of the chain of events that shattered so many lives. The story included here begins with the heart-rending cry of a little girl wanting her mother, and widens to show the scope of chaos and sense of loss after the accident.

Train riders thrown into eerie chaos

MARCH 17, 1999

By Bryan Smith

BOURBONNAIS—It was only by the glow of a wall of flames that Sheila Jaeger was able to see her.

The girl was small and crumpled and lying in a ditch and her tiny voice, a whimper really, was drowned amid the screams.

"I can't get up," she murmured.

"Shhhhh," Jaeger replied. "Lie still."

"But I want my mommy."

"It's OK."

It wasn't.

Because when Jaeger's eyes traced the little leg of the 8-year-old girl, they followed down to a foot that wasn't there.

Grabbing a policeman who had crawled into the wreckage, Jaeger pleaded: "Let me help. I'm a nurse."

The policeman pressed some bandages into her hand and Jaeger, just a passenger a moment earlier, went to work to save a life.

At least 13 people died and 116 were injured when Amtrak's *City of New Orleans* train slammed into a semitrailer at 9:47 p.m. Monday.

The survivors were left to wonder how a trip begun so serenely could turn tragic so quickly.

As the train roared toward Kankakee, Thomas Dixon had just settled down to a beer. A manager at the Cotton Club in downtown Chicago, Dixon, 53, was headed to Mississippi, looking forward to his once-a-year visit with his mom. Maybe he and his brother would get to do the thing that relaxes him most: fishing. For now, he and an acquaintance on the train just wanted to trade a few words over a brew.

Not far away, Jessica Switzer had pulled out a crossword. She and a few others from Covenant Christian High School in Jackson, Miss., had finished a ski trip in Quebec, Canada. Now, some of the others were asleep.

Her friend Shadia Slaieh was washing up in a bathroom.

Jaeger, a registered nurse from Mattoon, was starting to doze. She'd be home to her two children and her husband, Fred, soon.

Then came a jolt.

"All of a sudden, the lights went out," said Slaieh, 17.

"We were tipping over. I started screaming. Everybody started screaming. I didn't know where I was. I started banging around, then I was on my back. I heard somebody yell 'Fire!' and I started trying to unlock the door. I thought I was going to die."

Dixon didn't have time to think.

"It happened so fast," he said. "It was chaotic. I was sitting there having a beer, then the club car started sliding. The lights went out, and people were crying and yelling. People were trying to find their wives and husbands and friends. There was smoke and flames. People in the sleepers had their nightclothes. Outside, people were hurt and lying on the ground. Everybody was running around."

Switzer, 17, hurtled out of her seat, then felt bodies tumble on top of her. Nearby, flames licked upward, spewing curls of black smoke.

As if in a dream, she looked down at the hand that held the crossword pen. There, balled in a death grip, she realized she still clutched it.

It happened that fast.

Into the eerie swirl of smoke and flames, survivors clawed their way out. Among the jumble of rail cars, they saw bodies sprawled in the mud, medics huddled over them. Some of the victims were bruised and bloody. Some were without limbs. Some were dead.

Marcus Sykes, 19, of Maywood, who was on his way back to school, saw medics treating a woman who had lost part of her leg. Then he saw a man "whose back was all messed up." He tried to help, pulling people from the train, away from the smoke and flames.

After the noise and screams stopped, Slaieh found herself trapped in a bathroom, two cars back from the engines, fighting for her life. "The car next to us was on fire," she said. "I was calm until someone said that."

Unable to see in the dark, she punched the button on her illuminating watch to determine where the door was.

She banged on the door with her shoe. When that didn't work, she kicked at it. Finally, rescue workers pried it open. Then, she says, "I just kind of went blank."

Meanwhile, there was Jaeger. Dazed herself, she made her way outside and felt the wall of flame. "I've gotta help somebody," she thought. "These people have got to get off this train."

That's when she spotted the 8-year-old girl.

"I heard her whimper," she said. "I lifted her out of the ditch. Then I went to the hospital with her. I couldn't find her mom. I was going to stay with her. Then I found another family member."

She left without knowing the child's name, or if she ultimately survived.

The dozens of victims released from hospitals tried to rest in five hotels in nearby Bradley. But there was little sleep. On Tuesday morning, they wandered down, bleary-eyed and bewildered.

Some limped. One woman sat with a bag of ice on her head. Two little boys, perhaps 6, played at a table in their pajamas while their mother wept nearby, recounting her story to Red Cross officials. One passenger, Shalaine Johnson, 24, wandered the parking lot of the Hampton hotel, telling whoever would listen that she couldn't find her sister who was in the bathroom when the crash occurred. The wounded ranged from 5 months to a woman in her 80s.

As hard as it seemed to believe, some of those passengers were hoping to get right back on a train and complete their journeys.

Dixon, for one, still hoped to get home to his mom, even if that meant getting back on Amtrak. "I'm a little in shock, but I'm physically OK," he said, glancing down at an untouched doughnut in the hotel lounge at Lee's Inn. "I feel blessed and very thankful that I was one of the lucky ones."

So did Jaeger. But there will be no more train rides for her.

"Not soon, anyway," she said, her eyes red-rimmed and puffy from crying, just before her husband drove her home. "Not now."

Contributing: Lon Grahnke

Lessons Learned

BY BRYAN SMITH

I felt uncomfortable when I knocked, but I didn't know of any other way. So there I stood in the middle of a hotel hallway, ready to intrude on someone's trauma.

I'd been assigned to write the survivor story for the crash of Amtrak's *City of New Orleans* and the hotel was where passengers had been tucked away after the deadly crash.

Most of the other reporters hovered in the lobby, where a few survivors trickled down to be debriefed. I waited there, too, but no one wanted to talk. I couldn't blame them. The pack, though mostly polite, was a mass of mikes and cameras and notebooks, intimidating and hungry.

So I crept around the corner—no one said I couldn't— and down a hallway and began knocking.

The first door brought no answer.

Nor the second.

The third held people who were not in the crash.

The fourth was answered by a woman with puffy, red eyes and her husband's hand on her shoulder. Yes, they'd been in the crash. A nurse, she had helped a little girl who'd lost her leg. She'd only been able to see her by the light of the fire burning....

Thus came my lead, the most powerful image in my story and my first lesson learned—or rather, relearned—take a chance, be persistent. Look away from the pack. You might find gold.

And know when to bend the rules.

In some ways, I suppose, I admire reporters willing to get arrested crossing a police line or flouting an on-scene authority. But I've also seen many cases when doing so was simply foolish. We need to be intrepid, but smart. Bold, but not foolish.

The truth is, I actually did circumvent a police line in a way, taking to back roads, tromping through a muddy farm field, and walking along railroad tracks to observe families as they visited the crash site for the first time.

The access roads to the scene had been sealed off, but no one said we couldn't watch from this round-about vantage point. Doing so allowed me to write a lead packed with description and emotion rather than "The families of yesterday's Amtrak tragedy paid their respects by visiting the site for the first time..." kind of lead. I suppose I could have been arrested, though I felt it much more likely that I'd just be shooed away. The point is to pick your moments.

The one other lesson relearned was to give people a chance to talk.

As reporters, of course, we often walk the line between intrusion and insistence. Many people do not want to share their stories after such a painful, traumatic experience. But some, like the woman, do. It's a way for them to process the grief, to try to make sense of the pain. When they do want to talk, I believe we must treat them with as much compassion and empathy as we can summon. Put ourselves in their place. Yes, we have to ask about dead sons. It's the way we ask that's important.

I'm firmly of the school that says it's all right for reporters to feel, even to grieve, with someone who has suffered a loss. Not only does it comfort our sources, but I believe it elicits better information. And it honors our profession.

The one other lesson I would include is to always be on the lookout for an opportunity to tell a story. There's power in putting the reader in the shoes of someone who has been through such a disaster, a pathos that can't be found in a more traditional approach. Some will ask how you can tell a story with an event in which everyone already knows the outcome. The trick, I think, is that the reader doesn't know the outcome of the characters in the story, just the outcome of the event.

Lessons Learned

BY MARK SKERTIC

For me the lesson learned, or rather reinforced, is that in such a complex story someone near the top of the editor food chain must have a vision for how things are going to look tomorrow.

And, just as important, they need to be able to communicate that to the people in the field.

We knew what was needed in Bourbonnais, so each person could focus on his or her job rather than worrying whether the bases were covered.

Those of us out gathering the stories knew who was doing what, which stories were wanted, and who should be where. We built flexibility into the plan, but reporters had direction.

When it all came together that night, the result was a dramatic, vivid picture for our readers.

The Virginian-Pilot

Earl Swift, Diane Tennant, and Lane DeGregory covered the North Carolina flood for *The Virginian-Pilot*.

Finalist, Team Deadline Reporting

When Hurricane Floyd slammed into North Carolina and Virginia, *The Virginian-Pilot* in Norfolk dispatched teams of reporters and photographers up and down the coast. Earl Swift, Dianne Tennant, and Lane DeGregory headed inland, documenting the devastation in the flooded fields and farmland of North Carolina. With meticulous reporting and compelling anecdotes, they convey the heartbreak, and sense of hope, left behind in the wake of the storm.

Hamlet measures recovery an inch at a time

SEPTEMBER 22, 1999
By Earl Swift

BELVOIR CROSSROADS, N.C.—First light on Tuesday found this swamp-ringed settlement northwest of Greenville less a crossroads than a confluence.

Water turned brown and gritty with soil swirled over the town's namesake intersection, hiding the roads that cross here, lapping into stores and homes, stealing diesel fuel and gasoline from inundated storage tanks and sweeping them in rainbow-colored patterns into the surrounding thickets and tobacco fields.

A mile to the southwest, the Tar River flowed fast, debris-clogged and swollen miles wide, and everything between the settlement and the river's normal streambed —dozens of houses and mobile homes, acres of corn-rows and cotton, forests of sweetgum and maple and loblolly pine—lay in its grasp.

Fog obscured the treetops. Cold rain fell from low, dark clouds. The air was sharp with diesel fumes. It was a sullen beginning to Belvoir Crossroad's fifth day after Hurricane Floyd.

And the morning carried little promise of a rapid change for the better. Just south of the crossroads, the floodwater had fallen a little over 2 inches overnight.

In places, it had 8 feet to go.

For most of its history, Belvoir Crossroads has been a busy little place, with service stations on three of its corners, a truck-rental outfit a half-block from the corner, a used-car dealership.

The main road passing through its center, State Route 33, links Greenville, a university town, manufacturing center and Pitt County's seat, 7 miles to the southeast, with Tarboro, a locus of hog, turkey and tobacco farms 15 miles to the northwest.

Smaller roads form an asterisk with 33: Route 222, which takes off to the southwest; Stokes Road, which runs down toward the river; and Porter Road, which skirts the Grindle Pocosin, a trackless blackwater swamp just to the northeast.

On Tuesday, however, Belvoir Crossroads was empty, its houses and businesses abandoned, their interiors sodden and smeared with greasy brown scum. Coffee-colored water, opaque and stinking, filled the unsold sedans and pickups at the used-car lot.

The only sound was the periodic hiss of a warehouse's electric pump.

The only ways into town were by canoe or johnboat.

A half-mile south on Stokes Road, water raced, gurgling, through the heads of tobacco plants and corn-stalks, topped stop signs, devoured a trailer park. Mobile homes had become islands of twisted and punched aluminum, their interiors neck-deep in water, furniture and clothing afloat and ruined. Behind one, a white sedan, completely submerged, loomed amber through the flood's gloom. Dozens of other cars and trucks were scattered nearby, windshield-deep or deeper, glass fogged.

Here the Tar pulled at its edges. The floodwater streamed in riffles among the trailers, rasped against sunken mailboxes, spilled over rapids created by unseen, submerged obstructions.

Just down Route 222 from the crossing, Tony Coggins and his wife, Vicky, sat on the front porch of their yellow-brick rancher late Tuesday afternoon, eyeing a plastic snow gauge they'd affixed to the base of a silver maple in the yard. The gauge announced that the flooding had dropped another inch during the day.

"The way it's dropping," Coggins said, "I believe that by tomorrow afternoon, we'll be able to get that black Jeep out."

He pointed toward an SUV perched, with three cars and a riding lawn mower, on a grassy island on the yard's edge.

"Of course," he added quietly, "I don't know where we'll go."

Indeed, the real heartache for Belvoir Crossroads may lie in the days ahead, after the water drops far enough that vehicles like the Coggins' Jeep are able to clear the water that on Tuesday still blocked all of the town's approaches.

A wave of optimism seemed to sweep over people gathered at the flood's edges late in the day, as it became clear that, even with the day's rain, the water was no longer rising. But many have not seen their town since last week; they've stayed with friends elsewhere in the county, or at public shelters, or at the Gum Swamp Free Will Baptist Church up Porter Road. When the water gets low, they'll walk unprepared into the flood's aftermath.

And, as is the case with many inland floods, this one was particular about whom it struck around Belvoir Crossroads, targeting the poor and the self-employed.

"The saddest thing to me is that we live in a farming community," said Vicky Coggins, shaking her head. "Not only has it taken away people's houses, it's taken away their livelihoods. They have no way to make the moves, now, to get back on their feet from this."

"I used to joke that if the river ever flooded this far, it meant the good Lord was coming back to us," said her husband, who repairs farm machinery for a living.

"I guess he's come."

Lessons Learned

BY EARL SWIFT

When Hurricane Floyd passed over downtown Norfolk on Sept. 16, 1999, *The Virginian-Pilot*'s offices were minus much of the paper's staff. Reporter-photographer teams had been dispatched up and down the coast—along 120 miles of North Carolina's Outer Banks, where wind and water were expected to land their heaviest punches; at the Virginia Beach oceanfront; along the curving south shore of the Chesapeake Bay.

But no one from the paper witnessed what occurred in Edgecombe and Pitt counties, N.C., a quiltwork of hog farms, tobacco spreads, and villages 100 miles to our southwest.

Both lay well west of the path taken by the storm's eye. No one figured that Floyd would loose a downpour of biblical proportions on the counties, nor that the region's principal river, the Tar, would jump its banks. Nor that the Tar's waters, tainted with animal waste, fertilizers, and diesel fuel, would swallow up towns and farms downstream, drowning people by the dozen and livestock by the thousands.

By the time the scope of the disaster was clear, the *Pilot*'s North Carolina reporters were utterly exhausted; all had been working around the clock for days. The editors cast about for a fresh team to send southward. They settled on three feature writers—Diane Tennant, a West Virginia native, 15-year veteran of various *Pilot* news teams, and two-time Pulitzer nominee; Lane DeGregory, who'd written and edited in the *Pilot*'s Outer Banks bureau for nearly seven years; and me.

What we learned:

■ **When covering a flood, be willing to get wet.**

Diane made for Tarboro, the center of the government's response to the flooding. Lane headed for a Coast Guard base at Elizabeth City, N.C., hoping for a helicopter ride over swamped farms and villages. Photographer Ian Martin and I were ordered onto the flooded river itself, so we borrowed a canoe, strapped it to the top of my Toyota wagon, loaded up on camping gear and freeze-dried food, and struck into North Carolina.

We were able to get near Greenville before the roads became impassable. We were left with only one real option: abandon the car and carry the canoe nearly two miles to big water.

So, both of us sweating and swearing, we dragged the 65-pound canoe along the swamped backroads of Pitt County, N.C., fording chest-deep water in places, nervously tiptoeing past unfriendly farmyard dogs to the edge of a small settlement called Belvoir Crossroads.

Firefighters blocked the road just north of town, and we could see that they were turning back traffic, keeping everyone away from the water.

We had to get past them. We couldn't get the story we wanted any other way. So Ian and I made a pact as we neared the flood's edge: We would wind up in the water, or wind up in jail.

■ Don't ask permission.

We wordlessly marched past the assembled uniforms, pulled on our life vests, started walking the canoe into the shallows. One of the firefighters ambled over. "Can I help you?" he asked, arms folded across his chest.

"I don't think so," I replied. "Thanks."

He watched us prepare to shove off. "What do you think you're doing?" he scowled.

Ian climbed aboard at the bow. I held the boat steady. "We're from *The Virginian-Pilot*," I told him. "We're reporting a story."

The firefighter glanced over at his colleagues, seeking backup. They all seemed to freeze for a moment, unsure about what to do. Before they could sort it out, I threw my leg over the gunwale and pushed us into the deepening water, and we paddled like mad for the town center.

■ Don't wait until news breaks to cultivate sources.

Lane, meanwhile, had fishtailed her way down flooded U.S. Route 17 to the Coast Guard base, where she waited for a seat aboard a rescue chopper. The Coast Guardsmen kept putting her off. Seven hours passed. She and photographer Vicki Cronis talked about bagging the place.

But the base—and the Coast Guard's rescue operation—underwent a shift change as Lane's patience ebbed, and among the crewmen coming on duty was a rescue swimmer who'd figured in a big story Lane had written just a few weeks before. He got her aboard an H-53, and we got a great story.

Diane, far to the west in Tarboro, had been assured by reporters hanging around the city's emergency operations center that no one could get into Princeville, a nearby African-American community that had been hammered hard.

Then the photographer with her, Steve Earley, noticed a Coast Guard convoy pulling away. They ran to catch it. The public-affairs officer with the group recognized Diane's name from some routine stories she'd done with his help, and introduced her to the convoy's chief. He, in turn, invited Diane and Steve to come along.

Joining the convoy got them past the police roadblocks, after which they landed places in the Coast Guard's rescue boats. A short while later, the team was motoring among the rooftops of devastated Princeville.

■ **Make sure everything works.**

The *Pilot* leased several dozen cellular telephones and redistributed the newsroom's laptop computers to the reporters leaving town as the storm approached.

Lane, outbound on the fly, learned on reaching the flood that her laptop wasn't charged, and that there was no place to juice it up for miles around. Both she and I left Norfolk with cellular phones that had to be used once in Virginia before they could be used in North Carolina. Alas, neither of us knew that, and discovered too late that the devices were worthless.

Diane, wiser than we, checked out the laptop she'd been issued, and found that it didn't work. It took her awhile to scare up a replacement, but by the time she ventured into the flood zone, her gear had been thoroughly tested.

■ **Remember that in the midst of disaster, you don't much matter.**

The most important lesson we took away from Floyd was this: At times you have to stop being a reporter in favor of pulling a stint as a human being.

When a distraught flood survivor tearfully asks you to hold her muddy dog, put away your notebook and do as she asks. When a frantic homeowner asks for a five-minute ride in your canoe to check out what's left of his ravaged house, remind yourself that he needs those five minutes from you more than your editors do. When you approach people who've lived through hell, bear in mind that your deadlines, your story, your needs are pretty damn low among their priorities, and that they're doing you a favor just by acknowledging your existence.

They don't much feel like talking? Don't dare push them. As Diane put it: "I suppose I learned that people are gracious in the midst of tragedy if you are sensitive to their plight. Nobody turned me down for any kind of information. Then again, we didn't come barging in like we owned the place."

Bottom line: You can't expect to write a story with feeling if you feel nothing yourself.

Cynthia Tucker
Commentary

Cynthia Tucker holds what has historically been one of the most influential jobs in American journalism, that of editorial page editor of *The Atlanta Constitution*. She is also a frequent commentator on CNN and on PBS's *NewsHour* with Jim Lehrer.

In her capacity as editorial page editor, Tucker guides the development of the *Constitution*'s opinion policies on everything from foreign policy issues to gun control to local school board races. She also has considerable reporting experience covering local governments, national politics, crime, and education. She has filed dispatches from Africa and Central America.

Tucker graduated from Auburn University in 1976, and was a Nieman Fellow at Harvard University during the 1988-89 academic year. She is a member of the National Association of Black Journalists and the American Society of Newspaper Editors.

Born in Monroeville, Ala., a town famous for its writers, Tucker has developed a distinctive editorial voice, one that allows her to cover a range of issues. As these columns reveal, her range includes the ability to be serious and humorous, theoretical and practical, tough and gentle—sometimes in the same piece. In addition to her five award-winning columns, we've included one on colon cancer, which she discusses in her interview.

—Roy Peter Clark

Jackson and Milosevic:
Tricky business

MAY 5, 1999

As an ordained Baptist minister, the Rev. Jesse Jackson is required to have faith in the power of redemption. It's in the job description.

Perhaps, then, it is no surprise that Jackson would chide his buddy, President Bill Clinton, for "dehumanizing" Yugoslav President Slobodan Milosevic. Perhaps it is to be expected that Jackson would bow in prayer with Milosevic. Perhaps it is not so startling that Jackson would grasp Milosevic's hand, as if they were soulmates on a shared mission. In Christian theology, even Milosevic is not beyond salvation, no matter his crimes.

But as a longtime civil rights leader, Jackson has also had close-up, face-to-face experience with human evil. He has seen the savagery of seemingly ordinary, church-going folks who did not flinch from lynching, beating, bludgeoning, firebombing or fire-hosing their fellow citizens just because they were of a different color. And Jackson has not hesitated to call that evil by its name.

That same evil finds fertile ground in Milosevic. It has been written that he is not a madman but rather a shrewd politician, not so much a hater as a survivor. The distinction hardly matters. He has presided over a pogrom in which women have been gang-raped by his soldiers, young men marched from home and shot in the back of the head, children driven from their houses just as his soldiers set the buildings afire. All because they were a different people, of a different religion, than Milosevic is.

Jackson missed an opportunity to call that evil by its name. Milosevic is no different from the Philadelphia, Miss., murderers who killed three civil rights workers and buried them in an earthen dam. He is no different from the politicians who declared "Segregation now, segregation forever," giving cover to the crazed haters who bombed a Birmingham church and killed four girls.

Milosevic complained to Jackson about being portrayed by the Clinton administration as Satan, but there is a good reason for the portrayal. Milosevic has turned much of the former Yugoslavia into a bloody killing field, attempting to "cleanse" the land of as many Muslims as he can. For years, if not decades, human rights workers will be digging up mass graves that bear witness to the massacres Milosevic's men have carried out. Kosovo is just the latest stop in his campaign of genocide. It started, you will recall, in Croatia.

There is undoubtedly a tension in the minister's mission—hating the sin while loving the sinner. Jackson's mission had a host of tensions. If he wanted to gain the release of three American prisoners of war, he could hardly afford to condemn Milosevic loudly and repeatedly.

The significance of Jackson's accomplishment, especially with a hard case such as Milosevic, should not be underestimated. He has not only brought home three weary young men and eased the fears of their families but also taken away one of Milosevic's bargaining chips. The Clinton administration no longer has to keep the soldiers' safety in its calculations.

More important, it just may be that Jackson has helped nudge open the door for negotiations between NATO and Milosevic. Like the other religious leaders in his delegation, Jackson always believed that Milosevic could be moved by moral appeals and that peace should be given another chance. There is no more important role in the world for preachers than encouraging peace.

Still, even preachers ought to be wary of getting so close to evil that they are seduced by it. There was something about Jackson's handholding with Milosevic that was discomfiting, as if Jackson had forgotten what the man has done. Would Jackson have been as warm and cozy with the murderers of Medgar Evers or Martin Luther King Jr.?

Writers' Workshop

Talking Points

1) The writer says the columns that work best are those with a passionate voice. How does Tucker convey passion in this column?

2) Note the use of repeated phrases in this column: "is no different," "call that evil by its name." What is the effect of such repetition?

3) This column examines the conflict between speaking out against acts of evil and embracing the person behind the actions. How does this tension affect the tone of the column?

Assignment Desk

1) Write a column supporting Jesse Jackson's actions. Include your response to the arguments Tucker makes in her column.

2) Research what happened to those accused of killing Medgar Evers and Martin Luther King Jr. Write a column comparing their fates to that of Slobodan Milosevic.

Jefferson's kin ought to accept black relatives

MAY 16, 1999

As a veteran of family reunions, I can tell you they are often fractious affairs. Folks get their feelings hurt.

"Uncle Junebug hasn't spoken to Uncle Pink in 32 years, and he isn't about to talk to the stubborn old fool now. So who sat the two together at the banquet table? Aunt Lillie Bell never did care for Aunt Coot's sweet potato pie, and she never tires of telling her so. So how did the two of them end up in the kitchen together? The descendants of old Jim Tucker have felt slighted for decades by the descendants of old Jack Tucker—a bossy, elitist crowd. So who allowed Jack's clan to substitute a museum trip for the traditional fish fry and casino night?"

Given my experience with these affairs, I've got a little advice for the members of the Monticello Association: If the first gathering of the black and white descendants of Thomas Jefferson doesn't go all that smoothly, don't give up on it. You're just acting like family.

After DNA tests supported centuries-old claims that Jefferson had fathered at least one child with his slave Sally Hemings, the Monticello Association—a group of 700 officially sanctioned (read "white") Jefferson descendants—had little choice but to include the African-American heirs. Their first inclusive gathering, which goes through Monday, has no doubt been lively.

The invitation to Hemings' descendants started as a small act of rebellion by one white member of the Jefferson clan. Lucian Truscott IV told the Hemings descendants that they should gate-crash the gathering, held every May at Jefferson's famous Monticello estate in Charlottesville, Va.

When the association heard of the plan, they issued two dozen Hemings descendants an official invitation. Said Monticello Association President Robert Gillespie, "I want them to realize they are welcome by the entire group, not just Lucian Truscott."

But not too welcome. The Jefferson descendants are

squabbling over whether the black kin will have full membership in the Monticello Association and the privilege of burial in the family graveyard at Monticello, where Jefferson is buried. "We need to start the process of determining if they are descendants. There is some indication that they are, but we need to get more evidence," said Gillespie.

I have news for Gillespie and the other white Jeffersons: The evidence is in. DNA cannot be denied. While Jefferson defenders try to hide behind caveats of science (the DNA report only stated definitively that a Jefferson male was father to Hemings' youngest child), prominent white historians have given up trying to protect Jefferson's legacy.

So Gillespie needs to adjust to a bit of reality I have learned to live with: You can't choose your relatives. Every family reunion I attend subjects me to at least a couple of kinsmen I'd rather not be associated with, but the genes have already been cast. Those folks—arrogant jerks or drunks, officious busybodies or scam artists—cannot be excluded.

Indeed, the Monticello Association has led me to think of extending my family's reunions to include my white relatives. Like many African-Americans, I've got white kin.

Getting them to accept an invitation should not be difficult. After all, none of my white ancestors was a Founding Father, with a significant historical legacy to try to protect from the irony of black blood ties. The white Tuckers have been farmers, merchants, slaveholders. There was a Confederate officer or two. Mostly, they're ordinary folk.

So if the Jefferson clan does not end up in a drunken brawl (or even if they do), I might just issue a renegade invitation to the other Tuckers: "Y'all come!" Breaking bread together would be a good way to get to know one another, and I expect we'd learn that we have more in common than we knew. I expect that the Jeffersons will learn that, too.

Writers' Workshop

Talking Points

1) The writer's use of "I" and personal experiences gives this column a different tone. Study the effectiveness of such a tone.

2) This column compares two reunions—the Monticello Association and the Tucker family. Why does the writer use a comparison rather than commenting solely on the Jefferson family?

3) The writer's voice in this column has a distinctive Southern tone with such phrases as "Y'all come." Find other language that contributes to the tone in this column. Discuss whether such a choice might not appeal to readers in other regions.

Assignment Desk

1) Rewrite this column without the personal experiences. How does it change the strength of the column?

2) Write a column comparing your own family to the Monticello Association.

JFK Jr. legacy: He was role model for the elite

JULY 21, 1999

He was the perfect canvas on which to paint our larger-than-life fantasies—well-born, charming, rich, and handsome. So, upon his untimely demise, many Americans are also mourning the death of their own dreams, all those things they had hoped for that John F. Kennedy Jr. can never become: ambassador, senator, president.

If some of the speculation on the achievements of a middle-aged JFK Jr. seems a bit far-fetched given a young man of relatively meager accomplishments, it also seems inevitable.

In a culture that values wealth and celebrity over all else, the golden boy at the heart of Camelot was bound to captivate us. The myth of Camelot, after all, was fueled not just by the glamour of a youthful president, John F. Kennedy, and his wife, Jacqueline Bouvier Kennedy, but also by the sense of promise in their public service.

Still, there are other Kennedys to carry on the family political dynasty. Kathleen Kennedy Townsend—daughter of Robert F. Kennedy and lieutenant governor of Maryland—is talked about as a likely gubernatorial candidate. Robert Kennedy Jr., a New York attorney, would make an attractive candidate. Patrick Kennedy, son of Ted Kennedy, is making a name for himself in the U.S. House.

What the culture needed instead of more politicians was just what John Jr. gave us—an enormously privileged guy who knew how to bear the burdens of fame and wealth with grace. If his greatest accomplishment was his refusal to act like a jerk, that ought to be given its due.

It is rare enough. The headlines and airwaves are full of tales of the coddled and privileged behaving badly, of the scions of the famous pimping their family names, of celebrities whining about the burdens of fame while plotting furiously to stay in the spotlight. There is much too much of overpaid athletes leaving trails of cocaine arrests and paternity suits, of vain and self-important actors who mistake their celebrity for influence, of ego-maniacal billionaires who assume the normal rules of law and civility do not apply to them.

John Jr. was a refreshing contrast to all that, an easygoing guy who wasn't just like the rest of us but worked at making it seem so. He was often seen with friends bicycling in Central Park or playing touch football. Rather than relying on an assistant to place his phone calls ("Would you hold for Mr. Kennedy, please?"), he dialed himself ("Hello, this is John Kennedy"), recalled a friend of mine who knew him.

His grace was all the more rare because his celebrity *was* a burden. From adolescence he was stalked by paparazzi, his every stumble recorded. An early failure to pass the New York bar exam was noted with the headline "The Hunk Flunks." His love life, especially his courtship of Carolyn Bessette, was red meat to the sharks of the entertainment media. Yet he kept his cool.

Kennedy seemed a self-possessed young man, comfortable with his pedigree but not captive to it. He knew how to play off his celebrity without exploiting his family name. He founded a celebrity-tinged political magazine, *George*, in which he once posed nearly nude. Yet he turned down an appeal to run for a U.S. Senate seat from New York, apparently because he understood that he was not yet ready for a prominent political post.

The better we came to know John Jr., the better we also came to know his mother, Jackie, who reared John and her daughter, Caroline, to bear up under the white-heat of intense scrutiny without meltdowns. If the only thing he leaves us is a decent role model for the privileged, that will have to be enough.

Writers' Workshop

Talking Points

1) Study how the writer connects one man's death and the dreams of her readers. "So, upon his untimely demise, many Americans are also mourning the death of their own dreams, all those things they had hoped for that John F. Kennedy Jr. can never become: ambassador, senator, president." Discuss the reasons for making such a connection.

2) Outline the column and study the transition from the introduction to the placement of the theme.

3) The writer uses italics to emphasize a point. "His grace was all the more rare because his celebrity *was* a burden." Are the italics necessary? What other tools does the writer use to support the theme?

4) Study the column's conclusion. Does it reinforce the theme or unnecessarily repeat it? What makes it effective?

Assignment Desk

1) Research the death of another prominent public figure. Write a column about that person's legacy.

2) Note the amount of background information about John F. Kennedy Jr. What research was necessary? Evaluate the amount of research in your columns.

Kings defend rogue
who sullied famed name

SEPTEMBER 22, 1999

Sometimes the price of loyalty is just too high. Sometimes, when you attempt to pull a worthless friend out of the hole he's dug for himself, you end up covered in mud, too.

Such was the case last week, when Coretta Scott King used her name and prestige in an apparent effort to persuade a jury to go soft on a scoundrel named Ralph David Abernathy III, the son of Martin Luther King Jr.'s close friend, civil rights leader Ralph David Abernathy Sr. For her trouble, Mrs. King and her entourage are now being investigated by the Georgia Bureau of Investigation for alleged jury-tampering.

Abernathy III capped an ignominious career as a state senator with an indictment on charges of stealing $13,000 from his state-funded expense account. Last week, his trial on those charges ended in a hung jury. While jurors say Mrs. King did not influence them, she has nevertheless sullied her name, giving the impression that she supports rogues and miscreants.

The prosecution seemed to have solid evidence on some of the charges, including a taped conversation in which Abernathy admitted to his PR adviser, Zee Bradford, that he forged her name on expense vouchers and never gave her the money he received. He begged and badgered her to lie, telling her, "Let me tell you this, if you don't lie, it will be your reputation."

For those who've followed Abernathy's high-profile flameout, the theft charges came as no great surprise. His previous career low-lights included smuggling marijuana into the country in his underwear on a return trip from Jamaica; wandering into a women's restroom in a state building but failing to wander promptly back out; and insulting police officers who pulled him over for driving 60 mph in a 30 mph school zone.

Even when he wasn't in trouble with the law, Abernathy was less than impressive as a legislator. His six-year tenure was characterized by laziness, absenteeism, headline-grabbing and attempts to get by on his father's good name. His legislative career was finally ended, mercifully, last year, when he bounced the check he submitted to pay a qualifying fee to run for re-election.

Mrs. King has undoubtedly kept up with Abernathy's troubles. Over the years, despite occasional tensions, the Abernathys and Kings have remained friendly. And, when Abernathy was indicted, Mrs. King may have thought of her own two sons and their struggles to come to manhood in the shadow of their father's famous name. Neither Martin Luther King III nor Dexter Scott King has ever been indicted, but both have tainted their father's legacy with their endless profiteering.

So, last Wednesday found Mrs. King in a hallway outside the Fulton County courtroom where Abernathy was being tried, praying with a group that included the defendant's mother, Juanita Abernathy, state Rep. Tyrone Brooks, New York activist Al Sharpton and Mrs. King's two sons. As the jury prepared to leave the courtroom for lunch, a sheriff's deputy asked the King entourage to leave the area. They ignored him, the deputy said.

When a deputy took the jury out through a different exit, the King entourage followed and barged through the group of jurors. While Mrs. Abernathy claimed it was "an accident," it looked like an attempt to impress upon the jurors the fact that Abernathy III had the support of the King family.

Mrs. King should have left Abernathy III—who will probably be retried—to face the consequences of his reprehensible conduct. Instead, she lent him her reputation in an effort to help him salvage his family name. It's unlikely that Abernathy III appreciates her sacrifice, since he clearly cared so little for the family name himself.

Writers' Workshop

Talking Points

1) Once again, the writer analyzes the thorny issues of family loyalty and legacy. Are Tucker's comments in this column consistent with those in the previous columns?

2) Analyze your reaction to this column. Does it affect any preconceptions about African-Americans' views of the King and Abernathy families?

3) Note the use of second person in the lead. Is it more effective or less effective than the traditional third-person voice?

Assignment Desk

1) Research and write your own column about the legacy of the King and Abernathy families.

2) Read *The Autobiography of Martin Luther King, Jr.* edited by Clayborne Carson.

South honors fatal culture of violence

NOVEMBER 28, 1999

Over in my home state of Alabama, they might shoot you for looking at 'em funny. The law doesn't get too exercised over it. In court, the she-was-looking-at-me-funny defense may sway a jury.

If you don't believe that, consider the public discourse that has followed a case of road rage run amok on an interstate highway south of Birmingham. After one suburban mother shot another suburban mom dead in a roadside confrontation earlier this month, a surprising amount of public sympathy has flowed to the shooter.

It all started in a way that is frighteningly commonplace, with a scenario that would be recognized in any major metropolis in the country. On Nov. 8, in the grinding bumper-to-bumper traffic headed south on I-65 toward Birmingham's fast-growing Shelby County suburbs, two women started jockeying with each other for position—chasing, maneuvering, gesturing. Tempers flared.

When they both took the same freeway exit, the stage was set for confrontation.

As Shirley Henson's lawyer tells it, Henson was frightened for her life when Gena Foster jumped out of her car spewing obscenities, with—as one witness says—her arms out and "her eyes wide open." So, when Foster approached Henson's sport-utility vehicle, Henson stuck her .38 out of the window and shot Foster in the face.

Never mind that Foster was not armed. Never mind that Henson, according to the prosecutor, had room to drive around. Never mind that Henson had a cell phone and could have dialed 911. Never mind that Henson had her *window rolled down*. Foster was gesturing, cursing and generally looking at her funny.

Perhaps because the incident involved two women, both white, suburban mothers without criminal records, it has drawn national headlines, underscoring the spread of the phenomenon called road rage beyond the testosterone-charged tempers of male motorists. But the reaction to the shooting has also drawn attention to a peculiar Southern code of conduct which elevates the gun right alongside the Bible and takes pride in violence described as "self-defense."

Consider the comments on Birmingham talk-radio stations following the shooting. According to published reports, one caller said: "If there is aggressive behavior, somebody come after you, not only do you shoot 'em, you get out and shoot 'em again." Another caller, a woman, said, "If I'm in my car and somebody comes running up to my car, I sure would shoot them. That's just the way it's gonna be."

Even the prosecutor, Shelby County District Attorney Robby Owens, is taking a soft-edged approach to the case. Though Henson has been charged with murder, Owens says, "If they [the jury] were to come back with self-defense, I could accept that." Sounds like he's advocating that, since he made the statement to a local newspaper.

The odd notion that a verbal assault represents a threat to be fended off with violence has a long tradition in Southern culture, according to Dov Cohen, a psychologist at the University of Illinois at Urbana-Champaign and co-author of a book, *Culture of Honor*, which examines Southern violence. "The South has a culture of honor in which insults and affronts often are responded to with violence," he said.

It's not just Yankee academics who have discerned a hair-trigger temper in the mind of the South. Duke University sociologist Kenneth Land believes that the early Scottish and Irish settlers who are the ancestors of many white (and some black) Southerners passed on a quarrelsome nature that was part of a "herding tradition."

Whatever the cultural causes of the mindset, the tendency to overreact boils to bloodshed because of widely available handguns. Alabama law enforcement officials estimate that at least half of all Birmingham area motorists carry handguns in their vehicles.

And as long as the common culture holds guns and "honor" in high regard, there'll be lots more mothers—and fathers—dying the same senseless deaths.

Writers' Workshop

Talking Points

1) Note the writer's voice in this column. "They might shoot you for looking at 'em funny." Why does the writer use "'em" rather than "them"? Does this conversational tone carry throughout the column?

2) In the third paragraph the writer uses a string of active verbs to describe the situation between the two drivers: jockeying, chasing, maneuvering, gesturing. What is the effect of so many verbs?

3) The writer repeats the phrase "never mind" in the sixth paragraph. What is the effect of the repetition? How does it tell the story of the shooting?

4) Note the number of sources cited and the amount of reporting included in this column. Do the quotes from experts and callers to a radio show affect the pacing and tone of the column?

Assignment Desk

1) Do you think the South is more prone to violence? Research and write a column about your views.

2) The writer uses road rage as the starting point for a discussion of regional culture. Find an example that reflects the culture of your area and write a column.

Personal loss teaches lesson about cancer

MARCH 12, 2000

He died 16 years ago this month, and nothing has been the same since. No family photo is taken, no family reunion held, no special occasion celebrated when he is not missed. My father's death at the age of 57 remains the greatest loss of my life.

It was colon cancer that claimed him—a disease that sneaked up on him, showing very few symptoms until it was too late. My father had always been healthy and vigorous, never overweight, never sick, never absent from his job as a junior high school principal. He took pride in staying in shape. A treasured photo shows him at a backyard barbecue playfully standing on his head to show he could still do it. He was in his 50s then.

There was bitter irony in his untimely death. He had tried so hard to stay healthy. He quit smoking cigarettes when I was in elementary school, tapering off to cigars and then pipes before finally quitting altogether. He ate my mother's less fatty meals as she tempered her old-style Southern cooking (if it ain't fried, it ain't food) to follow the latest health trends.

None of that saved him. By the time his cancer was diagnosed in January 1984, it had already undergone extensive metastasis. Seven weeks later, he was dead.

What neither he nor my mother knew was that he should have been getting regular screenings for colon cancer. Even though my mother was conscientious about keeping up with the latest trends in diet and exercise and medicine, she had never heard the recommendations issued as early as 1980 that middle-aged men and women should have regular colon exams.

Now we know. And so should you: If you are over the age of 50, insist that your doctor screen you for colon cancer. If someone in your family has had the disease, you need to start getting screened by the age of 40. When detected in the earliest stage, colon cancer has a cure rate of 90 percent. Now is a good time to get that screening done: March is National Colorectal Cancer

Awareness Month.

There. I've said it. Colorectal. Colon. Rectum. As a nation, we're so sophisticated about sex that we watch casual bedroom romps on daytime TV, but we're still prudish enough to be embarrassed by certain body parts. It is that embarrassment, apparently, that suppresses public discussion of colon cancer, though it is the second-leading cause of cancer deaths (behind lung cancer) among men and women.

Colons don't have the glamour associated with breasts or the machismo associated with prostates. So, while women have rallied to raise funds for breast cancer research and men have finally begun to publicly discuss prostate cancer, colon cancer remains undiscussed. And, unfortunately, undetected.

NBC *Today* show host Katie Couric, whose husband, Jay Monahan, died of colon cancer two years ago at the age of 42, aims to change that with a public awareness campaign. I'd like to join Katie's crusade. After all, it was her husband's death that prompted me to finally have my first colonoscopy.

Funny how that works. After I watched my father's painful death, I had promised my mother I'd have my first colon cancer screening by the time I was 40. But my 40th birthday came and went without my giving it a second thought. Then Monahan—a man around my age with access to the best health care—died just a few months after his diagnosis. That got my attention.

I don't have Katie's courage. I wouldn't have shown my first colonoscopy on national TV. (She did that as part of a weeklong *Today* show series, "Confronting Colon Cancer.") But I will tell you this much about mine: It didn't hurt. And while there are less invasive screening tests for colon cancer, the colonoscopy is recognized as the "gold standard."

I will always miss my father, but he left me much that I value, including a work ethic, a good name and a sense of responsibility for my own health. I'll be getting that colonoscopy regularly. I hope you will, too.

A conversation with
Cynthia Tucker

ROY PETER CLARK: I've read and studied these winning columns.

CYNTHIA TUCKER: Oh, oh. You've read and studied them. That's frightening. Thank you, really, but I don't want to have somebody renowned as a writing teacher and coach studying my columns. I have to tell you that's very unsettling. But thank you anyway.

Does this mean you're an insecure writer?

Yes.

Tell me about that. Tell me about the nature of your insecurities.

Well, I think I am a pretty good writer. I don't think I'm a brilliant writer, by any means. And I'm certainly not the kind of writer who can summon up her best work on any given day. On the days that my columns seem to come together, it is a complete and utter mystery to me how it happened. Now, I have tried to think about what are the common things on those days when the columns seem to come together. One of them is very basic. If I have a day full of terrible distractions, it's probably not going to work very well. But the other is having a subject I am genuinely, deeply interested in. Having something to say, basically. I mean, there are those days when I think I ought to be saying something about a subject simply because it's an important issue or it's out there and it's what everybody is talking about. But the simple fact of the matter is I couldn't care less, and so I sit down to write and I usually produce something. But it's just not very good.

Would you describe your best work as having "passion," those moments of real deep connection with the subject matter or the issue?

Absolutely. And I have used the word myself. I spoke last year at the National Writers Workshop, jointly sponsored by Poynter and the *Atlanta Journal-Constitution*, and that's one of the tips I gave: Write about subjects about which you are passionate. And it really doesn't matter if it seems arcane and obscure to other people. If you feel passionately about it, I think it comes through.

Let me see if I can put this in context. I wrote a column a few weeks ago. When I was 28 years old my father died of colon cancer. He was 57. Needless to say, that remains one of the most traumatic experiences of my life. And I have been haunted by the colon cancer issue since then, both in an abstract manner and in an emotional sense, since I now have a family history and I'm supposed to be tested and all this stuff. Well, a couple of years ago Katie Couric's husband, who's very close to my age, died of colon cancer. And this is basically something I try not to think about. I put it in the back of my mind. But a few weeks ago, she did this five-part series every single morning on the *Today* show, including her own colonoscopy on TV, which I can tell you I would not have the courage to do. But I thought if she can talk about this, I can, too.

So I wrote a column about my father's death and about the need for people to be tested for colon cancer. You're figuring there are very few people out there who really want to hear about being tested for colon cancer, but there was something about my talking with genuine passion about the death of my father that people who still don't necessarily care about colon cancer were moved by the column.

That is a sign of the power of the writer to transform that personal passion into something that has a community or civic value.

Right.

That's really well said. Are you a fast writer or a slow writer? Where on the spectrum do you think you fall?

I'm a pretty fast writer, actually. That may or may not be

born of necessity. I am an editorial page editor, and at the biggest newspapers in the country, being an editorial page editor and being a columnist are two separate jobs. But I do both. Every single day I have to manage two opinion pages and so that means, for better or for worse, I don't have a whole lot of time to spend on my column. Having said that, let me also say that I may just be a creature of bad habits going back to high school. Because there have been those rare occasions when I had time to think about a column. I have known I was going to write about a subject for a week in advance. I tried to get started on the column a couple of days early. I couldn't do it. I simply couldn't do it.

You're the kind of student who used to pull all-nighters or something?

There you go. The term paper is due. Now I had no problems reading the book. I'd get the book read in plenty of time. But writing is hard brain work. And I just could not turn my attention to it until the very last minute.

Do you experience those periods when you're not writing as procrastination or as preparation?

I am almost certain in my heart of hearts that it's procrastination. But I do manage to justify it as preparation.

You're thinking about it.

I'm thinking. The day before, I've at least tried out a couple of leads in my head, and I'll keep reading on the subject, particularly if it's something technical. I write a lot about gun control. You never want the gun lobby to catch you with any little fact wrong. So I may know a week in advance that I'm going to write about the NRA or gun control, but I will keep collecting magazine pieces and think-tank pieces and CDC reports and all that kind of stuff and keep reading, knowing again I'm not going to start writing until the very last minute.

When you do sit down and start writing, can you de-

scribe what happens? Do you write a draft all the way through?

No.

Do you have to get the lead just right?

For me there are two very hard parts to the column. The lead—just getting it started. My column tends to be a little bit short compared to a lot of syndicated columnists. And so the lead is hard, but there is a point, maybe a third of the way through, that is transitional. You have introduced the subject, but now you've got to say what you believe needs to be done. You have to begin introducing your conclusion, and that transition is also very difficult for me. It needs to be deft, needless to say. It can't be abrupt—or it shouldn't be. It should flow naturally from the introduction, and that can be difficult.

Once I get the lead down—I've sweated bullets over the lead—I get up and I have a cup of tea. I have a very short attention span. There is no doubt that if, when I was a kid, teachers were teaching the way they do now, they would have diagnosed me with ADD and I would have been on Ritalin. I cannot sit still. And so I get my lead down and then I get up and I wander out and I have a cup of tea and I talk to people. And then I come back here, and if the lead is decent, the next six inches or so flow because I'm warming up to the subject. But then again comes that point when I have to have a transition to whatever my conclusion or solution is going to be. And that's hard. So then I get up and I have another cup of tea and I walk around and pace and come back and tackle that. And then the conclusion, the last paragraph, is hard for me. How do I wrap this up?

You know Susan Sontag says that writers suffer from attention surplus disorder.

Paying attention to too many things?

Yeah, right.

Maybe that's it. You've got all of these things floating

around in your head and you're trying to connect them in a column. You know, sometimes I do have the problem in a single column of trying to say too much. I think I have managed to discipline myself over the years. It's a little like Bill Safire years and years ago who wrote a brief piece in *The New York Times Magazine* about how to write a speech. There was something essential that I took from that that I boiled down a bit on how to write a column, and that's essentially just to try to make one point. You know, don't go all over the place. You don't have room for this. This is not an essay in a literary journal. This is a newspaper column.

What I like about what you're saying, Cynthia,— and what's really different from the way most writers have described this process—is that most writers seem obsessed about getting the beginning and the end right. You've introduced an important new area of writing: the middle. And the problem with a lot of writers is that...

They're not paying the middle any attention.

Yeah! And it's an invitation to readers to say, "Oh okay, this is one of those sagging middles."

Yeah, right, and you wander away.

Absolutely. People use the word "voice." Does that mean anything to you?

One of my remaining insecurities is that I'm not sure that I yet have a voice, or at least one. I mean *just* one. For example, I am not persuaded that even the people who know me best, the people who work for me, could pick up a bunch of columns without bylines, mine and some other people's, and pick mine out. Now is that a good or a bad thing? I don't know. But everybody says a good writer has a voice and I'm not sure I have one.

Well, I thought that in these columns you can definitely hear the echoes of your voice from column to column. I thought the most interesting place—the

place where I think I could hear your conversational voice, the one that I'm listening to now—is the column on Jefferson's kin, because you have the ability to write in a voice that is able to move from a kind of newspaper issues perspective to a down-home kind of voice. And that's very unusual to be able to combine those in a single column. Some people are able to do one…

One or the other?

…or the other. But I think it may be one of your gifts that you're able to combine these two so that I really feel like we're chatting over a table but we're talking about serious stuff, even though we're doing it over a cup of tea or a sandwich or something like that.

Well, let me say a couple of things related to that, one about that column in particular and one about the general idea that you just mentioned.

About that column, two things. First of all, while I think that it is a very serious subject, I also think that there had been far too much divisiveness in the conversation about whether Thomas Jefferson was the father of Sally Hemings's children, and so I wanted to bring a perspective to it that brought the volume down a bit, if you will. But it is absolutely true that I have white lineage in my ancestry, as is very common for African Americans, especially in the South. But I also know families. And it is perfectly possible to have a group of family members sitting around a table and nobody is arguing about whether you're kin or not, but you still can't have a civil discussion. And so somehow I wanted to bring that aspect into it.

As a more general matter, I run a page whose politics are center-left in a market that is center-right. I am a black woman, one of the few in the country even now and the first to be editorial page editor here. Atlanta is in many ways a progressive city, but we're still in the South. And I realized that there were going to be many readers who were, if not put off, at least suspicious of the paper's having appointed a black woman as editorial page editor.

When I first took this job in 1992, I was having a conversation with someone about the late great Ralph McGill. It may have been Jack Tarver, who was the publisher here during the McGill years. And Tarver had long since been retired. But every now and then he would wander in, and by this time he had all white hair and a long white beard and looked a little like Father Time, but he was great to talk to. He and I were talking one day—he had come by to congratulate me—and he was talking about McGill and how McGill managed most of the time to keep his readers with him by varying his tone and subject matter.

He said when McGill had to say something very serious that he knew people would hate, he just said it. Those were usually the columns advocating desegregation. He said McGill would also remind his readers that he was one of them, a Southern boy, by writing a column about barbecue or his dog or something like that.

I have kept that advice very much in mind. And so sometimes I just want to remind my readers that I'm a woman who grew up in a small town in the South, I have many things in common with them, even if our politics are very different. And so there are times when I'm searching not just for that subject matter, but for that voice that communicates with readers in a slightly different way.

And you're willing to use—without being patronizing—language that is familiar to you and familiar to them.

Exactly. I mean I don't think I'm patronizing because that language is familiar to me. Maybe it would seem different if I didn't come from a very small town, maybe it would sound different, but I grew up in a place where people talked like that.

So when you say, "I've got white kin," or call one of your relatives "a stubborn old fool," it's just you and who you are.

Exactly.

And it's a way to build a bridge with readers.

I'm very interested in the way in which you begin some of these columns by challenging readers to think. Before you get down to the specifics, sometimes you're writing on the level of ideas. In the column on John Kennedy Jr., you say, "He was the perfect canvas on which to paint our larger-than-life fantasies in a culture that values wealth and celebrity over all else."

These pieces not only are grounded but they also gain altitude because you're willing to go up the ladder and connect with readers on the level of their ideas, their minds, not just their emotions.

I have on occasion sat down and looked at the columns that I thought worked and tried to figure out what they have in common. So from time to time I do that and again one of the things I keep in mind is that these pieces are short. You have got to get in and get out. So you want to introduce your readers to the larger idea first. They may have no idea where you're going with this, but give them the general idea first, and then when you narrow to the specific—if you're any good at it— they may say, "Ah ha, I see where she's headed."

I want to ask you, Cynthia, and it's a question I've been really looking forward to asking you for some time, even before you won the contest, and it comes out of having had many conversations over 20 years with Gene Patterson, who I guess is another predecessor of yours.

Absolutely.

He ran the editorial page at the *Atlanta Journal-Constitution*.

He did.

And I'm starting to read the daily columns that he wrote from 1960 to 1969.

By the way, daily columnists amaze me. He had one,

McGill had one. I'm just in awe of that.

Isn't that amazing?

It's astonishing.

I don't know how it's possible.
But one of the things that Gene said is that he
thought one of his most important jobs was talking
to other white Southerners. And to persuade them
that a certain way of life was no longer tenable, that
segregation was profoundly corrupt. I don't know
enough about Atlanta to know how different a city it
is now than it was 35, 40 years ago. How do you
imagine your audience? Among these columns
you're writing about race, you're writing about the
Abernathy family, about the King family. Are you
writing for them? For white folks? For black folks?
For the larger community?

What an interesting question. I think to answer that I
would have to begin by going back to what Tarver said
about McGill knowing that some days he was going to
infuriate his readers, so on other days he would want to
go back and soothe them a bit by saying, "Look, I'm
one of you." Although in many ways Atlanta is a very
progressive city and has better race relations than many,
I also do keep in mind that I have a readership divided
along racial lines. Some days I'm writing for all of
them. Again, a column like the one about my dad easily
brings all my readers together. That's intentional. I'm
trying to look for subjects that cut across all lines. No
matter who you are you can relate to this.

Other times I am intentionally trying to soothe my
white Southern readers. Other days if I write a column
about the Confederate flag, I am writing very strongly
out of my own personal beliefs and passions, and if
some of my readers are offended, that's too bad. This
has to be said. Now it happens that that's probably going
to be a column a lot of my black readers like. But I'm
not even thinking about it in those terms. There are
those issues out there about which I feel strongly, and
I'm just going to write on those subjects no matter what.

They may not win me a single friend, but I'm going to say it anyway.

And then there are those moments when I think that I have a special responsibility as a black woman editorial writer to do exactly the same thing McGill and Patterson were doing, but it works out to be the flip side of it. That is to say to my black middle-class readers that some things are hard for them to hear but need to be said. If, in fact, McGill's courage lay in his decision to sometimes infuriate his friends, his peers, by saying to them some difficult things that needed to be said, the same is true for me except that my friends and peers are different. I mean it is easy in the year 2000 in Atlanta to talk about racism. For a black woman editorial page editor? That requires no courage of me at all. But it does require at least a tiny bit of courage, or at least a tiny bit of foolish recklessness, for me to say to the King family, "You are selling Martin Luther King Jr.'s name by your behavior."

Yeah, I'll say.

And I also understand very keenly a white male editorial page editor would be unlikely to get away with that. All the more reason this is my special burden. I'm not cynically choosing various categories of subject matter. "Okay, today I'm going to infuriate my black readers." This is something I feel passionately about. I mean I go down to the King Center and I notice what they're doing. I keep up with the activities of the King family. You know, I grew up with Martin Luther King Jr. as my hero. So I had certain expectations of what his heirs would do. And so some people in my position might choose to think these things and never say them. I happen to believe that it is part of my special responsibility in this job to say those things.

Did you write about John Rocker (an Atlanta baseball player quoted as making ethnic slurs)?

No. And maybe it's because I just pulled my punches there. But you know what? That was one of those days—and this is rare for me—I couldn't figure out what I thought of it. I honestly could not decide what I thought of the John Rocker mess. And quite frankly, while I was utterly appalled by the things he said, the more outrageous commentary there was from his detractors, the more I thought we were paying this 24-year-old jock far too much attention.

I know you're a busy person and I know that you do a lot of reading for your column. Do you have any time to read for pleasure?

Absolutely. But I don't have nearly enough time for those things. First of all, let me say that I think it is the coolest thing in the world to be in a job where you get paid to read the newspaper. Right? So if my boss walks in and I'm reading the paper at my desk, I don't have to try to hide it. Isn't that a cool thing? I just think that is so cool.

Even the funny pages.

Right. Exactly. I'm reading "Doonesbury" but, hey, he thinks I'm political. I need to know this. So I think that is the coolest thing in the world. I mean, who would have thought? When I was a kid I was such a reader. I was encouraged by my parents, of course, and there wasn't much else going on in Monroeville, Ala. We didn't have a mall and we didn't have cable. But my mother—this is a literal, true story. If you ask her about this, I think she would confirm it. My mother would send me into the bathroom with some Ajax and some Clorox to clean the bathroom. She would come in and find me reading the labels and reading the old newspaper she had given me to wash the windows with.

That's a great story.

Now I think she was ambivalent—both appalled that two hours later the bathroom was not clean, but also pleased that I was such a reader. And so all of that is by way of saying what a cool job this is.

This goes into the category of those people who think

that people become writers so they don't have to do manual labor.

Right. But I have far more reading. It is my goal to read, or to at least skim four newspapers every day: to read mine comprehensively, to read *The New York Times* comprehensively, and to at least skim *The Washington Post* and *The Wall Street Journal*.

My favorite stuff when I have my brain turned off is mystery novels. You know, I just inhale it and so when I'm at the gym on the treadmill, I usually have some mystery novel going. I have just started—I realize I'm late but so many people have said you've got to read it—I just started *Angela's Ashes*. One of my favorite writers at the moment is Gabriel Garcia Marquéz. And I have just finished *One Hundred Years of Solitude*.

I didn't know that you were from Monroeville, Ala.

I am. Home of Harper Lee (author of *To Kill a Mockingbird*).

That's what I was going to ask you about. I mean what's in the water in Monroeville?

Well, Monroeville has just named itself the literary capital of Alabama. Now do bear in mind we're talking Alabama here. So we're not talking a fast league when we say literary capital. I'm from there, so I get to say these things. But they have made it a whole industry. But it is true that Harper Lee was there. Truman Capote spent a lot of his childhood there. They were best friends. Mark Childress (author of *Crazy in Alabama*) went to high school there. And so I would like to think I am the next best. You know, they're in one league and farther down, there I am.

Did you and Harper Lee grow up in the same Monroeville or in a different Monroeville?

Both the same and a different one. I was in the generation when schools were integrated. Now they were integrated late in secondary school, not until 11th grade, but things were changing pretty fast in my childhood. On the other hand, absolutely related to some of the ways of life and ways of being that Harper Lee described. But, heck, my father could identify some of the actual characters in the novel.

In *To Kill a Mockingbird*?

Absolutely. Like Boo Radley. My father said, "Oh, yeah, you know there was this man who lived over here who was retarded," and my father would point to the place where the house had been. "His house was right there," blah, blah, blah. Yeah.

That is really fun. Well, Cynthia, this is a fabulous interview. You're doing great work. You're making it so easy for me. Do you want to say anything else about writing or reading?

Can't think of a thing. I just feel tremendously honored to have won the ASNE writing award. And there have been so many really, really good newspaper writers honored. I just am thrilled.

The New York Times

Gail Collins

Finalist, Commentary

Gail Collins joined the editorial board of *The New York Times* in September 1995 and has hosted the *Times*'s cable news program, *This Week Close-Up,* since 1997. She is on special assignment as an op-ed page columnist, writing a twice-a-week column on the 2000 campaign season. Previously she was a columnist at New York *Newsday* and the *New York Daily News*. Collins has a bachelor's degree in journalism from Marquette University, Milwaukee, and a master's degree in government from the University of Massachusetts, Amherst.

Collins is a serious student of American political history and the author of *Scorpion Tongues*, a book about gossip and scandal in U.S. politics. She brings the mind of a scholar and the eye of a skeptic to her columns about current politics. Collins weighs in on the presidential campaign with a blend of entertainment and instruction, stretching the language to illustrate the bizarre and the absurd in the 2000 race.

Introducing Campaign Y2K

OCTOBER 1, 1999

The millennium was at hand—only three months away and counting. Everywhere Americans turned, they saw harbingers of great change. There was flooding in North Carolina, pestilence in New York. The first sex controversy of the 2000 Presidential race turned out to involve Gary Bauer and Steve Forbes. The first great issues debate centered on the advisability of getting into World War II.

Al Gore, in his new identity as Underdog, became the first Vice President ever to run away from home. Donald Trump described himself as a natural candidate for "the working men and women in the center." Warren Beatty declared he was the Democratic Party's liberal conscience, and also possibly a drum majorette. In Iowa, unconfirmed reports held that it was raining toads.

People, who said this was going to be a boring election?

Jump-starting a candidacy that has already been remade more times than *A Star Is Born*, Mr. Gore came to Manhattan to announce that he has finally figured out how to run for President. He has begun, he said, "hearing the music of the campaign." He failed to provide any details about exactly what his campaign sounded like—something by John Cage? Nine Inch Nails? But he was very clear on the new form, which would be all about "grass roots" and hearing "the heartbeat of America." In a word, the Vice President is planning to reinvent the Listening Tour. "I'm going to spend my time from now on having open meetings with voters, talking about their hopes and dreams," he said spunkily.

With his overstuffed campaign hemorrhaging cash, Mr. Gore fled our nation's capital, hoping that at least some of his expensive consultants would be unable to track him down in his new Nashville headquarters, particularly if he refused to pay moving expenses. He was going to keep his ear to those grass roots, hang out at the local Kmart, and try to figure out where all his money went.

"I don't think the polls count for much," said the man who, until recently, employed at least five different polling organizations.

In New Hampshire, a calf was born with two heads.

Meanwhile, Bill Bradley was roaming around the country, unveiling a health care proposal even more ambitious than Mr. Gore's and calling for drastic campaign finance reform. He advocated the licensing of all handguns and repeatedly discussed the centrality of racial justice to his campaign. All this inspired Warren Beatty to suggest that he might be forced to run for President because there were no liberals in the race.

In a much-anticipated speech this week, Mr. Beatty began to give advice to an imaginary majorette, who was apparently a stand-in for a 62-year-old actor torn between a desire to run for President and a dislike of actually meeting the public or press. "Look, drum majorette," he lectured himself, "there's no harm in thinking about this—however unlikely it might be. But whatever you do, go ahead and speak up. Speak up for the people nobody speaks up for."

In Oregon, graves opened and statues wept real tears.

Over on the Republican side, Gary Bauer, the family values candidate, dragged his own spouse and children to a press conference so they could stand next to him while he announced that he was not an adulterer. "I have not had any physical contact with anyone in my campaign or out of my campaign other than my wife," he informed the 99.999999 percent of the population that had no inkling his monogamy had ever been called into question.

Mr. Bauer's followers say he was forced into this humiliating display by gossip spread by supporters of Steve Forbes. You do not want to hear all the details of this argument. But the crux of the squabble was that Mr. Bauer has been having unsupervised talks with a female aide.

"In a post-Clinton-Lewinsky world, pro-family leaders cannot be spending hour after hour after hour with young women staffers behind closed doors," said Charles Jarvis, who used to be Mr. Bauer's national campaign chairman. Mr. Jarvis quit recently and went to work for Mr. Forbes as an unpaid adviser, thus becoming one of the few unpaid people within a mile of the Forbes organization.

"What's wonderful about Steve Forbes," said Mr. Jarvis, "is that he will never be alone with a woman. Period."

In St. Louis, the Mississippi River began running backward. Babies began to speak in tongues.

Lessons Learned

BY GAIL COLLINS

Writing a column isn't necessarily a learning experience, but it's always an exercise in self-examination. When I look back on a campaign, or even just a piece of one, I'm usually amazed by how much actually happened, and heartened to realize I actually enjoyed it.

This particular essay is mainly about the peculiar things that happened during the early months of the 2000 presidential race. I like to remind people that politics, although frequently perverse, doesn't need to be depressing. In this case, I found it cheering to see how entertaining it had all been.

The Washington Post

Colbert I. King

Finalist, Commentary

Colbert I. King is an editorial writer for *The Washington Post* where he writes commentary on national, local, and international topics and a weekly column. Before joining the *Post* in 1990, King was a banking executive, U.S. representative to the World Bank and a deputy assistant secretary of the treasury in the Carter administration, and a U.S. Senate staff member. He has a bachelor's degree from Howard University where he did graduate studies in public administration.

King brings fearless honesty to a wide range of subjects, from racism and crime to government and human relationships. In the column included here, he reveals a different voice with the same unflinching tone—the anguish of a son whose mother has just died. In examining his own grief, he rebukes the media for their quick and callous coverage of death and dying, and he offers solace to those left behind.

Other people's sorrow

NOVEMBER 6, 1999

My mother, Amelia, died on Monday. I never knew it could hurt so much.

As a writer, I have composed what seems like volumes of brave words about other people's sorrow. But now I know for myself what they, and millions like them, are going through each day. A survivor's world is filled with secret sorrows. And this week, I tasted that grief.

Reporting on death and dying is one thing daily journalism does well. A golf celebrity dies in a downed aircraft, a professional football Hall of Famer loses his life to cancer, office workers are shot and killed by a lone gunman, a passenger-filled jumbo jet crashes at sea, two teens are gunned down returning from a church Halloween party: These are the kinds of events that we in the press go to great lengths to present in your morning paper or on TV and radio news.

We may not be great shakes at explaining why this and not that person died. But when it comes to describing the who, what, where, when or how of a Payne Stewart's sudden death, the horrifying end to 217 souls on board EgyptAir Flight 990 or the gentle fading away of a Walter Payton, we can dig up more details than most people would ever want to know. And newsgathering doesn't stop with our reporting on the way people die.

We are at our best when it comes to telling you all about the somber songs that get sung, the funeral gloom, the sighs, the falling tears, the sad farewells. But those stories don't stay on Page 1 or at the top of the news very long. When the eulogies end, the hugging stops and the day draws to an end, we in the press can be found gearing up for the next news event.

And here's the part that doesn't get told so well: Grief, so dutifully reported but not really felt by us, stays behind.

Sorrow lingers with those people we conveniently

tuck under the catchword "survivors." They are the wives and mothers, husbands and fathers, the sons and daughters, the friends left to pick up the pieces of their shattered lives and go on. They are the ones we expect to eventually get back up to speed, to continue to function, prosper even, after the death of a loved one. And we hardly give you time to know them before we make them disappear from our pages and the airwaves altogether, lumped in with yesterday's stories.

Survivors make it easy for us to get on with the next big national or local story. Our last view of them is usually an image of people standing tall, managing wan smiles as they greet well-wishers at the post-funeral reception. Their bravery or stoicism in the grip of grief allows us to overlook their hidden misery. But they put a lie to the saying that suffering ends with death. It certainly is not true for the living.

And so today, my thoughts are with those men, women and children who make up the rest of the story.

I now know why Deborah Ford still cries when she holds the picture of her 15-year-old slain son, Rowland, wearing his football uniform. I can ache for Tammy Jackson as she describes her son, Doniell Smith, who with Rowland was killed in a hail of bullets last Sunday night. If Tracey Stewart; her children, 13-year-old Chelsea and Aaron, 10; or Connie Payton, son Jarrett and daughter Brittney speak of heartache, I'll understand.

The dying will continue. There will be more shocks, and tragedies, and tears and tributes. But this time around, I'll not only report and comment on the pain: I'll feel it too.

Mike Littwin

Finalist, Commentary

Mike Littwin is a columnist for the *Denver Rocky Mountain News*. In his day job he writes a sports column (three times a week) and then moonlights as an op-ed columnist every Sunday. Littwin came to Denver three years ago from the *Baltimore Sun*, where he worked for seven years as a sports columnist and five years as a general columnist. He began his career at the now-defunct *Times-Herald* in Newport News, Va. From there he moved to *The Virginian-Pilot* in Norfolk and then to the *Los Angeles Times*.

Littwin takes an offbeat approach, finding the humor and irony in the news of the day. Even a rock concert comes under his microscope. With wit and warmth, Littwin analyzes the fans, young and old, who seek meaning in the music of his youth.

The rock is classic, but I'm feeling old

JUNE 13, 1999

In case you have trouble spotting a trend, we are embarking on yet another round of boomer-mania, and not just because Bill Clinton has won himself a war. (This just in from the White House: You can officially change that resume to read "draft-dodging, pot-smoking, carpet-bombing butt-kicker.")

And not just because Austin Powers is back to remind us that some people in the '60s really did wear platform shoes. See his next movie: *The Spy Who Tripped Me*.

No, what we have here is the summer of classic rock music, and just in time for the millennium. This can't be a coincidence. Our parents always warned us that rock music was a sure sign of the Apocalypse. This could be the last time?

I already saw the Stones last winter at $150 a pop—the concert in which rock 'n' roll finally converged with the Dow Jones. Tours still to come: Springsteen. Petty. Crosby, Stills, Nash, Young and somebody who can actually harmonize. Isn't it time for another Monkees reunion?

I bring this up because I just saw—ladies and gentlemen, hopefully together for the last time—the Bob Dylan-Paul Simon concert, in a double dose of '60s iconography. Separately, they were great. Together, well, let me ask you if you've been waiting for that *Dylan Sings Garfunkel* album.

The music wasn't the problem, though. The music, taken one icon at a time, was as good as ever. It is the post-concert dread I still haven't shaken.

The whole point of being a boomer, we're constantly reminded, is to pretend you never have to grow up, as if Peter Pan played Fillmore East. Dylan is not just grown up—he's 58. Remember when Dylan had the famous motorcycle accident? This time, you worry he might fall off a golf cart.

And Simon now has a band so huge I kept waiting for

him to introduce his musical director. This has always been my greatest fear: that I'd wake up one day to see my music idols had turned into Jerry Vale.

This is the problem with nostalgia. If you go to a concert looking for your youth, you'd better bring a time machine. When I looked at Dylan and Simon together on stage, I saw two old guys who looked as if they could have been waiting for a bus. Either that or posing for a wax museum.

That's OK for them, but what does that say about me? I think I know. I got my first clue from this young woman at the concert with rings pierced through her lips who's saying, "I can't believe I'm here with my dad. I never hang out with him." I'm not looking at her, though. I'm looking through her—or through the rings, anyway—at her dad.

I can see why she wouldn't hang with him. I wouldn't either. He's rocking to this great arrangement of "Tangled Up in Blue"—Dylan is so energized I think I saw an eyebrow twitch—and my mouth is open wide in horror. Not because this guy, this dad, looks, well, stupid, singing about the lace of his shoe. But because I suddenly sense that I must look exactly the same way.

As I look around the hall, there are many people my age, 40-somethings and older. But the majority were much younger. This is, in part, because Paul Simon—every generation throws a hero up the pop charts—made a lot of the new fans with *Graceland*. Many of these same people might have thought Dylan was that singer for the Wallflowers.

But it wasn't the music that brought these kids in their tie-dye sportswear to the concert. This was an anthropology field trip. This was a chance to see people who had been to Haight-Ashbury. This was a chance to ask Uncle Bud what he did during the revolution. I thought I was going to see some music, and instead I was in danger of turning into an oral-history project.

I have had this sense before. I was taking my daughter and her then-boyfriend—they were too young to drive—to a Simon concert. The boyfriend, trying hard to make small talk with the father, said, "Mr. Littwin, how long you been into Paul Simon?"

"From the beginning," I said, without missing a beat.

I should have learned these lessons by now, but they never seem to hold. I had gone to Woodstock II, with a cell phone, a Gold MasterCard and a VIP parking pass clutched to my breast. Because it was Woodstock, nudity became the central theme. And when this young woman climbed naked onto the shoulders of an available guy, all I could think was that I hoped her parents hadn't bought the pay-per-view.

It started to rain—who'd have thought Mother Nature was nostalgic?—and the bands had to leave the stage. I was standing in a baggie, trying to stay dry, when they piped some Neil Young over the loudspeaker. He was singing, "Old man, take a look at my life."

How could I have known that he was talking to me?

Lessons Learned

BY MIKE LITTWIN

The problem with writing a column for a living is that it's no way to live a life. Not that it's hard work—it's not. The pay is good, the hours are short, and my hands are callous-free.

But if you write a column, as I have for more than half my adult years, you inevitably begin to see everything through the lens of your role as observer/critic/cynic. You don't watch movies; you deconstruct them. You don't have friends; you have source material. The column—to be written three or four times a week—demands constant care and feeding, and preferably at the best restaurants. On your good days, the column is a nagging presence in your life. On the others, it *is* your life.

A good example is the column included in this book. I go to a concert not just for the music—although Dylan and Simon are both charter members of my personal rock pantheon—but to simultaneously record my reactions to the music. When I notice this guy with the bejeweled daughter, I find, with mock horror, not only a mirror on my life, but a readily available metaphor. Boy, we kill for a readily available metaphor.

I'll make a terrible admission here (yes, that's part of the columnist repertoire—the apparently sincere admission of guilt). When my daughter was graduated from college, I wrote a (blush) moving account of dealing with my little girl growing up. And though the moment was genuinely moving, I can, even now, see myself watching myself being moved and thinking how best to convey it. When my daughter left the line of happy graduates to hug her grateful dad, my great regret, as I wiped away the tears, was that I had failed to bring a notebook.

Good columnists report. Good columnists understand context. Good columnists know how to examine a topic logically. Good columnists know how to persuade a reader to at least consider the argument they're making. And though some columnists never use the "I" word and preach the dangers of the cult of personality, the columnists I admire are the columnists I know. I know them from reading them. I know what makes Russell Baker laugh. I knew what made Mike Royko scream. I know the epiphany Maureen Dowd experiences each time W. retreats to his room with his favorite pillow. I know the tears behind the jokes when Tony Kornheiser pokes fun at his father's losing battle with age.

And while most of my columns are not about me, they all say something about me. They are the ever-accumulating evidence either for or against me. I like to say that a good column should read like a conversation, which ends when the reader and writer hop simultaneously off their respective bar stools. That's one reason why I try to use humor for all but the most serious topics. Any good conversation should include a few laughs. Even at wakes—maybe especially at wakes—you end up laughing as much as crying.

In this column, I'm not crying for my never-to-be-regained youth. I'm laughing at what I see when I look in the mirror. What I'm saying is, you should have seen this middle-aged schlub at Woodstock II in the baggie in the rain. I looked exactly like a raisin. And if you see me at a friend's wake, I'll gladly tell you the whole story and, if I'm lucky, steal a moment of truth back from you for the next day's paper. After all, what are friends for?

Dianne Donovan
Editorial Writing

Dianne Donovan was in her sixth year as an editorial writer for the *Chicago Tribune* when she produced the work that won this year's Distinguished Writing Award for editorial writing. She has since become the paper's senior editor for staff recruitment.

Donovan came to the *Tribune* in 1979 from the copy desk at the *Chicago Sun-Times*. In two decades at the newspaper, she has worked on the national and foreign desks, been a Sunday news editor, literary editor, and op-ed page editor. She is a member of the board of the Chicago Tribune Foundation, the newspaper's philanthropic arm, and chairs the journalism advisory committee of the foundation.

Donovan is a native of Houston, Texas. She graduated from Spring Hill College in Mobile, Ala., in 1970 and has master's degrees from the University of Missouri and the University of Chicago. She has taught journalism and literature courses at the University of Oregon, the University of Illinois at Chicago, and Northwestern University.

Editorials are collective judgments—the voice of the newspaper—but individual writers produce these instruments of persuasion. Donovan's work demonstrates how skillfully she balances her respect for the form as an institutional expression of conscience and her own beliefs, passions, and individual voice. Perhaps only a Texan could wax so rhapsodic about the Houston Astrodome in the Chicago Cubs hometown, while it took a lifelong reader and book editor to remind readers of the merits of Ralph Ellison's contribution to literature, before and after his death.

Her pieces also reflect the challenges of a job that requires knowledge and understanding of complex subjects, such as the controversy over the growing trend to treat children who break the law as adult defendants, on a daily deadline. Beyond their beat specialties, editorial writers need the flexibility to respond to the serendipity of news. Witness Donovan's whimsical reflections on the phenomenon of blue moons, an editorial that delights as well as informs. Whatever the topic, she brings the journalist's craft: independent reporting, careful yet graceful writing, and above all, the clear thinking that helps illuminate the issues of the day.

—Christopher Scanlan

Out of the blue,
a mystical moon

MARCH 31, 1999

Did your newspaper land on the front porch this morning instead of out by the sidewalk or under the bushes?

Has someone from the bank called to tell you that they made a mistake and you have a lot more money than you thought?

Did today's mail bring a note from your son in college returning that check you sent because he doesn't need it after all?

No, it's not the Twilight Zone; it's a blue moon. That rare phenomenon will appear Wednesday night, and— scientific minds assume—will be heralded by all those things that happen…well, once in a blue moon.

Those are not so rare, of course, as things that occur only when hell freezes over, but they are not nearly so common as things that happen every time you turn around.

A blue moon, as popularly understood, is the second full moon in a month. Most years, there are 12 full moons, one in each month, and the whole thing works out quite tidily.

But when there are 13 full moons, one month gets the "blue" one. It isn't actually blue in color, though it's possible that dust particles in the atmosphere can make it appear so, just as with any other moon. We could as accurately call it "another white moon" but, musically speaking, we'd be the poorer for it.

Oddly enough, Wednesday night's blue moon is the *second* one in 1999, January also having had two full moons. And if that makes you suspicious as to just how genuine these so-called rarities are, you're in good company.

According to *Sky and Telescope* magazine, there's been a terrible misunderstanding due to a simplified definition of blue moons that appeared in a 1946 issue of the magazine. Reportedly the magazine's editors, firm adherents of the better-late-than-never approach, plan to run a correction in the May issue.

In fact, what that long-ago definition *should* have said was that a blue moon is the third full moon of a season in which four appear if 13 full moons appear in a 12-month period.

Got that? Neither did a lot of other people, which is why just about everybody considers the second moon in any month a blue moon. For the record, the next by-the-book blue moon will be on Feb. 19, 2000.

But if the paper did land in the bushes, the bank hasn't called and the check isn't in the mailbox, it's most likely because good fortune is a stickler for details.

Writers' Workshop

Talking Points

1) This editorial opens with a series of three questions. How does the number of questions affect the pacing of the editorial? How would two questions, or four, affect the pacing?

2) The use of questions in a newspaper lead generally is discouraged. Does it hook the reader or would statements have been more effective? Why was it used here?

3) Rather than the traditional use of the phrase "once in a blue moon," the writer says "...well, once in a blue moon." Is this difference necessary? What tone does it convey to the reader?

4) The writer explains a complicated scientific concept and follows it with "Got that?" Why ask the question?

Assignment Desk

1) Rewrite this editorial without the questions in the lead and elsewhere. How does it affect the tone and pacing?

2) The public assumption about the frequency of blue moons is based on a decision made in a 1946 issue of *Sky and Telescope* magazine. Read a recent issue of the publication and find another topic on which to base an editorial.

Ralph Ellison, visible once more

MAY 30, 1999

"I am an invisible man." It has been almost half a century since readers were introduced to the genius of Ralph Ellison with those words, with which he began *Invisible Man*, his now-classic novel of an African-American searching for individual identity.

By turns angry, comic, lyrical and raw, calling on influences as disparate as André Malraux and Leadbelly, the story brilliantly delineated the world of a black man in mid-century America who was determined to live his own life, not one projected upon him by the expectations of a race-based society.

Invisible Man garnered critical praise and popular acclaim, and it was the only novel Ellison ever published—until now. Next month, Random House will publish his second, and it is cause for celebration.

Titled *Juneteenth*, this new work is a heavily edited version of the massive saga Ellison labored over from the early 1950s until his death in 1994, when the manuscript was still unfinished. And though scholars and critics are already sparring over whether editor John F. Callahan has preserved the author's vision or defiled it, readers can be thankful that, after all these years, Ralph Ellison's fictional voice, so resonant and true, is heard once again.

Callahan has turned almost 2,000 pages of sometimes apparently unrelated narrative into a comparatively compact 386-page book about a black minister and the racially ambiguous boy he raises, a boy who grows up to become a white race-baiting politician.

Some critics argue that the novel's linear frame doesn't reflect Ellison's style or intent, and others say too much of the original work was left out, or the wrong elements were included. Such debate is welcome, because it's a healthy intellectual exercise and because the attendant publicity may well serve to introduce Ellison's work—early and late, fiction and essays—to a new generation of appreciative readers.

After all, Ellison was no stranger to controversy during his lifetime. He wrote about race as a central reality of American life, but his writing was neither polemical nor even overtly political on the subject. His "invisible man" was an individual first, an American second, and a black American third, a characterization that incensed some black activists, particularly in the 1960s and '70s.

Similarly, Ellison wisely perceived himself as an American artist who wrote from the depth of his experiences, which happened to be those of a black man in a race-conscious society.

What sad irony that today, in a major national bookstore chain, *Invisible Man* is still invisible in the section labeled "Literature," where books by far more dubiously "literary" white authors are quite at home. For anything by Ralph Ellison, a reader must go to the shelves labeled "African-American."

Perhaps after the publication of *Juneteenth*, all of Ellison's works finally will find their rightful place in the American marketplace. And even though this cobbled-together posthumous novel may not be "pure" Ellison, for those eager to renew their acquaintance with a master of the language, it is welcome nonetheless.

Writers' Workshop

1) The writer previously was literary editor of the *Chicago Tribune*. How does that experience influence the reporting and tone of the editorial?

2) Note how succinctly the editorial summarizes the life of Ralph Ellison and the effect of *Invisible Man*. What are the major milestones covered in the section? Is more information needed for the reader?

3) In the third paragraph, the writer makes the transition from background information about Ralph Ellison to the news about the release of *Juneteenth*. Would the editorial be more effective if the news were in the first paragraph? Explain your reasoning.

4) Readers usually expect a sense of finality in the ending of an editorial. The closing paragraph of this editorial uses conditional words such as "perhaps" and "may" rather than a concrete conclusion. Is this effective? Why do you think the writer chose that approach? Would a stronger summary be appropriate here?

Assignment Desk

1) Read or re-read Ellison's *Invisible Man* and *Juneteenth*. Write an editorial that follows up on the premises of this one.

2) Visit a local bookstore and see where Ellison's works are located. Write an editorial in support of their placement at the store.

3) Research one of your favorite authors. Using this editorial as a model, write three to four paragraphs summing up the author's life and work.

A boy's right
not to understand

JUNE 6, 1999

Okay, quick: What does "counsel" mean? How about "waive," or "consult"? What's an "attorney"?

Maybe you're not stumped. But maybe you're not 9 years old. And maybe it's not after midnight and you haven't been sitting alone in a room half the night.

It is foolish to think that any 9-year-old child, even a well-rested one, could comprehend the meaning of the Miranda warning explaining his rights to remain silent and to have a lawyer present while he is interrogated by police. And it is absurd to think he could understand those rights well enough to voluntarily relinquish them.

Yet that is what prosecutors are claiming in the case of a boy, now 10, accused of killing his 5-year-old foster brother last year. The boy, who was taken to the police station about 8 p.m. on March 8, 1998, denied involvement in the killing when he was first questioned by police.

But almost five hours later, when a detective, a state's attorney and his mother joined him, the boy's Miranda rights were explained to him, after which he allegedly implicated himself. How do you "explain" legal rights to a kid who tests at the level of a 6-year-old? The assistant state's attorney thinks she knows; she says she explained the whole thing to him.

We'll never know the secret of her success because it wasn't videotaped, and no one took notes during her "explanation" or his alleged statement. But he asked her no questions and whenever she asked if he understood he said "uh-huh" or nodded his head, so he must have grasped the concept of his rights and the implications of waiving them, right? Uh-huh.

The case against this child rests on the validity and legality of what he said in that room. Yet it is doubtful that even an *adult* with such limited experience and understanding would be held accountable for his statements under those circumstances.

If one of the youngest children in Illinois ever to be

charged with murder is tried on so tenuous a basis, then the juvenile justice system, founded here 100 years ago for the protection of children, had better change its name.

Writers' Workshop

Talking Points

1) The tone of this issue-oriented editorial is much different from the previous editorials. How would you describe the writer's tone? How does she convey her passion for the argument put forth?

2) The editorial starts with the words "Okay, quick." Is this necessary? How does this affect the reader's pace in reading the rest of the editorial?

3) The editorial itself is quick—only eight paragraphs. Does the opinion in the editorial seem complete or does it seem hurried? What is the relationship of length to clarity and impact?

4) Notice the use of quotation marks around "explain" and "explanation." What does that technique signal to the reader?

Assignment Desk

1) In eight paragraphs the writer includes four elements of an editorial: a lead, a transition, the newspaper's opinion of the events, and a conclusion. Outline the editorial and note the location of each element. Study how economically each element is used to convey the concept.

2) Ask several 9-year-olds to define "counsel," "waive," "consult," and "attorney." Write an editorial based on their comments.

Sense and nonsense in youth justice

JUNE 28, 1999

It's not easy being a kid.

If you're, say, 10 years old, you can't join a mail-order club to get CDs or videos. That's because the state doesn't think you're mature enough to understand the binding nature of a contract.

You can't buy cigarettes or order a beer. That's because the state doesn't think you are knowledgeable enough about long-term cause and effect to comprehend the harm those substances can do your body.

And you can't get in by yourself to see *Shakespeare in Love* or *Saving Private Ryan*. That's because community standards (as reflected in the movie rating system) presuppose that your cognitive skills aren't yet developed enough to fully distinguish the real from the imaginary, and certain images might be harmful to your brain.

In short, you are subjected to all sorts of protections, and properly so, because you lack maturity, knowledge and experience. Until you are suspected of a crime, that is.

That's when the laws of the state and the mores of society cut you loose, and all those assumptions about the limitations and vulnerability of youth are left outside the stationhouse door. That's when someone reads you your Miranda rights and asks you if you want to waive them—and claims you know what in the world they are talking about.

It is utterly astonishing that in most states, including Illinois, children as young as 7 or 8—children who don't even walk to school without the aid of crossing guards—are expected to understand, to intellectually *absorb*, not only what their constitutional rights are when they are questioned by police, but the consequences of waiving them.

That flies in the face of common sense and of an impressive body of research as well. In the largest study conducted on the subject, involving more than 400 juveniles, Dr. Thomas Grisso, now director of forensic training and research at the University of Massachusetts Medical School, found that children 14 and younger are significantly less capable than adults of understanding the concept of rights and the implications of waiving them. And the younger the child, the more confused he is.

Grisso also found that, because of cognitive difficulties and emotional and mental disturbances, kids who are 15 to 17 years old don't necessarily understand what's going on either, even when compared to adults with low intellectual capabilities.

Based on what we know about the intellectual and emotional development of children and adolescents, his findings should come as no surprise.

In fact, *no* juvenile in police custody should be given the option of waiving his rights to remain silent and to representation by a lawyer. That is not to say that a juvenile should not be questioned, but a lawyer acting on his behalf should be present during the questioning. It's just that simple.

The protections society offers its young people represent a well-founded recognition of the fundamental differences between the experience and knowledge of children and adolescents and those of adults.

To deny those differences at what could be the most critical moment in a juvenile's life is disingenuous and hypocritical. Indeed, the image of a state's attorney getting a youngster—eyes wide, legs swinging—to waive his Miranda rights would be ludicrous were it not so sickening.

Writers' Workshop

Talking Points

1) The editorial hinges on the comparison between everyday limits on children and youth and the disregard for those limits in the justice system. Are the comparisons effective? What other examples of limits would illustrate the point?

2) How many paragraphs are in the lead of this editorial? Where does the transition to the opinion begin? Does the editorial take too long to make its point, or is the length necessary?

3) Note the use of second person in the examples cited in the lead. How does it affect tone, pacing, and impact compared with the traditional use of third person?

4) The writer says that the ending of an editorial should be a "punctuation mark on your opinion." Does the ending in this editorial serve as a punctuation mark? Compare the ending with those of the other editorials.

Assignment Desk

1) Write an editorial supporting a youth's ability to waive his or her Miranda rights.

2) How many sources are cited in this story? Interview other experts about this issue and write an editorial based on their opinions.

3) Rewrite the ending of your recent editorials to put a "punctuation mark" on your opinion.

Back to the future in Houston

OCTOBER 11, 1999

Big and ugly and squatting in the heat, the haze and the dust of Houston's south side like something that had either just hatched or just landed, the Astrodome was hailed as the Eighth Wonder of the World when it opened for business on April 9, 1965.

Now it's history.

But though it didn't come close to outlasting the seven other wonders, or even lots of other ball parks, the Dome, which on Saturday saw the last game of its final season, has left its mark on baseball—for better or for worse.

It began as the brainchild of Roy Hofheinz, a politician and dealmaker who pioneered the dubious art of public-private funding partnerships. Taxpayers got the bill and Hofheinz got a palatial suite overlooking the playing field. He dubbed it a "sky box."

The Astrodome itself was pure Texas: oversized, gaudy and making up in sheer brashness what it lacked in taste. Houston was thrilled; Dallas was jealous.

This was a watershed moment in mythic imagemaking: The old name of Houston's baseball team, the Colt .45s, brought to mind six-shooters and malt liquor. The *Astros*, a bow to the new-in-town NASA crowd, looked ahead to the space age—and they needed a ball park to match.

But the Dome was never a park, and it was always more than a baseball field. It was all things to all comers. Mickey Mantle played there; so did Elvis. The Astros didn't always draw a big crowd, but Roy Rogers and Dale Evans packed the joint.

The idea was, you didn't have to like baseball (or football—the Oilers also played there) to go to the Dome. In fact, it was sometimes better if you didn't.

The Astrodome sported chandeliers, red carpet and upholstered cushion seats. It had a 470-foot-long electronic scoreboard and 4,500 skylights 208 feet overhead. More to the point, in a city so humid you can hear your hair curl, it had *air conditioning*.

But it didn't have sunlight or fresh air or a cozy feeling of camaraderie. It lacked the tease of looming thunderheads and the refreshing feel of an unexpected breeze. And after they painted over the acrylic skylights because players kept losing fly balls in the glare, all the grass died and it didn't have that either.

But other cities scrambled to copy Houston's success story. Domes sprang up (in Canada!) and AstroTurf became a household word.

Now the city that started it all has come full circle, and when the Astros open their 2000 season, it will be in more intimate surroundings—for Texas anyway. They'll play ball on real grass, and when the weather is fine and the stars are bright, somebody will shut down the a.c. and retract the roof.

It won't be Wrigley Field, but it will be progress.

Writers' Workshop

Talking Points

1) Compare the number of words in the first paragraph with the second paragraph. Is this pacing effective? Defend your answer?

2) Examine the use of comparisons in the editorial. "Mickey Mantle played there; so did Elvis. The Astros didn't always draw a big crowd, but Roy Rogers and Dale Evans packed the joint." What reporting was needed? How do the comparisons contribute to the main theme of the editorial?

3) Note the use of italics for emphasis in the editorial. How does this affect the tone?

4) This editorial about a sports arena in Houston was published in Chicago. What techniques does the writer use to make the history and fate of the Astrodome relevant to *Tribune* readers? Is she effective?

Assignment Desk

1) The writer describes the effect of the Astrodome on baseball. Write an editorial about whether you support that effect on professional sports.

2) Note the balance of news and background information. Rewrite the editorial with a summary lead.

A conversation with
Dianne Donovan

CHRISTOPHER SCANLAN: Are you a Chicagoan?

DIANNE DONOVAN: No, I was born in Houston, Texas. That's the genesis of the Astrodome editorial. I came to Chicago because, at that time, Chicago had five daily newspapers and a lot of healthy suburban weekly papers. It just seemed like a good place to come looking for a job.

That was 1975. I worked at an Earth Shoe store for a while. Remember Earth Shoes? I once had 13 pairs. But my feet lived through it.

I did get a job on a suburban weekly and you know how those are. I was a reporter for three months and then they made me managing editor. As managing editor, I wrote an editorial once a week. I did that for a couple of years; then I went to the *Chicago Sun-Times* as a copy editor. I came to the *Tribune* in 1979 as a copy editor.

How did you learn to be an editorial writer?

Writing comes pretty naturally to me, always has, and I think that's because I've always been a big reader. I think if you read a lot, you learn how to write. I went to the editorial board as the op-ed page editor, which is not a writing position. It was very helpful for me to have that first year as the op-ed page editor because I was also responsible for reading and editing the editorial. High-falutin' copy editing is what it was. So I spent a year reading three editorials carefully every day. It'd be hard not to be able to write an editorial at the end of that time.

For an editorial writer, reading is just extremely important because you have to know about so many things. You have to have a breadth of knowledge, if not of experience, which most of us don't. That allows you to be able to see a lot of different viewpoints and also to be able to come up with a lot of different things to write about.

How do you view editorial writing? As a craft? As an art?

I've always thought of journalism as a craft.

What makes it a craft?

A craft is something that requires skill but not a Ph.D., and it's something that you get better at with practice. Craftsmen are people who work at something and get better and better at it but don't necessarily need to be licensed or degreed or anything else to do it.

Did you have a beat as an editorial writer?

At the *Tribune* each person has a number of what we somewhat laughingly call areas of expertise. It's our job to be particularly up in those areas and we're expected to write about them. My areas were education, everything from vouchers to school prayer to test scores to higher education to rising tuition costs at state universities versus private schools. All of that stuff. At that time, I was the only woman writing editorials. By default I took on what you might call family issues. I didn't like to call them women's issues, because I always say that *all* issues are women's issues. Maybe there are a few out there, like Viagra or something. No, even that's a woman's issue.

That also happened to dovetail with the big push for welfare reform, which is definitely a family issue, and so I took that on and also early childhood development. And Northern Ireland and Ireland and Britain, because I had spent a lot of time in Ireland.

Last year juvenile justice issues came on my radar screen, originally because this was the 100th anniversary of what was then called the Children's Court, which was the genesis of the separate juvenile justice system, which started here in Chicago. The more I looked into it, the more I realized that the system is headed in the wrong direction. I actually wrote about 14 or 15 editorials on the juvenile justice system.

How was the editorial writing job?

In editorial writing, you're very much a part of a group within the paper. I mean, the board is pretty much one organism. It's a truly collegial group. We were like a family. We'd squabble among ourselves but don't anybody outside dare say a word against another board member to one of us. And I really enjoyed that.

What is an editorial?

An editorial expresses the institutional opinion of the newspaper. It's not a personal opinion. If you think of the institution of the newspaper as an institution in the community, as a bedrock of the community, but one that has perhaps many, many voices, there are times when people should be able to look to that institution to say, "Well, you've got all these resources. What do you think?" And the editorial answers that question.

There has been a move to have signed editorials. Part of it is that we all want to get personal these days. And people want to know who wrote this opinion. We do not do that and I would hope that we never would, because I think it's difficult enough for us as editorial writers to make readers understand, or even our neighbors understand, that I may write this but it's not on that page, in that position, because it's *my* opinion. That's the *Tribune*'s opinion.

Now, of course, if I play my cards right and I can make my arguments at the board meeting, then ideally my opinion becomes the *Tribune*'s opinion. That's my goal. But that doesn't always happen for a number of reasons. History, tradition, bad arguments. I've had my mind changed in there. Somebody has a better argument. But that's what an editorial is. It's not an individual's opinion. It's what this institution believes about issues.

Obviously, sometimes an editorial is an entertainment. Like the Astrodome thing. Readers like to read that stuff, too. I think you like your institutions to be occasionally whimsical and that's what that shows. We aren't just all bearded guys smoking pipes and thinking great thoughts. We can be whimsical as well.

Where would the Ralph Ellison editorial fall?

Another function of the board or of an editorial is to acknowledge some things that might go unacknowledged
or to analyze something in a way that might not be evi-
dent to the reader on the face of it. It wouldn't have been
so important to write that editorial if this book had come
out and it had been a huge success and everyone had
said it was the second *Invisible Man*. That didn't happen, and a lot of people said, "Ralph Ellison blew it. He
wrote one great book and a lot of essays and some other
stories." But I think it was important to say, "Let's step
back and look at this guy."

**What is the process by which an editorial is pro-
duced at the *Tribune*?**

We have a board that meets four mornings a week, from
10 to 11 usually, in this wonderful old room with oak
paneling and cool pictures on the walls and you can see
the gargoyles outside. And we sit around a big wooden
table in these big green leather chairs. This sort of im-
parts this feeling of *gravitas*, which doesn't last long.
I'm making it sound like we all march in to "Pomp and
Circumstance" and that's not true at all. We all sit
around and talk and laugh and drink—I drink tea and
everybody else drinks coffee—and chat about sports
scores or something goofy in the paper or the acquisi-
tion of a major other newspaper company. We each are
expected to have read about four papers before the
meeting.
  And then Don Wycliff, the editorial page editor,
starts going around the table. I'll pitch something.
"Here's the issue and here's what I think we should say
about it," and you make your argument. Eight times out
of 10, there is no argument. Two times out of 10, people
are just short of throwing things at each other. But you
say, "Here's what I think we should say and here's
why," and are always extremely mindful of where we
have been in the past on this issue. If we have said one
thing, we're not all of a sudden saying something else.
We have a past that we hew to pretty carefully. We do
make some U-turns, but it's like turning an aircraft car-
rier. They take a long time.
  What we're going for is consensus and we usually

get it eventually. If we don't come to a consensus, then either we'll decide to put it off, give it some more thought, or Don will say, "Here's what we're going to say." Sometimes Don will say, "Are you comfortable writing that?" and you can say no, and then someone else will write it so that you don't have to grit your teeth. This is really only a problem with real visceral issues, something like abortion. Sometimes you want to be writing about what you believe and you want to be passionate about it, but sometimes it's just a paycheck, and they pay you to write something and you write it.

And then I go back to my office, and probably make phone calls. This is the other part of being an editorial writer that some people don't understand, and I know a lot of reporters don't understand, but we do our own reporting. In order to protect ourselves in the paper, we get on the phone and make all the phone calls.

What is the landscape of the editorial page? How many editorials a day?

Usually three a day. We have the cartoon up at the top. The editorials are stacked underneath, always in order of importance. It's just like structuring a story or a page. You know you put the most important one at the top. Usually that's the longest one.

Viewing an editorial as a writing form, could you describe the elements or characteristics of an editorial?

I would compare it to a good newspaper story, though not necessarily the traditional, inverted pyramid news story. I'm a great fan of the inverted pyramid news story. I'm very conservative that way. But I think I would compare it more to a good news feature story. The first component of an editorial—and it's the biggest hurdle for an editorial writer—is to draw the reader in. That, of course, is the challenge that faces every writer. But with editorials, because they're short and because they're frequently about things people think they have absolutely no interest in, you've really got to figure out a way to pull a reader into that editorial. I realize that is true for all writing, but a lot of people think that you don't need that with an editorial because all you're trying to do is give an opinion. But that opinion is worthless if no-body's reading it.

The lead is the hardest part. Once you're in there, you're gone. I mean, you know, your fingers just go. Sometimes it just comes to you and sometimes you walk about eating peanut butter M&Ms for a long time, and wander into people's offices, and look out the win-dow, and then you eventually sit down.

If I were to shape an editorial, the lead would draw readers in by doing something that they don't expect ed-itorials to do. Maybe by using a specific example of a person just as if this were a feature story, or by saying something surprising, or posing a question. Everyone says you're not supposed to have question leads, but if it's a question that somebody actually might think about for a minute or puzzle them somewhat, then why not?

You wrote: "Did your newspaper land on the front porch this morning instead of out by the sidewalk or under the bushes?

"Has someone from the bank called to tell you that they made a mistake and you have a lot more money than you thought?

"Did today's mail bring a note from your son in college returning that check you sent because he doesn't need it after all?

"No, it's not the Twilight Zone; it's a blue moon."

That's right. That one had a bunch of questions.

Here's another lead: "Big and ugly and squatting in the heat, the haze and the dust of Houston's south side like something that had either just hatched or just landed, the Astrodome was hailed as the Eighth Wonder of the World when it opened for business on April 9, 1965.

"Now it's history."

In an editorial you can't just say the Astrodome, which was this big deal, isn't going to be there any more, be-cause people already knew that. Part of the problem with an editorial is that you're usually writing off of the news, frequently a couple of days after. Nobody's going to read this to find out what happened. They know what happened.

Why are they reading it then, if not to find out what happened?

They're reading it to find out what the *Tribune* is saying, what in the world is new here. You want to make a reasoned case and you want to do it in a flowing way, so that people feel like they're really listening to someone talking about it. Not someone shaking their finger at you.

How about this for a lead: "Okay, quick: What does 'counsel' mean? How about 'waive,' or 'consult'? What's an 'attorney'?
   "Maybe you're not stumped. But maybe you're not 9 years old. And maybe it's not after midnight and you haven't been sitting alone in a room half the night."

That's using that same thing but with an issue-oriented piece. And I think then you go on to have a transitional paragraph in which you tell the reader what you're talking about.

This editorial continues: "It is foolish to think that any 9-year-old child, even a well-rested one, could comprehend the meaning of the Miranda warning explaining his rights to remain silent and to have a lawyer present while he is interrogated by police. And it is absurd to think he could understand those rights well enough to voluntarily relinquish them."

That tells the reader exactly what we think. I think in an issue-oriented editorial, it's really important to tell the reader what you think somewhere in the first third of the thing. You can't write the editorial chronologically and have your opinion be the kicker. You have to let them know quickly.

Why?

Because that, after all, is the point of an editorial. You're writing to inform readers of your opinion, of the paper's opinion, and perhaps to change their minds. You can't count on them getting to the bottom. That's like burying the lead. One, they may never get there, or two, by the time they get there, maybe they don't care. You draw them in; you give them an explanation of what it is you're talking about, which is your transition; then you tell them exactly what you think of it. The rest of the piece is telling them why.

I think there are times when being really pissed off helps an editorial, and this is probably one of those cases.

But even so, it's outrage controlled by language and pacing. That editorial was only eight paragraphs.

That's a short one. I think readers will read something if it doesn't look like it's a huge chunk, and also you just write them and they're done. There are people who say it takes much longer to write a short one than a long one, but I have never been that kind of person. This probably took me maybe an hour and 15 minutes to write.

We always talk about the Miranda rights and we pretty much know what it means, but I decided that I wanted to read exactly what someone would have said to this child. So I called the morgue and asked them to ship me up a copy of Miranda.

Now for our younger readers, what's the morgue?

Oh, that's the library. Well, now wait. Library is old now too. It's not the library any more. I don't know. Now it's probably the multi-cyberspace storage intergalactic facility...

Do you all call it the morgue there?

Those of us who are elderly do. The morgue is where you keep dead stories.

So I called and asked them, and they sent it to me so that I could stand there and read it to myself. Actually that's where that lead came from. When I read the thing out loud, I immediately thought this kid doesn't know what counsel means because he probably wouldn't know what an attorney is—lawyer maybe—attorney, probably not. Waive? You say waive to a kid, you know they either think of Lake Michigan or somebody's going bye-bye. So that lead came from looking at the Miranda document and thinking how a 9-year-old would handle it.

Do you make outlines?

Oh, no. Rarely do I write any more than two lines more than I have to. I have colleagues who write twice as much and then trim, and my argument is, you could have written two editorials. Efficiency is everything.

You get your lead, then it basically writes itself.

No, no, no. I didn't say that. The next step is to tie that in. You have to tell the reader fairly quickly so then you get your transition, which ties it in so the reader knows what you're talking about. And then the third step is telling them what your opinion is, and then the fourth step is telling them why.

And then have you essentially finished ?

Yeah.

What's the last part of the story you work on? Is it the ending?

Every now and then you'll come up with a sentence in the middle, and you'll think, "Ooh, that's a good ending." Generally speaking, I just write start to finish. Sometimes if you really can't come up with a lead, you can start after the lead and worry about the lead later.

You're not wedded to the notion, "I've got to have my lead"?

No. Sometimes if you're stuck and, if you can, you just start writing the rest of it, out of that will come the idea for the lead.

How important is the ending?

Very important. It does have to end in the way that a story does. It can't just end—it needs the kind of finality that a good short story has. That's sometimes very difficult, too. Sometimes what you do is find your ending sentence somewhere up in the piece. Sometimes, sadly, it's the lead.

What do you do if that happens?

By the end of the time I was writing editorials, if I came up with a sentence in the middle of the thing and I thought, "Oh, that's the end," I would just move it down to the end and then write everything in between. Sometimes if you're stuck for an ending and you go back and you read it, you say, "Oh, that's a good ending right there," you move that down and then figure out how to fill in that sentence that you just took out. If it's the lead, unless you can think of another lead, I just leave it as the lead and try to come up with another ending. Because it's more important for it to be the lead than the end, you know.

What do you want an ending to do?

The ending is the punctuation—it's like when Mary Lou Retton did that flip and landed and stuck. That's what the ending does. There's no wavering here, there's no question. What this ending does is put the last punctuation mark on your opinion, on what you think and why, and it leaves the reader with the feeling that this is intelligent, this is correct. And sometimes that requires an emotional sort of ending. I mean, it requires some passion and sometimes it just requires a very thoughtful coda, I guess.

What do you want people to do when they finish your editorial?

Buy another *Tribune*.

Anything else?

I want them to agree with me, of course. That's what editorials are all about. Or agree with us, I should say. Often, especially with a paper like the *Tribune* and especially on local and state issues, you're not always writing to the reader. You're specifically addressing, though you don't say this in the editorial, lawmakers or opinion makers. Frequently you really are writing because you know that people in Springfield or the city council or Congress or wherever are going to be looking at what you think. We know that because over the years we've been influential, and we also know that because sometimes we'll get a call for help and someone will say, "We're taking this up tomorrow. I would love to be able to put on everybody's desk in the chambers an editorial." And so your readers are reading it, but you're not always just addressing your everyday reader.

Are you interested in inspiring action?

Yeah. So that a certain action will come about.

After the editorial about the boy's right not to understand Miranda, the case was thrown out in court. Do you know whether your editorial had any impact?

I know that the judge read the editorial.

Can you say how you know that?

No. But I know she did. I mean, someone told me who knew.

How'd that make you feel?

Wonderful. In a number of these cases, I think that we at least gave judges pause. In a couple of cases, we were successful in keeping the state's attorney from going after kids that they would ordinarily have gone after if they didn't know that we were on their case.

What was the origin of "Out of the Blue"?

A little piece explaining what a blue moon was, but it didn't exactly say why. I mean the first question you would say is, "Wait a minute, if these are all so rare, how come we just had two of them?" So that kind of started me. You can't write about welfare and juvenile justice and really deep, grave issues all the time. You need a change of pace. It's a boost. It gets me out of the rut of writing on the same issues over and over again, and I think it helps the reader. I think this kind of piece is a refresher for the reader who's expecting doom and gloom on the editorial pages.

Was this something you did in a day?

Oh, yeah.

Were you an expert on blue moons?

No, I never knew what a blue moon was.

So how did you get up to speed?

Well, I called the morgue and said send me everything you can find that's been printed about the blue moon in the last year, and then one of those clippings from *Sky and Telescope* magazine came up, and I double-checked with them. These days with Lexis-Nexis and stuff like that you can get all kinds of information on stuff.

What is the story behind the *Juneteeth* editorial?

I had, of course, studied *Invisible Man* and read Ellison's later essays, and I thought that this was certainly worthy of some recognition and acknowledgment and also to reconcile. There were people on either side, academicians—you know, the academy is second only to the church in terms of vitriol and acerbic confrontational modes—so there were major scholars having big fights over this. I just thought it was important to say, "Let's cut through this and talk about how important he was and what it means that a new work has finally come out."

Do you write the headlines?

At this paper the editorial writers write the headlines.

At what stage do you write the headline?

After the editorial is done. Sometimes you think of a really good headline and you just slap it right on there before you've written the editorial. But usually that's last.

Do you like having to write the headline?

No. It's just hard to do because sometimes editorials are difficult to bring down to three or four words.

Who edits you?

Don Wycliff, the editorial page editor.

What does the editing involve? What happens?

Usually not much. If he has problems with the piece, he'll put it in notes mode. Maybe a question: "I'm not sure I understand what you mean by this," or "Don't we need to say what happened last Thursday?" or something like that.

"Back to the Future in Houston." Why did you write this one?

Frankly, because I'm from Houston, Don's from the Houston area, Steve Chapman, who's on our editorial board, is from Austin. We've got a lot of Texans on this board. Sometimes you write something because you don't know if the readers will care, but you hope they'll be entertained.

This is a big baseball town with not even arguably any more the best ball field in the country, that being Wrigley Field, and we're proud of that. And so the Astrodome was the antithesis of Wrigley Field—everything Wrigley Field is the Astrodome wasn't. And I think readers would relate to that.

"They'll play ball on real grass, and when the weather is fine and the stars are bright, somebody will shut

down the a.c. and retract the roof.

"It won't be Wrigley Field, but it will be prog-ress."

What did you want people to do when they fin-ished this editorial?

Weep.

Do you read other editorial writers?

Well, I read editorials of other papers but not to read specific editorial writers.

If somebody said to you, "I'd like to write editori-als," what advice would you give them?

Editorial writers generally come from the staff. They're people who have excellent writing and/or editing skills. So I would say hone your skills because you're going to need all of them if you want to be an editorial writer. Make sure that you are known as a good writer, as an ac-curate reporter, and that you show versatility in your work.

Do you miss editorial writing?

I sought out my new position because I felt that I was ready for something different and this is about as differ-ent as it gets. But I haven't adjusted at all to this.

What are you still doing?

I'm still taking my same early train in the morning and reading four papers. I haven't adjusted to not having an almost diurnal deadline. In fact, Don and I were in a managers meeting today and I whispered to him, "Gee, you know, Seamus Heaney's translation of *Beowulf* is now on *The New York Times* bestseller list." I said, "I sure wanted to write because that would make a lovely editorial." You know the whole thing about every col-lege and high school student these days just in terror of *Beowulf*—I'll take any course that doesn't require *Beo-wulf*—and now Seamus Heaney has put it on the bestseller list. I suspect that, like some other books, it will be bought but rarely read. It just sounded like it would be a fun editorial to write. But I don't write them any more. But that doesn't mean that I have to stop thinking about writing them.

What would be the point you'd want to make?

I don't know. Sometimes on these kinds of things, you don't really know what the point is until you write them.

Can you really not write that editorial?

Oh, no, I wouldn't do that.

You can't.

No.

What a shame.

I know. Just look at what the world has missed.

The New York Times

Verlyn Klinkenborg
Finalist, Editorial Writing

Verlyn Klinkenborg began contributing nature editorials to the editorial page of *The New York Times* in 1996 and then joined the board in 1997. Born in Colorado, Klinkenborg was raised in Iowa and California. After graduating from Pomona College, he completed a Ph.D. in English literature at Princeton University. For 20 years he has taught creative writing in various places, among them Fordham University, St. Olaf College, Harvard University, and Bennington College.

Klinkenborg brings a poet's voice and painter's eye to his craft. His distinctive voice rises above the familiar terrain of editorial writing. In his observations about the death of John F. Kennedy Jr., Klinkenborg examines what the burial at sea says about death and dying.

From the water's edge

JULY 24, 1999

In 1799 a London cartographer named William Heather prepared a map of coastal New England. On Heather's chart the Atlantic Ocean is a blank, a generality of uninked paper. But Martha's Vineyard and Nantucket, home of fishermen and whalers in those days, are surrounded by shoals of numbers, each one the result of a depth sounding taken with lead and line paid out over the gunwales into a troublesome, unsteady sea. To that same sea, so well sounded and still so restless two centuries later, the Kennedy and Bessette families have restored the ashes of their children, John F. Kennedy Jr., his wife, Carolyn Bessette Kennedy, and her sister Lauren.

The flat summer light on the water, the deep, metallic vibration of the Navy destroyer U.S.S. *Briscoe* under power, the swift lessening and final disappearance of what the families gave back to the ocean current—these are things we can only imagine. But the grief of the Kennedy and Bessette families requires no imagining, nor does their desire to console themselves with ceremony. For people of a certain age, it was impossible to watch that ship without remembering the sight of a flag-draped coffin being drawn by horses through the streets of Washington nearly 36 years ago. The procession replays itself in the mind with preternatural clarity, right down to the chill in the air, the weightless sunlight.

But where that interment honored the public and national loss, this one brings us closer somehow to the mystery of death, which is something we all honor privately, if in common. This interment dramatizes both the dissolution of the body and, in a sense, the immensity that reclaims the body.

There is no more forcible emblem of the unknown than the sea, no clearer demarcation of the abruptness with which life passes into death than the border between the warm, moist July air on Nantucket Sound and the cold ocean current on which it rides. Consigning the ashes of these three young people to the sea in which they died is a way to express not only grief for the dead but the humility of the living, too.

Sailor after sailor has taken a measure of the home waters around Martha's Vineyard, but there is obviously no sounding death. Like the blank Atlantic on William Heather's chart, it is featureless. We build upon its shore, we walk its beaches. From time to time we stop looking inland, where life is, and turn to look out over an immensity that frightens us and gives us, at the same time, a certainty in which there is much consolation. The moment passes, but grief remains part of us.

StarTribune

Kate Stanley

Finalist, Editorial Writing

Kate Stanley joined the *Star Tribune* as an editorial writer in 1980. She studied English literature at the University of Minnesota and served as editor-in-chief of the college newspaper, the *Minnesota Daily*, in 1979-80. Stanley's editorials for the *Star Tribune* address legal issues, social policy, international affairs, and medicine. Her 1997 editorial series on medical care at life's end, "Learning to Die," was recognized with several national awards, including the ASNE and Society of Professional Journalists distinguished writing awards.

Direct prose and clear language are the hallmarks of Stanley's editorials. She's not afraid to say Minnesota's governor is ignorant about the issue of suicide. She uses her editorial to dispel myths about mental illness and teach her readers, including Gov. Jesse Ventura, ways to respect their fellow citizens.

On suicide: A lesson Ventura must learn, and teach

OCTOBER 11, 1999

Feather boas notwithstanding, Jesse Ventura is a common man, plagued by common foibles. He speaks from his heart, yet sometimes is heartless. He says what he thinks, yet can be thoughtless. He's clever, yet prone to occasional fits of unenlightened candor. And being a common man, it's no surprise that Minnesota's governor is seized by common misapprehensions. Take his thoughts about suicide, for instance.

Ventura thinks people who succumb to suicide are weak. He was quoted as saying so in the latest *Playboy* magazine. "I have no respect for someone who would kill himself," the governor said. "If you're to the point of killing yourself, and you're that depressed, life can only get better. If you're a feeble, weak-minded person to begin with, I don't have time for you."

A few things can be gleaned from these comments. Ventura isn't depressed. He isn't well-informed. He's parsimonious with his respect and his time. And he's not particularly compassionate about the suffering of the mentally ill.

None of this is surprising. Ventura's sentiments about suicide are shared by many of his constituents—perhaps most. He calls the suicidal "feeble" not out of malice, but out of ignorance. He belittles them as "weak-minded" because he imagines that suicide reflects a failure of will.

But Ventura imagines wrongly, as do many of his fellow Minnesotans. If he'd listen, neuroscientists could give him the facts. They could tell him that suicide is the tragic endpoint of a physical illness. They could describe the chemical basis of the disease, and show how depletion of crucial neurotransmitters leads to unfathomable despair. They could explain that this brain disease can't be reversed by "bucking up" any more than diabetes can be cured by smiling.

Depressed people need medicine to change their brain chemistry. They need therapy to nudge them toward recovery. They need these things just as diabetics need insulin to normalize their metabolism and special support to stay healthy. The treatment works; it saves lives.

People suffering from depression need something else, as well—something other sick people enjoy as a matter of course, but that Gov. Ventura says he can't muster for the suicidal. They need simple respect. If they had it, they might be able to shake off the preposterous notion that depression is shameful. They might be moved to seek treatment. They'd certainly find that the people around them—newly enlightened about the source of their suffering—would be eager to help them recover.

Wouldn't it be something if Minnesota's governor—its top common man—got the message about suicide? Wouldn't it be great if he realized—as he's fully capable of doing—that he ought to take back the uninformed things he said? If he did, he could help replace a common misunderstanding with a life-saving truth: Suicide victims aren't weak; they're sick. They deserve treatment, not contempt.

Michael Dobie
Diversity Writing

Michael Dobie covers sports for *Newsday*—but he doesn't consider himself a sports reporter.

"I consider myself a reporter who happens to cover sports," he says. "And a reporter who covers people who happen to do sports."

It bothers Dobie, who began covering sports at *Newsday* in 1987, when people categorize him as a sports reporter. He knows many people conjure up an image of the sports fanatic Oscar Madison in *The Odd Couple* play by Neil Simon that became the popular television series. Or they think of the character in the TV show *Everybody Loves Raymond*. He prefers people view what he does as journalism.

The 44-year-old Dobie never started out to be a sports reporter. He began as a math major at Notre Dame, switched to engineering to sociology to political science to philosophy, before ending up with an English degree from New York University.

But while he loved math, and still does, he found himself more fascinated by people and ideas. That led him to writing. As an NYU economics research center administrator, he wrote short stories and screenplays.

Luck made him a journalist. He had a New York friend who moved to Oregon and lamented a lack of information about New York teams.

So Dobie wrote him letters—during the pre-Internet days—using an urban, sassy, hip, off-the-cuff take on the local teams. He left such a letter on his desk one day and an NYU professor looked at it and said, "Hey, did you ever think about going into journalism." That's how it started.

Dobie's interest in issues and people, coupled with his many years of covering high school sports, made him the right reporter to do *Newsday*'s series on "Race and Sports in High School."

In order to tackle such a volatile topic as race, he needed to understand where people were coming from and where they were going. He also recognized he needed time, context, familiarity, comfort, knowledge, and insight into the inter-relationships among the people, the school, and the civic environment. The opportunity to immerse himself in both the community and the topic resulted in a series that shows the human face of both race and sports.

—Aly Colón

Friends 'forever'

MAY 16, 1999

Like many sports seasons, this one began long before the first game. Like many friendships, theirs began long before they understood what they meant to each other.

They were five football players from Glen Cove High School, and by last summer they were bracing for battle. They had high expectations for the upcoming season, their senior year.

So they took night jobs and joined one another at the high school by 9:30 every morning. They lifted weights. They worked on plays. They ran sprints, ran the bleachers, ran two miles and ran the bleachers again. They went to malls and clubs together. And in the course of preparing for the season of their lives, they discovered something else was happening.

"I didn't think we could get tighter, but we did," Andre Devone said.

They even gave themselves a nickname—the Fabulous Five.

Dustin Grosso was the quarterback, Matt Capobianco the tailback, Doni Baskin the fullback, Guido Penafiel the slotback and Devone the wide receiver. Manning the five offensive skill positions, they knew their performances would in large measure determine Glen Cove's success or failure.

Their nickname, brewed with a bit of bravado, was meant to reflect those exploits. But it also described something far more important that was happening off the field. The five friends were hurdling the barriers of race.

Devone's mother is white, his father black. Penafiel's father is Hispanic, his mother white. Baskin is black. Grosso and Capobianco are white.

Devone and Penafiel met in first grade and played on the same kickball teams. Capobianco and Grosso cemented an early friendship with games of touch football in the street. Capobianco and Devone played youth baseball together. Devone became closer to Baskin and Grosso after they were teammates in eighth-grade football and basketball. Outside, the five played endless games of pickup football.

By the time they reached high school, they seemed of a piece: Teammates—plus, as Devone said, "all best friends."

"We think of each other as a family," Grosso said. "I like having that. I like being able to play sports and not having to worry about any racial stuff."

Certainly, sports is no cure-all for racial ills—well-documented economic, political and social barriers remain on and off the field. For athletes of color, life outside the games is fraught with the same kinds of prejudices and restrictions common throughout society.

But spend a year at one of Long Island's most diverse high schools, visit the locker rooms and playing fields, interview scores of athletes, coaches, fans and parents, and you can see up close the power—and limitations—of sports to affect race relations.

Sports at the high school level can provide an undeniable opportunity for some athletes, such as the Fabulous Five, to get to know each other. As they do, the barriers among races often begin to crumble.

It is a message clearly visible at Glen Cove High School, from the moment one enters the front door. Walk down a long hallway and look to the left; there is a showcase for the track and field team. Behind the glass is a photo of a record-setting girls relay: Four smiling faces—one Hispanic, one Asian, one black, one white.

Continue down the hallway and turn right. Running along the corridor outside the gym is the Wall of Fame, a collection of 8x10 glossies of every Glen Cove athlete who receives all-county honors. There are 119 players on the wall—65 white, 36 black, 17 Hispanic, 1 Asian.

But even at a school where so much goes right, athletes discover that sports sometimes can harden racial divisions and perpetuate corrosive stereotypes. There are sports still identified as "white" and "black." There is perplexity when a Hispanic boy plays point guard for the basketball team, or a Chinese girl breaks sprint records on the track team. There are pressures and expectations of boys basketball fans, who together revel and suffer with their team's fortunes, yet often sit separately in black and white sections.

To stand at the intersection of race and sports is to stand at a juncture rife with contradictions. At Glen Cove, students from nearly 35 ethnic backgrounds speak 14 languages. Nearly half of the students are people of color. But all 28 coaches are white.

The same ugly, racial epithets that sometimes are used by the opposition to taunt Glen Cove players are used casually in the locker room by teammates as a sign of camaraderie.

The most gifted athletes of color, many of whom are strong on-the-field leaders, are often the most isolated in the classroom.

And while it is an article of faith among most Glen Cove athletes that through sports they can make friends—often friends of different races, friends they never would have made in the classroom—it is equally an article of faith that few know for sure if those friendships will last.

As the Fabulous Five's final season as teammates began to unfold, Penafiel began to wonder: What would happen to them once they did not have sports to bind them?

"Each year we get closer," Penafiel said. "I hope to be friends with all of them for a long time. It's kind of hard, though, you know? After high school, they can go to college and then come back as a different person. You just move apart."

Sometimes kids do go their separate ways. Sometimes being on a team does little to crack the cliques that exist outside sports. And sometimes everything goes gloriously right. Sometimes there is a Fabulous Five.

By the end of September, they were beginning to believe they were on the verge of something special. Penafiel's worries were something to be wrestled with as graduation approached in the spring. In those balmy days of early autumn, it was football first. And there they were, basking in a 2-0 record, a start few at the school imagined would lead to the most memorable November in Glen Cove in nearly half a century. But the Fab Five knew.

PLAYING IN HARMONY

They were coming off a season in which they had

won but a single game, yet they found the bedrock of success in their belief in one another. In football, they shared a single dream; off the field, their personalities were as different as their backgrounds.

Grosso, who shared co-captain duties with Capobianco, lives to play sports. Hard-nosed and highstrung on the field, he wears his athletic pride on his sleeve and cheerfully admits he would play sports and do nothing else if he could get away with it.

Baskin is pragmatic. Affable and easygoing, a man among boys on the field, he hopes for a football scholarship to college. But he takes auto mechanic courses in the afternoon, just in case.

Within the group, Penafiel and Devone are best-of-best friends. Both are products of mixed marriages. When the pair are out with Devone's mother, people assume she is Penafiel's mom. Where the soft-featured Devone is earnest in a disarming sort of way, Penafiel is intense—frighteningly so during games. One of his nicknames is "The Psycho." They want to go to college together.

"We're always hanging out together," Capobianco said. "We're all different races, and I think it's cool that we could all hang out real well like that."

Simultaneously sweet and street-wise, Capobianco has an everyman quality that allows him to relate to kids from all sorts of backgrounds. He is, as one classmate put it, the student in Glen Cove who most easily crosses every racial barrier.

Raised in an atmosphere of openness and tolerance, Capobianco has played with black and Hispanic friends in and out of school for as long as he can remember. His older sister was a member of the high school's African-American Culture Club.

He and his four friends find in their families a similar quality. As Capobianco put it, "They don't care what color you have just as long as you have that nice attitude."

Off the field, they often travel in a pack.

Wander into the cafeteria at lunchtime; chances are the five are sitting together at a table in the middle—unless they're out cruising Glen Cove in one of their cars. Visit Penafiel or Devone or Capobianco on a Monday night in autumn; the same five will be there, sprawled on couches, watching football together.

When Penafiel's family moved across town last summer, they rented a van and the Fab Five plus two other friends spent a hot July day packing, carrying and ferrying boxes back and forth across Glen Cove.

Their friendships set the tone for a Glen Cove team that thrived on closeness. With help from a core of veterans, including Jason Watson, Angelo Filippone, Ian McCloskey, Dave and Paul Graziosi, Ricky Johnson and kicker Juan Hernandez, the Big Red began the season in impressive fashion.

Capobianco and Baskin had two touchdowns apiece and Grosso and Penafiel each added a score as Glen Cove trounced Roslyn, 49-21, in its opener. The first home game was a 17-7 win over Lynbrook. Afterward, the dreadlocked Johnson held court outside the locker room with a group of white friends as a ragged pickup game broke out on an adjacent practice field among a dozen little kids from a variety of ethnic backgrounds.

Week 3 brought Roosevelt, a longtime nemesis, and one of Long Island's top running backs in Jerone Pettus. It also brought the victory that began to convert doubters into believers as Glen Cove emerged with a pulsing 33-32 victory. Capobianco scored two touchdowns, Grosso threw for three and Filippone forced a fourth-down Pettus fumble that was recovered by Johnson deep inside Glen Cove territory in the final minute.

As the Big Red rumbled off the field, boisterous fans formed an alley of whooping backslappers. Victories followed over Bellmore JFK and West Hempstead—the latter a 49-30 win that featured three touchdowns apiece by Baskin and Capobianco. Going into homecoming weekend, Glen Cove had a 5-0 record and was Nassau County's highest-scoring team.

The surge paralleled that of another local team that profited from the trust shared by its multiracial teammates—the Yankees, who won the World Series two days before the homecoming pep rally. Baskin was among those impressed by the postgame celebration.

"It's not about they're white, black, Spanish," Baskin said the day before the Glen Cove pep rally. "It's about how they're celebrating how they won the World

Series…We want to celebrate like that and not, like, hey look, I'm hugging a white guy, hey look, I'm hugging a Spanish guy."

They had been friends for so long, Baskin said, that they barely recognized their own diversity—until, that is, they were seniors.

"Then we started really looking, like, yeah, I never thought about that, because before we looked past each other," Baskin said. "When I'm with them I don't even think about their color. It's just, 'He's my friend,' and that's it."

AFTER THE WHISTLE

Often, friendships made in sports are neither as simple, nor unconditional.

Rohini Sahni had many friends from her years on Glen Cove's soccer, basketball and softball teams. On bus rides, she said, she and her teammates talked about anything. Sometimes they shared secrets. On occasion, someone would ask about her Sikh religion and the new temple on Lattingtown Road.

"But then once you get off that bus, a lot of times some people just don't mix with other people," Sahni said. "Sometimes it tends to just be, like, oh, that's my soccer friend, you know? Sometimes it happens. It depends on how close you get to a person."

There are clues that stretch from the past. Some parents and alumni who played ball for Glen Cove in the 1960s and 1970s have kept almost no friends from sports. But many speak reverently of teammates they are tight with to this day. Many were in the stands last fall, sharing handshakes and memories as they watched the team sparked by the Fabulous Five.

"The friendships go on for years," said Albert Granger, who played football and lacrosse and ran track at Glen Cove in the late 1970s. "So many guys, both white and black, are in different circumstances in their lives. Some are working for public works in the city, police department in the city, all different. But when we see each other it's just like it's back in high school. White, black, it doesn't matter."

Chris Thaw finds the process intriguing. A black defensive back and honors student who transferred from

Brentwood in 1997, Thaw has made many friends of many races at Glen Cove. But he also wonders how real some of these sports-based relationships are and whether acceptance that is granted in the locker room is genuine or superficial.

"It depends on the person," Thaw said. He spoke softly but forcefully. "It definitely changes their view of a person. I'm not sure if it changes their view of an entire people or group. But in some cases I think it proba-bly...opens them up to change. That person might be more willing to give another person a try."

And if that's all there is?

"That's a start," he said.

HOMECOMING

By late October, the football team was drawing a growing crowd that blurred long-standing racial lines in Glen Cove.

A Gold Coast estate town where waves of immi-grants once poured in to work on magnificent properties owned by the Morgans and the Pratts, Glen Cove is a city of staggering but segmented diversity. It is home to the Holocaust Center of Nassau County, a Sikh temple, Lech Walesa Place and the Napoli Soccer Club. There is Christopher Columbus Avenue and Marcus Garvey Mall, the Order of the Sons of Italy in America and Glen Cove Soul Food.

For the most part, the population is separated geo-graphically along racial lines. Most blacks live on The Hill. Most Hispanics live in the Lower Orchard (the Up-per Orchard is mostly Italian). The Landing is the most racially diverse part of the city. Those three neighbor-hoods—The Hill, The Orchard, The Landing—are the three sections with the highest concentration of people of color. Ask kids from the predominantly white sec-tions of town where they live, and they invariably name the street since that part of town has no label.

But labels had little relevance by Homecoming Sat-urday, when the crowd that numbered a scant 400 for the Lynbrook game swelled to nearly 2,000, the largest home crowd in years.

The fans—mixed and mixing, like the team it had come to cheer—were rewarded with a 42-6 win over

Great Neck North in which Grosso scored three touchdowns and Capobianco, Baskin and Jeff Rudloff all rushed for more than 100 yards. But the victory was costly. Capobianco, the Big Red's leading scorer, was carried off the field by Baskin and Watson with an ankle injury.

It was an ominous ending to a week infused with energy and an enthusiasm that reached its first climax with Friday's pep rally. That morning, the grounds of the high school were pinstriped with thousands of toilet paper rolls that streamed down from every tree on campus.

Inside the gym, spirit squads entertained an overflow crowd of students, parents and alumni. The football team sat at one end of the gym on a small set of bleachers, the Fabulous Five side by side in the first row. And when the five-boy, five-girl homecoming court was announced, four of them were in it—Capobianco, Devone, Grosso and Penafiel.

Capobianco was elected king. When their selections were announced, each sprang from his seat and raced across the floor to thunderous applause.

Their closeness was obvious as they clowned around with Baskin, bouncing off one another in adolescent frenzy. Capobianco relishes that camaraderie and the fraternity that now comes so naturally to him and his friends.

But he wants more. In the school's popular "Minority Experience" class, Capobianco and other students discuss attitudes toward race and ethnicity with a frankness he finds missing in football. Often, classroom discussions are so intense that students break down and start crying. Sometimes, the class does sociological experiments, as it did when it sent interracial couples to Roosevelt Field Mall and observed people's reactions when those students held hands.

Capobianco thinks some athletes are missing out.

"You really get to know what people are like," Capobianco said of the conversations in class.

He doesn't see that type of dialogue taking place in football—not on the bench, on the bus, or in the locker room. He would like to know, for example, what life really is like for Ricky Johnson on The Hill, the most misunderstood neighborhood in Glen Cove. Or what life and sports were like in the Dominican Republic for safety Victor Hidalgo. He calls it a missed opportunity.

"It would be cool if people brought it up more: What's it like over there? You guys have football over there? I don't think people bring it up as much as they could," Capobianco said. "[Sports] has helped out a lot and I think it definitely could do more."

THE 'PEOPLE CLUB'

While the Fab Five drove through the regular season with its eye on a title, Guillermo Martinez often paced the sideline, keeping an eye on the quarterbacks and helping refine their technique. A Colombian emigre and now a sophomore at Nassau Community College, Martinez quarterbacked the Big Red until his graduation two years ago. His closest friends remain a group of white and Hispanic high school teammates.

Sports, Martinez said, is different from the African-American Culture Club or the Spanish Club. He calls sports the "People Club," and said nothing else is like it.

"When you see other groups hanging out, it's mostly Hispanics hanging out with Hispanics, blacks hanging out with blacks, whites hanging out with whites," Martinez said. "When you see it in sports, it's mostly a mix. That's the grand thing about it."

David Boyajian, a running back who played with both Martinez and the Fabulous Five before graduating in 1998, agreed that sports promotes mixing. "But after the season is over, people don't say hi to you anymore," said Boyajian, who also was an all-county wrestler. "They don't hang out as much as they used to. It's weird. I don't know. It's like during the football season we all talk to each other and…after practice is over everybody goes to the little groups, everybody goes to their branch."

Some athletes do go their separate ways to their separate parts of town. But when the basketball team plays, Penafiel and Capobianco arrive together to watch Grosso, Devone and Ricky Johnson. Penafiel often drives Johnson home to the The Hill.

There is no magic involved, Martinez said. It begins with one person making an effort to reach out to another. Sometimes it works. Sometimes it doesn't. Sometimes they connect and stay that way.

When that happens, Martinez said, "It's all just one. It's beautiful."

Most athletes buy that—some only to a point. Sharon Lopez, a former volleyball player and Glen Cove's valedictorian in 1995, believes some sports-related friendships can be superficial. Lopez, who is black, gravitated toward people in her classes. She rarely called a teammate to hang out on Friday night.

"That's why I'm saying superficial," Lopez said. "You're friends at the time and even friends later, you talk and say hello, but it's not like a lasting let's-go-out kind of friendship."

Whether or not their friendships last, most of Glen Cove's athletes say sports has done more for interracial bonding than anything else in their lives. Relationships among athletes are better, they say, than those among students in general, and students in general get along better than people in the community. The fact that all of their relationships might not last doesn't mean that sports has not had an effect.

"I think it carries over, I do, into their other lives," said Thom Ruckert, a former lacrosse coach who has been teaching English at Glen Cove since 1969. Ruckert also co-teaches the "Minority Experience" course.

"Do they go and have dinner together at each other's houses? Maybe in a couple isolated incidents. Should it be more? Well, of course, it should be…To a certain extent I think it works. There's more of a tolerance. I don't think we're all going to love each other. You just have to be understanding."

PLAYOFFS AND PARADES

As November crept in and the postseason approached, the crowds saw that the football team had a chance to make Glen Cove history.

With Capobianco on crutches on the sideline, the Big Red lost its final two games to Mineola and Wantagh. But its 6-2 record allowed it to sneak into the Nassau County Class III playoffs, where it traveled to Hofstra University to meet longtime rival and perennial power Bethpage.

With his ankle still tender, Capobianco returned to

play wide receiver and scored the Big Red's first touch-down. Freshman Zhivargo Simmons scored twice and Dave Graziosi broke a 20-20 tie with a 47-yard inter-ception return. After Bethpage roared back to score, Penafiel knocked down a two-point conversion pass with 21 seconds left to guarantee a shocking 27-26 up-set. When the horn sounded moments later, teammates and fans quickly joined in celebration.

Piles of players and followers were everywhere. Carmine Portaro, a white lineman, carried Devone onto the field. Johnson ran along the base of the bleachers, slapping hands with fans of every color. Glen Cove players began hurling themselves up and into the stands. After the postgame handshake with Bethpage, the Big Red gathered at the north end of the stadium and raised their helmets to the sky, their arms a mosaic of white, black and brown.

The following weekend, Glen Cove defeated Floral Park for the school's first county championship in 49 years. Back at tailback, Capobianco ran for two touch-downs, Hernandez kicked a 33-yard field goal and Pe-nafiel forced a critical fourth-quarter fumble in the 17-13 victory, which sparked another raucous celebration. A few days later, the team gathered at Glen Cove City Hall to receive citations from Mayor Thomas Suozzi and the city council.

While the players waited patiently in the back of the room for the ceremony to begin, Capobianco and com-pany gathered over on the side, smiling at a photograph of a youth team some of them had played on as 12-year-olds.

"The best teams are the teams that get along the best, on and off the field, and these guys are an example of that," Suozzi told the audience. "They not only won a football championship, they brought us all together."

Yet for the Fab Five, it would be a defeat that under-lined the depth of their friendships.

BEYOND THE WINS COLUMN

The season's final week was a jarring roller coaster of joy and sadness. Between classes and practice, Capo-bianco, Grosso and others rushed off giddily with coach Pete Kopecky to do various radio and cable television talk shows. Baskin was embraced by his mailman one day, emblematic of the hug the team was receiving from all of Glen Cove. There were moments that put it all in perspective, however.

After the City Hall ceremony, the team trooped off to Dodge-Thomas Funeral Home to attend a wake for classmate Felipe Barbagelata, a Glen Cove senior and the team's mascot. Barbagelata, who wore the school's knight costume and patrolled the sideline brandishing a sword and shield, died the morning of the Floral Park game from a sudden seizure.

"It was a great feeling when we won but when we found out he had died, it was kind of hard to smile," a somber Devone said the morning of the wake. "We wanted to believe it was just another rumor."

Said Grosso: "I bet he had the biggest heart of anybody in the whole school."

The morning of the Long Island championship game against Sayville, the team learned that popular physical education teacher and boys cross-country coach Mark Hasen had died the night before from lung cancer. A moment of silence was requested before kickoff to honor the pair; several Glen Cove players had tears in their eyes.

The somber beginning contrasted starkly to the sense of anticipation the Fab Five had carried with them throughout the season. Back in September, Penafiel had enunciated what seemed then an impossible dream: The Fab Five wanted to play Sayville for the Long Island championship, a wish born that summer after Glen Cove beat Sayville in a hard-fought and controversial 7-on-7 passing league championship game.

Together for the last time as teammates, the five friends took the field at Hofstra, but the team quickly found itself overmatched. Sayville led 16-0 by the end of the first quarter and kept pouring it on until the lead grew to 51-0 in the fourth quarter. Still, the Big Red fought gamely to the finish, and when Grosso finally scored with 21 seconds left to make it 51-6, it was difficult to tell whether anyone had lost.

The team returned to town with a police escort, players perched atop three fire engines, sirens blaring. A crowd of about 800 greeted them with chants and signs as Suozzi welcomed them to a podium.

"This team was special because we were one team and we respected one another," Grosso told the crowd.

And as Nat King Cole's "O Holy Night" wafted overhead, team and crowd dispersed into the dark.

What lingered among a season's worth of images was the sight that night of the five best friends in the center of the group that surrounded Suozzi.

Wins and losses were one thing, friendship another.

"When we first went to fifth grade, [they were] inseparable," said Hilary Dorfman, the senior class president, "and that's how they are now…They stayed friends for a long time and I'm sure they'll stay friends throughout."

A brisk breeze blew up School Street as nighttime settled in. The fire trucks were gone. The crowd had vanished. An occasional shopper strolled past the deserted courtyard. The celebration, so joyous and so vibrant only moments ago, seemed almost a mirage. That was Penafiel's worry—that the bond they shared so strongly might dissipate with time.

At that moment in another part of town, a party was about to begin. Friends and families celebrating a season, with five teens in the middle again, as youthfully optimistic as they were back in September: Their friendships were special, just like this season.

Would they last?

"Definitely," Capobianco said, "they'll last forever."

Writers' Workshop

Talking Points

1) "Like many sports seasons, this one began long before the first game. Like many friendships, theirs began long before they understood what they meant to each other." Study this introduction and define the theme for the story. How does the writer develop the theme through the course of the story?

2) The writer says this was one of the most difficult stories of the series to write. The structure changed several times before finally being written in a narrative style. Outline the structure of this story. What other structure could you use?

3) How does the writer establish the theme of the series? Is it clear? Is it effective? Is it necessary?

4) What tools does the writer use to describe the atmosphere at the high school? How does he convey a sense of place?

Assignment Desk

1) Rewrite this story using a different story structure.

2) On your next assignment, practice writing more effectively about a sense of place. What descriptive elements help you write effectively?

Expectations

MAY 17, 1999

Todd Johnson says he knows the deal. He's a good player. Then again, he has to be.

Because he is black. Because the sport is basketball. Because the Glen Cove High School star knows what would happen if he couldn't cut it on the court. If he lost his starting spot to a white kid, for example.

"I'd be the talk of the town. My teammates, the people who played with me before, would be, like, 'Dang, you don't know how to play no more? What happened?' " Johnson said.

Sports can bring kids together. It also can pull them apart by feeding the misconception that race predetermines what athletes can or cannot do.

Blacks are good in basketball. White men can't jump.

Such phrases often are uttered without second thought—or any thought. For players such as Johnson, these labels can hurt in unexpected ways. Stereotypes create expectations. Expectations create pressure.

Basketball, perhaps more than any sport in the country, is polarized by racial stereotypes that place a burden on both black and white athletes. Images of the predominantly black NBA only reinforce assumptions about race.

The message, Johnson says, is clear:

Excel, or you're a failure.

Whether Johnson would succeed was a question mark in November for a Glen Cove team that graduated three starters, including leading scorer Michael Thurmond. Johnson was the heir apparent, and eagerly awaited his chance at stardom.

The two players differ in personality and style. Johnson is more boisterous and given to a stream-of-consciousness style of speaking; Thurmond was more measured in thought and conversation.

Johnson, who likes to wear do-rags off the court, will hit a shot, then point to opposing fans and put his finger to his lips, as if to shush them; Thurmond, whose concession to style was a left sock he sometimes wore pulled up, played a quieter game.

As it turned out, Johnson did not fail. A starter as a sophomore last year, he blossomed during the 1998-99 season into one of the best players in Nassau County. As the team's leading scorer, Johnson led Glen Cove to the Class B semifinals and was named to the all-county team.

But success did not eliminate the pressure Johnson had felt long before he pulled on a varsity uniform.

Even in gym class, Johnson said, classmates showed what they were thinking when they chose sides for pick-up games. "People who don't know me will be, like, 'I want to be on your team,' " Johnson said. "Like, you don't know whether I can play or not, but you want to be on my team?"

For Johnson and Thurmond, who also is black, basketball is filled with expectations—score a lot, dunk when possible, look good doing both.

The flip side is what they are expected to avoid—getting shown up by an opponent, particularly a white opponent. Even someone such as Brian Bachman, whom Thurmond faced last year when Glen Cove played Jericho in the Class B quarterfinals. Like Thurmond, Bachman was an all-county player. But get beat by Bachman, Thurmond said, and he would be slammed, especially from black fans.

"Yeah, definitely," Thurmond said. "I've seen people in the community say racial things on the courts—'That white boy bust your ass!' "

As it turned out, both Thurmond and Bachman played well, and the two seniors ended the game with a hug at midcourt.

According to Johnson, being beaten by a white player is "the worst thing" that could happen to a black player—"except losing."

"And getting dunked on," added senior guard Cliff Davenport, who is black.

For a white player, it is a world turned upside down.

"It would look better if I rebounded over a black guy than a white guy," said Keith Hansen, a 6-8 senior center who is white. "It makes you feel so good. If you can beat the black guy, you must be pretty good, that's what they're saying."

Again, there is the flip side: When less is expected, respect can be harder to earn. Hansen said he knows what would have been said had he beaten out Tad Williams, a black player who also was 6-8, for a starting role on last year's team: "Either I must be pretty good, or it's because we have a white coach."

TURNING THE TABLES

The players say they don't buy into stereotypes. It's other people, they say, who believe in them. "Just like they say that white people can't jump, but they say white people can shoot better than black people," Davenport said.

But stereotyping is not that simple. Athletes, for example, often size up opposing teams along racial lines.

"When we look at a white team, we'll be, like, 'Oh, we've got to watch out for the shooting. Oh, we have the boards,' " Davenport said. "Watch the picks, because they're going to have the picks because they listen to the coaches. A black game, like you see an all-black team, it's like a fast-paced game, you go up and down the court. It's just all about athletics."

So, stereotypes are tough to shake.

"Yeah," Davenport said.

Johnson and Davenport have seen a difference in some of their teammates before some games—this year's squad had eight white, four black and two Hispanic players—depending on the race of the opponent. There are few jitters before playing a predominantly white team.

"If we see an all-black team, the white kids will be, like, 'Oh, they're good. Oh, we can't beat them.' White kids tend to do that," Davenport said. "I'm, like, come on, you've got to think positive. They're not all good."

Black opponents, Glen Cove's black players said, sometimes prey on that apprehension and try to intimidate their white Glen Cove teammates. "There's a couple of our guys on our team and the black guys on their team are, like, 'If you shoot the ball I'll kick your ass,' and things like that," Thurmond said, "and people will be intimidated."

Donny Seaman, program director at the predominantly black Glen Cove Boys and Girls Club, said black players also can fear black opponents. He schedules certain teams for his club squads with that in mind.

"If we went up against Syosset's ninth-grade team, though Syosset has a solid program, the kids would not shy off as much because they're all white," Seaman said. "Now, if we went up against Roosevelt's ninth-grade team, there would be a little bit of nerves rattling."

Glen Cove varsity coach Jon Dolecki believes things are changing, however. The Big Red could win games 10 or 15 years ago "because we were black," he said. "I don't think that's a factor anymore."

Glen Cove's last game of the 1997-98 season was a playoff matchup against predominantly white Jericho. As one Jericho supporter entered the gym, she spotted Glen Cove warming up, gasped, and said with awe, "Oh, my God!"

Tad Williams thought she was commenting on his height. Virtually everyone else from Glen Cove said she simply was counting heads—Williams and nearly half his teammates were black.

Jericho won.

PRESSURE COOKER

For many of Glen Cove's black players, the pressure begins at home. That usually means the housing project known as The Hill. Located in the mix of apartment buildings and townhouses, some well-kept, some run-down. Most blacks in Glen Cove live there.

The Hill is isolated from the rest of Glen Cove. The vast majority of white residents never go there. Ricky Johnson, a reserve on the basketball team, said some white classmates will drive onto The Hill to give him rides; for others, he must walk down to a "certain spot where they can drop me off and pick me up so they don't have to worry about anything."

On an autumn morning, the area is quiet. A woman with a walkie-talkie patrols the grounds around the townhouses known as Kennedy Heights. Workers enter and leave an apartment building across the way. Nights—at least some nights at some apartment buildings—are a different story. Ricky Johnson's mother, Cathy Potter, jerks her head disdainfully toward those buildings and calls them "Wild Kingdom" because "they go crazy over there." Youths, she says, hang out in front, drinking and smoking and harassing others. Most of the white people she sees there at night, Potter said, are looking for drugs.

"this side of town," Seaman said sadly, "is almost like a closed door."

Thurmond, like many of the great black players before him, grew up on The Hill. Most of his basketball education took place at the Boys and Girls Club, a low-slung building whose stone facade shows wear from the ravages of time.

The Hill, Seaman said, always has put its athletes on a pedestal, especially its male basketball players. That creates different pressures for black players such as Todd Johnson and Davenport, who do not live on The Hill. When they go to the Boys and Girls Club, they must prove they can play with blacks from The Hill.

"When I show my face there, it's, 'What are you doing down here? You come to play ball?' " Davenport said as Johnson laughed, recognizing his tone of mocking dismissal.

Both players said some white classmates expect blacks from The Hill to be better players, too. If he turned out to be as good, Davenport said, "They'll be surprised."

Glen Cove players—black, white and Hispanic—say there is a strong sense of ownership of basketball in the black community in general that fosters both pride and pressure on teens.

"They feel like it's their game," Dolecki said.

"It's like a tradition," Thurmond said, and new players are expected to take their place in a line that often resembles a family tree. One of Thurmond's older cousins is former Glen Cove great Anthony Penn. Todd Johnson's older brother and a cousin—Damon Garner and Michael Grant, respectively—were both all-county players. Davenport and Thurmond are cousins.

Seaman, whose son Allan is a freshman who was called up from the junior varsity for this year's playoffs, calls himself and other legends of the past the "elders." Young players are expected to test themselves against these veterans, a ritual that usually takes place at the

Boys and Girls Club. Taking advice is part of the package. Often during halftime at high school contests, one of the elders will come out of the stands to instruct a player in some finer point of the game. Thurmond, now a freshman at Dean College in Massachusetts, considers Seaman his mentor.

"There is history, he comes from somewhere and we're a part of where he comes from," Seaman said, proudly producing a photo of himself with a 10-year-old Thurmond.

There is no corollary in the white community, nothing analogous to Thurmond having his performances dissected by an assortment of alumni.

"You come home after the game, even if you lost, the older guys are, like, 'You should try this move like this next time,'" Thurmond said.

That support system often is not there when they go to college. Separated from their mentors, some Glen Cove alumni have found the going tough and quickly returned. Black athletes know the cynicism that awaits them after high school:

No matter how well you do at Glen Cove, no matter where you go to college, you will fail.

Dolecki said many white players and students in general also struggle and come home. But the sting of this label is felt most keenly by black basketball players, a point Thurmond made clear shortly before heading off to Dean last spring.

"There's a lot of people that went up to college and did really well the first year and they came back and they got into the wrong things, like drugs or whatever," Thurmond said.

He is determined to overcome the skeptics.

"There are people out there who are saying that," Thurmond said, "and I feel I would be just smacking myself in the face if I did that."

Thurmond, who has had a good freshman year on and off the court at Dean, wants to return to Glen Cove with his diploma and become a physical education teacher and coach at his old school. "It's like something you want to prove people so wrong," Thurmond said.

Most people who know him believe he will make it.

"He's different than them," said Vanessa Saavedra,

the leading scorer on the girls basketball team. "I think
he's going to go far. I don't think he's going to fall into
that trap like other people did."

THE FANS

In the stands at Glen Cove, it's blacks to the left,
whites to the right.

"I don't know how. I don't know why. But that's how
it looks," Davenport said. "It's always been that way."

It happens at every game. Black fans from the community cluster along the left side of the stands. White
fans, both Glen Cove's and the opponent's, move to the
center and right. There is more mixing among current
students, many of whom migrate to the top rows.

When the game begins, a group of black fans, mostly
young men, keeps up a loud and steady stream of commentary from opening tip to final buzzer—some of it so
outrageous and funny that people sitting nearby can't
help but laugh out loud. The fans pepper referees with
criticisms and coaches with suggestions. They yell out
to individual players until they get their attention, then
give the players instructions. They shout goodbye to de-
parting fans of the opposing team, when Glen Cove
clearly has the game in hand. White fans, Hansen observed, are more "organized" in their cheering, more
likely to produce "one noise."

Former athletic director Sal Travatello said the stands
have been split since he arrived in 1960. The players
grope for explanations. It's who gets there first. It's who
wants to be nearer the concession stand. It's who wants
to be at Glen Cove's end in the second half. Some say
it's a reflection of the city's cliquishness. No one finds it
particularly disturbing.

"I don't think it's really anything racial," Thurmond
said. "I just think it's the whites sitting with the whites
and the blacks sitting with the blacks."

More important to the players and their coach is
whom the crowd cheers for.

"The black community doesn't accept the white basketball player," said Dolecki, who is white. "You get
that just being in the stands and just listening to them
talk…We've seen that over the years because over the
years we've had a lot of white point guards and they are

unmerciful to them, and I'm talking before Jamie."

Jamie is Dolecki's son, last year's point guard and the only white starter on the team. Jamie was criticized harshly throughout his career, especially by black fans —something noted by white and black players alike.

"I remember one game," said Ted Caruso, a former player who frequently attends home games. "They were screaming, 'Take out the white boy!'"

Jamie Dolecki said such comments began in his sophomore year, but he was reluctant to blame it on race. Jamie said it was due "predominantly" to the fact his father was the coach.

Ashanti Douglas, a black student who graduated last spring, said: "There's definitely a lot of pressure on him. Based on Dolecki, his dad, or whatever…The guys, I hear them in the stands."

Thurmond said black fans—many of whom are former Glen Cove players—will cheer good performances by white players. "When I was in the crowd yesterday they gave Mike Puckett a lot of props, he was doing really well," Thurmond said after attending a game during Christmas break from Dean. Puckett, a junior, is white.

In truth, Jamie Dolecki's treatment was hopelessly entangled with the fact that his father was the coach. But both Thurmond and Jamie Dolecki said that black fans are less likely to tolerate mistakes made by any white player.

"That's how it is, it's always been like that," Jamie said.

"They don't forgive mistakes as easily, definitely a tough crowd," Thurmond said. "Jamie would do good and the crowd would still dog him. I think they would be harder on the white person. Why, I don't know, but I think they would be."

Thurmond—whose skill, open personality and engaging smile made him a fan favorite—said white fans are more likely to accept players of all colors, whether they are playing well or not.

Sometimes, however, it is just about basketball, like it was back in December, as a dispirited crowd watched Glen Cove's junior varsity lose a home game to Chaminade. With the clock winding down, a Chaminade player drove the lane and unexpectedly threw down a forceful dunk.

Instantly, a group of Glen Cove's black fans sprang to their feet in boisterous celebration. The Chaminade player was white.

In the end, perhaps, a dunk is just a dunk.

Writers' Workshop

Talking Points

1) Count the number of words in each sentence of the first two paragraphs. Examine how effectively this draws in the reader. How does it affect the pacing for the story?

2) Study the use of quotes to support the points made by the writer. "So, stereotypes are tough to shake. 'Yeah,' Davenport said." Find other examples in the story. How does this vary from a traditional approach to using quotes?

3) The writer spent eight years covering high school sports before he started this project. Is that experience reflected in Dobie's voice as he writes this series? Do you sense a greater voice of authority than from someone without that experience?

4) The writer uses italics for certain assumptions that are not attributed: *"Blacks are good in basketball. White men can't jump."* Why do you think he used this format?

Assignment Desk

1) Examine your own writer's voice. Do you write with authority? When is it appropriate to do so?

2) In this story, students battle the expectations they face when they are stereotyped. Research and write about expectations and stereotypes in another setting: an office, a college, a restaurant.

3) Have you ever felt stereotyped? Write a personal essay describing and reflecting on the experience.

Balancing act

MAY 18, 1999

The Glen Cove gym, 6 p.m., Oct. 23, 1998:

The game is over and so is the season. Having defeated Great Neck North, Daisy Sanchez and the rest of the Glen Cove High School girls volleyball team begin to disassemble the net for the final time. But first they have to deal with Brandon Villa. Released from the confines of the stands, the 3-year-old dynamo is running amok. He attaches himself to the net, hanging from it as if it were a chin-up bar.

Daisy, Brandon's older sister, finally pries him off and the girls lower the net to the floor. But Brandon attacks again, sprawling across the net, making it impossible to fold. Exasperated yet entertained, Daisy and her teammates laugh and try dragging the net, which gives Brandon a nice ride but does nothing to dislodge him.

And there he lies like a millstone—which, now that the season has ended, is what he has become to Daisy. She never would choose to see it that way—this is her brother, after all. But family ties cannot obscure the fact that caring for him and his sister, Cynthia, will keep Daisy tethered to home for the next two seasons.

What she wants to do is join the rifle team in the winter and play softball in the spring. What she has to do is go straight to a job when classes are over in order to help support her family, then go home to take care of Cynthia, 9, and Brandon.

"I feel cheated," she says. "I'm happy…to help my family. But I still feel cheated because I still would like to do so many things but I'm not able to do them."

Daisy, a junior, was born in Colombia and arrived in Glen Cove in time for fifth grade. In many respects, her story is not unusual among immigrant Hispanics, the fastest-growing segment of Long Island's population. Her experience illustrates the many economic and cultural barriers that stand in the way of participation in high school sports by immigrants in general, and by Hispanics in particular.

Sports can be a powerful tool for newcomers looking for acceptance. But for the burgeoning population of Hispanic immigrants in Glen Cove, many obstacles can lie in the way—language differences, cultural expectations about the role girls play in family life and, perhaps most powerful of all, economic pressures.

"I saw a lot of kids who had talent who could have helped us, but basically were forced by their parents or had pressures economically to quit," said Eddy Linares, who emigrated from the Dominican Republic and played football and baseball at Glen Cove.

The phenomenon is not unique to Glen Cove.

"The notion of both males and females contributing to put bread on the table continues to be a predominant problem for young immigrant students," said Hector Garza, director of the Office of Minorities in Higher Education at the American Council on Education. "There is a huge economic gap between Hispanic immigrants and other U.S. citizens, so you find the parents often are engaged in two or three jobs...So the responsibility falls on young people, high school students, to get home early from school to cook dinner or take care of the children. It's just an expectation, a fact of life."

Hispanics hardly are the only students who forgo sports for after-school jobs. Though there are no statistics relating employment with athletics, Glen Cove officials believe the need to work affects Hispanics in disproportionate numbers.

"Absolutely," said Lori Austin, a Spanish teacher and moderator of Glen Cove's Spanish Club. "That's very common in the Latino families...These girls work at every store in town."

Austin said she started a soccer club that met right after school for the many boys unable to try out for the varsity team.

"In some cases, I told the boys, 'Let me see if I can get you on the team,' and they said, 'No, I absolutely have to work,' " Austin said. "By 3:15 or 3:30, they began to disperse because they had to go to work. It's such a factor. It's so real."

Lonnie Bresnick, boys soccer coach for 19 years, always has a contingent of Hispanic immigrants on his team. Four of this year's group emigrated within the past few years; all four work. One starter, El Salvadoran emigre Antonio Zavala, missed four games because of his job. As Glen Cove advanced to the Nassau County Class B semifinals, Zavala missed two of three playoff games, including the semifinal loss to Jericho.

"He had no choice," Bresnick said. "Family pressure."

A COACH'S OFFICE, 10:15 A.M.

Daisy plops down on a couch. Always effervescent and bustling, she seems even more so than usual this morning. Daisy careens through life on a normal day, spraying smiles and hellos like a politician on a caffeine rush. This day is special—Homecoming Friday. A pep rally will take place in a few hours. The volleyball match later this afternoon will feature a ceremony to honor the team's seniors, and figures to attract the largest crowd of the season.

Daisy's mother, brother and sister are coming. She says this is the second time they will see her play. Although she is excited, a hint of sadness creeps into her voice as she admits she longs for the opportunity to be a three-sport athlete like one of her best friends, Carmen Delcid.

Daisy's face is a kaleidoscope of expression and she summons some of those looks now. A wrinkle of her nose, a rolling of her eyes, a twisted mouth all provide insight into what she thinks and feels. The effect is heightened by words that fly from her mouth like pellets from a BB gun.

She says she came close to fulfilling her dream last year, when her mother gave her permission to join the rifle team. At the last minute, her mother, Rosa Bedoya, rescinded her approval. In spring, however, Rosa signed the permission slip for softball and Daisy attended the team's first meeting.

"I was so excited—softball I wanted to do really bad," Daisy says.

The night before the first practice, everything changed.

"I tell my mom I have practice and she's like, 'Oh man, Daisy, but I can't,' " Daisy says. "I was just, like, 'But Mom, it already started.' And then she was, like,

'I'm so sorry,' and I'm just, 'OK, OK,' " says Daisy.

She lets out a little chuckle, bittersweet and filled with chagrin. Daisy uses laughter like a tool. She punctuates the entire account of her near-brushes with rifle and softball with bursts of a soulful staccato that salves the most painful moments.

Those were the ones that came after softball season began.

"Ohhhh, I felt so sad," Daisy says. "I would hear them talking about the game in classes or something…And I'd be, like, ohhhhhh God, you know? But then I just don't say anything."

Not all Hispanic girls are burdened in the same way. Vanessa Saavedra, an all-county player in volleyball, also was the leading scorer on the basketball team. Delcid is on the volleyball, rifle and outdoor track teams. Neither Saavedra nor Delcid has younger siblings.

Melissa Castro does. She participated in cross country, cheerleading and track before graduating last June and said proudly, "It's basically Hispanic women have to stay home, go home early, take care of the housework…My family does not believe in that. My mom tells me to go out there, push for it, get what you want, get what you deserve, and that's what I'm basically doing right now. I'm breaking that stereotype. I don't go home after school."

But she did go home in middle school, when her sister and brother were too young to care for themselves.

Walle Johanson, who coached both the volleyball and softball teams until retiring in June, often accommodated girls in Daisy's situation by letting them bring younger siblings to volleyball practice. "We'd give them a ball and they'd play on the other side of the gym," he said.

Compounding the economic pressures are Latino cultural mores that root a Hispanic girl in her home. Hispanic parents, Daisy and her peers say, are far more protective of daughters than sons.

"With guys, [parents] don't care," Daisy says. "The girls they protect completely. It's like a flower blooming, and it's like the guys are like a weed."

"Nice simile," Delcid says, laughing.

Alicia Hormaza, a former all-county volleyball player, called home "your sanctuary" and said, "Oh my God, that's been the story of my life…It was really, really hard for me to get out there and play volleyball."

Hormaza got permission to play by slipping papers in front of her parents and asking them to sign, not explaining what they were. She covered up staying late for practice by saying she was at club meetings.

Sometimes playing sports comes with a price. Castro said although her mother's friends generally approved of her playing, "You can see in their expressions, even though they're happy, it's kind of iffy. Sometimes they criticize: How come I'm not helping my mom as much as I should be?"

THE GLEN COVE GYM, 4:30 P.M.

Daisy flits about the court before the game begins. She has donned a multicolored bandanna and painted her cheeks—BIG RED on the right cheek, MEAN GREEN on the left. She runs through drills, smiling all the while. Just short of 5 feet tall, she mixes a good serve with a feisty style and competes with the same infectious joy that marks the summer games she plays with Delcid at Pryibil's Beach. When warmups are over, Daisy joins in the applause as the team's three seniors—Saavedra, Erin Smith and Notoya Stone—are recognized.

But her cheerfulness masks the uneasy accommodation she has made with her mother. The family makes arrangements to get through September and October while Daisy plays volleyball, a popular sport among girls from Central and South America. When the season is over, Daisy returns to the fold. This year, that means an after-school job tutoring Hispanic children at the public library. Then she scurries home to Cynthia and Brandon to supervise the evening ritual of homework, dinner, relaxation and bed. On Saturday, she does office work for her uncle.

Rosa, meanwhile, works 12-hour days at a commercial laundry to support her family, then goes to night school to learn English and take a computer class.

Daisy began helping out immediately after being reunited with her mother in Glen Cove six years ago. When Daisy was 4, she moved to New Jersey to live with her grandmother until her mother and Cynthia emigrated to Glen Cove. Brandon was born here. Daisy's father remains in Colombia; the family lives with Cynthia and Brandon's father. At first, helping out was easy for Daisy.

"Then I started to realize it—that every time I tried to do something I couldn't because I had to go home and be with the kids or I had to go home and help my mom or something," Daisy says.

The problems intensified when Daisy joined the junior high volleyball team in seventh grade. Some days, Daisy went to practice without her mother's permission. Some days, Rosa arrived during practice and took her daughter home. Gradually, they came to an understanding—Daisy loved volleyball, Rosa needed her help.

As the game begins, Rosa settles into her seat in the stands. Like her daughter, she is smiling.

THE GLEN COVE GYM, 6:15 P.M.

Cynthia Villa, Daisy's sister, watches Daisy and her teammates as they pack up the volleyball equipment. A third-grader, Cynthia looks at her big sister with obvious admiration. Brandon, meanwhile, gambols about the gym. With five years separating Cynthia and Brandon, it is easy to imagine Cynthia someday taking care of her brother.

A few weeks later, on a brisk November evening, the three kids sit around the family's kitchen table. Having just arrived home from her tutoring job, Daisy immediately plunges into the business of checking Brandon's and Cynthia's homework. She alternates speaking English and Spanish because she worries they will lose part of their cultural heritage if she does not. Afterward, Daisy begins her own homework as Cynthia reads a Roald Dahl book and Brandon cavorts about the kitchen. Whenever Daisy reprimands her brother, which is often, he calls out in singsong fashion, "OK, Mommy."

By now, Daisy is tired. That morning, Brandon woke her up at 3:15 and vomited all over her room. At her tutoring session, she had her hands full trying to convince a girl with a loose tooth to stop chewing gum, come up with homonyms for a boy writing a poem for English class, and rummage for a calculator to check another kid's math homework.

Daisy holds her head in her hands as she tries to concentrate. Enrolled in Regents classes, her guidance counselors say she is hard-working and highly motivated. She would like to study marine biology in college and also is contemplating enlisting in the Army. She sits beneath a picture of Jesus and the Twelve Apostles that hangs on the wall by the table. Then Brandon misbehaves again. Daisy threatens to take away his television privileges and he quiets down.

Cynthia, who has been sitting quietly in her chair, says she likes to watch Daisy play volleyball. She says volleyball is her favorite sport. She never has been on a team but she plays with her cousin, Christina, who is 10, outside in the yard. In school, they practice with a soccer ball until their arms turn red.

"I like volleyball, basketball and soccer," she says dreamily, and adds that she wants to play those sports in school.

Daisy picks her head up and nods at Brandon. "She'll probably have the same problem I have—she'll have to take care of him," Daisy says.

Cynthia turns to study Brandon. It's clear she sees him only as a brother.

"Yeah," Cynthia says, "but I think he'll be old enough and he won't be a pain in the butt anymore."

* * *

Sometimes language is a barrier to playing sports. Immigrants for whom English is a second language often feel distant from schools and school sports, said Pascual Blanco, executive director of La Fuerza Unida de Glen Cove, a community-based social service agency. It was Blanco who hired Daisy as a tutor and office worker.

Sports teams, Blanco said, are an extension of school and "parents are not involved...in many areas of the school that affect the way the children are educated and the way the children might participate in extracurricular activities."

For those Hispanics who do participate, families are rarely in the stands. Bresnick said boys soccer games played at night at Pascucci Field, which is near the predominantly Hispanic section of Glen Cove called The Lower Orchard, will draw Latino fans. Afternoon games up at the high school will not.

"The Spanish kids who were there, their parents weren't there," said David Boyajian, a Venezuelan wrestler and football player who graduated last June. "They're working. They really don't get involved too much with the sports thing."

THE GLEN COVE GYM, 6:30 P.M.

Daisy and her family are ready to go home. Rosa smiles as Daisy says her goodbyes. Her mother might be pulling her away from sports, but Daisy refuses to blame Rosa.

"I don't think it's her fault," Daisy says. "It's something that happened and we just have to stick by each other and help each other out."

Daisy's athletic future is unclear. She is fairly certain rifle and softball will remain out of the question. She hopes she will be able to play volleyball as a senior. "I was planning to do a lot my senior year, but who knows," she says.

She wishes Brandon was older. "But," she notes with a rueful laugh, "it ain't happening."

So she keeps working—to earn money for her junior prom, to earn money for her mother and sister and brother. Lately, she has been wondering about whether she will be able to go away to college. She would love to—and thinks her mother would encourage her—but says she would feel guilty "because I can't leave them like that."

Then they are gone, out of the gym and into the parking lot. The hallways are nearly empty now. Back in the athletic department office, a piece of paper lies on a shelf just inside the door. It is the signup sheet for the rifle team. There are 13 names on the list.

Daisy's name is nowhere to be found.

Writers' Workshop

Talking Points

1) Study the structure of this story. The subheads indicate this story is a "tick-tock," a strict chronological retelling of events. Yet the scenes within each subhead weave background with chronology. How effective is this juxtaposition?

2) The writer authentically captures the voice of a high school junior with this quote: "I was just, like, 'But Mom, it already started,' And then she was, like, 'I'm so sorry,' and I'm just, 'OK, OK.'" Should it have been changed to include the traditional "she said." Does your news organization have a policy for changing quotes? What's the purpose of including a quote such as this, rather than summarizing the information for the reader?

3) The writer uses his own voice to describe Daisy through details, and uses her own words to help paint her portrait. Underline all the ways the writer helps the reader see Daisy.

Assignment Desk

1) The writer uses empathy to emotionally connect Daisy's life to the lives of readers. How can you use empathy in your stories?

2) The last two paragraphs provide the kicker that summarizes the theme of the story. Look for ways to incorporate these telling details in your stories.

Upon reflection

The pitch was seductive.

You should be with us, the coach said. I can get the best out of you.

Ashanti Douglas was on the track team at Glen Cove High School. The coach was from a rival school. Douglas never considered leaving Glen Cove, but she listened. Her specialty was the triple jump, an event the coach knew well. She knew she would improve under his tutelage. And there was one other thing:

He, like Douglas, was black.

Sitting in a classroom on a quiet spring afternoon, Douglas was firm in her convictions: Color does not matter when it comes to a coach. The best coach was the coach who could teach her the most.

But Douglas hesitated as uncertainty crept in. She stared out the window toward the Glen Cove track and tried to decipher the coach's hidden message: Was he appealing to her because he could have made her better in the triple jump, because they were the same race, or both?

After a long silence, she finally spoke.

"Umm, [it was] not necessarily racial," she said. "I don't think it was that. More or less it was because he saw that I had some talent in the event and he could push me to go so much further. The fact that he's black and I'm black and we're in this together was just another plus."

A plus that does not exist in any sport in Glen Cove. The district is among the most diverse on Long Island—55.2 percent of its enrollment is white, according to state Department of Education statistics, 15.0 percent is black, 24.7 percent Hispanic and 5.1 percent Asian and other ethnic groups.

But all of its coaches are white.

Partly, that is because 95 percent of the teaching staff is white: Glen Cove, like most high school districts, must draw its coaches from its faculty first. State regulations require schools to hire certified teachers as coaches; a school can look elsewhere only if no teachers apply for the position. Most districts, including Glen Cove, have additional stipulations in their local teacher contracts that lock them into hiring their own teachers first.

Glen Cove hardly is unique in the racial composition of its faculty. In Nassau County, 94 percent of the teachers are white, compared to 71 percent of the students. Suffolk has a similar disparity—96 percent of its teachers are white; 78 percent of the students are white.

Neither county has done a racial breakdown of its coaches. An informal survey produced these results: There is not a single black head coach among the 111 teams that play high school football on Long Island. Approximately 11 percent of the area's public school boys basketball head coaches are black; among their girls basketball counterparts, about 8 percent are black.

Cathy Gallagher, executive director of Section XI, the governing body of high school sports in Suffolk, said when she looks at the number of coaches of color, "It's probably not proportionate to the players who play boys basketball, specifically."

Both Gallagher and her Nassau counterpart, Todd Heimer, said the issue of needing more coaches of color has never been raised at any meeting they have attended.

In Glen Cove, administrators say they have been trying to increase the number of teachers of color by recruiting aggressively. The district is part of a consortium that actively recruits educators of color. Progress, they acknowledge, has been slow. Officials say the pool of potential candidates is small. Athletic director Mary Berhang believes the low percentage of teachers of color at Glen Cove may discourage others from applying.

"People will gravitate to where their own kind is," she said. "It's a comfort level."

Berhang recently had an opening for a physical education teacher and received 30 applications. "Not one," she said, "was a minority."

The lack of results has led to skepticism among some students. Even if Berhang had received applications from teachers of color, senior Theneshia Dixon said, "I don't think the district would probably hire them."

So the gulf remains.

What does it mean for a high school athlete?

"I think it's very important," Douglas said.

A former child model and an accomplished R & B singer who performed at Glen Cove's commencement ceremony last June, Douglas took a year off from school after graduating to travel to Atlanta to finish her first record. In the music business, she does not lack for same-race role models. High school was a different story.

"We need to have some more minority teachers. We need to have some more minority guidance counselors, minority coaches, all of that," Douglas said.

"It would be real beneficial for this school, for the students," said Golnar Nikpour, an Iranian emigre who is the No. 1 singles player on the girls tennis team. "It would bring a new vitality to everything. You can't underestimate what a different viewpoint can bring and that's not only in classrooms. It's in sports, anything."

Their concern, experts say, is understandable. People want to see themselves reflected in their environment. Whites see themselves nearly everywhere, but in many arenas, adults of color are hard to find. And if you've never had something, these psychologists say, you won't know what you're missing.

After looking into their own coaching mirror, several Glen Cove athletes admitted they never realized all of their coaches were white.

Many, on the other hand, are well aware of the composition of the coaching staff. Perhaps it is because they don't see any coaches of color in Glen Cove that so many athletes of color want to return to the high school and coach at their alma mater after graduating from college.

Guillermo Martinez called that "my dream." Martinez, a Colombian emigre who played football and baseball before graduating two years ago, is a student at Nassau Community College. He patrolled the sideline last fall, keeping an eye on the quarterbacks as Glen Cove's football team won the county championship.

Michael Thurmond, star of the 1997-98 boys basketball team, is taking physical education classes at Dean College in Massachusetts in preparation for what he sees as a career teaching gym and coaching in Glen Cove.

"I want to…show kids," Thurmond said. "They see this black face teaching gym. I want people to see that, show them they can do that."

Thurmond said many students of color grow up without a father—as he did. He believes he can offer more than someone who has not been through what he has experienced. "I feel I can get through to a lot of kids rather than some other coaches would, just for being black," he said.

Some of Glen Cove's coaches agree. Walle Johanson taught and coached a variety of sports from 1966 until his retirement last June. Shortly after the bell would ring at the end of each school day, Johanson would migrate to his office outside the gym. In the midst of the traffic swirling through the hallways, he would renew his duties as listener, adviser, and father figure. At times, he said, a different coach might have had more of an influence.

"They need to have some role models in their lives, someone who's been there, someone who can discuss what it's like to go down that road," Johanson said. "I can guide, but there's a different perspective and I think we need that perspective."

Football and wrestling coach Pete Kopecky said he often suggests coaching as a career to athletes of color, as he did with Martinez. "There is a need," he said, "especially in Glen Cove and areas similar."

One of those diverse areas is Freeport. Longtime girls basketball coach Ernie Kight, who is black, does not feel his race has been a benefit or a hindrance in dealing with his players. The best coaches, he said, have something in them as individuals that allows them to cross racial lines.

"I have white girls on my team, I have black girls on my team, I have Hispanic girls on my team, I have Haitian girls on my team," Kight said. "They all just treat me as a coach, Coach Kight, and that's it."

On the other hand, Kight agreed, there is merit to Thurmond's argument that simply being black means that he brings something extra to the table by virtue of shared experience. "He probably does," Kight said. "I'm not going to disagree with that. You have to see what he's been through."

When describing their version of an ideal coach, most of Glen Cove's athletes join Douglas in saying they want, first and foremost, the best coach available.

"Give me a coach who can teach me the game, I don't care about his skin color," said Chris Thaw, a black athlete who plays football and lacrosse. "There's some who need visual stimulus. I don't."

Many students are quick to dismiss the debate that has raged in the professional ranks over the need for more coaches of color. These students see pro coaches as figureheads, not teachers. Pros, they say, need to be motivated, not taught. So having coaches of diverse backgrounds aids in communicating with athletes of similar diversity.

It is only in high school, Glen Cove's athletes say, that real teaching occurs. So their priority in identifying the ideal coach is teaching ability. Complicating the issue for Glen Cove's athletes is that the overwhelming majority—no matter what race—give high marks to their coaches for being fair, open-minded, and good teachers and motivators.

But scratch the surface and it becomes clear that kids also are looking for someone to emulate. Sometimes, that someone can be white. Wrestler Joel Bolivar, a Peruvian emigre, and black football players Ricky Johnson and Doni Baskin all said they would love to coach someday; all pointed to Kopecky, who is white, as their inspiration.

But in the search for role models, many athletes of color also said they would love to play for a coach who looks like them.

Martinez believes a coach of color might have made a difference in the lives of several friends whose athletic careers were waylaid by things that took place outside sports.

"The minorities, the blacks, the Hispanics—they were led the wrong way," Martinez said. "They didn't have that role model. Maybe if they had a black coach or a Hispanic coach they would take the other path."

Nelson Rivera, a Hispanic baseball player, said having coaches of color would be important for symbolic reasons. "I'd like to see it, just like when they broke the barrier in the major leagues," Rivera said. "It opened a lot of doors for a lot of people."

White athletes agree that Glen Cove's teaching staff needs to better reflect the students' diversity. Many believe the presence of coaches of color would draw more athletes of color to tryouts. The absence of such coaches, some say, can harm one's self-esteem.

"When you see the janitors mostly coming from your heritage, the people in the cafeteria from your heritage, and you don't see a teacher or a person with a doctorate, that only can give a kid a negative image of themselves," said Julia Schneider, a white soccer player and cheerleader.

Earnest and concerned, Schneider spoke while sitting in an empty lunchroom. The school day was over. A few feet further down the hallway, a black janitor swept out a classroom.

Some find the view that only athletes of color need coaches of color far too limiting. Sharon Lopez, a volleyball player, was Glen Cove's valedictorian in 1995. Lopez, who is black, said white athletes need coaches of color, too, to change their understanding of black people.

"Most people look at it from the perspective that young black people need role models," Lopez said. "But at the same time, in order to change society's perception about what black people can do besides just running and jumping, it's important for everyone to see that."

Sometimes, an experience with a coach can have a profound impact on how an athlete sees herself.

That's what happened to Alicia Hormaza, an all-county volleyball player who graduated from Glen Cove in 1995. Hormaza, a native of Peru who moved into Glen Cove before fifth grade, said she always tried to see herself in an "objective manner" during her high school years. She was an athlete, she said to herself, not a Hispanic athlete.

That changed when she went to college, where she had problems with her volleyball coach. Speaking quietly at the kitchen table in her parents' home, Hormaza said the coach, who was white, did not understand her, could not communicate with her, criticized her style of dress and changed her position on the team. Finally, a sympathetic white teammate told Hormaza that she thought the dispute stemmed from the fact Hormaza is Hispanic.

By nature a warm and welcoming person, Hormaza grew more agitated while telling her tale. She said she quit the team at the end of her sophomore season. While continuing her studies, she has spent the last two years as a student coach at another university. She plays club ball on Long Island. In the summer, she plays in pro tournaments in Long Beach and throughout the Northeast. She would like to coach in high school someday. She still does not care what color a coach is, only that the coach is good. But she will never think of herself as "just an athlete" again.

"I've evolved to think of myself as a Latin athlete now because of my experiences in college, because of what that girl said to me," Hormaza said. "I had felt that it was a lot because I was Hispanic but I didn't want to think it was like that until she said that to me and I realized that everyone outside felt that. It wasn't just her. That's when I started seeing myself more as a Latin person."

Hormaza's experience was echoed in other Glen Cove voices. Thurmond, for example, sees himself as a black athlete because he believes that's what others see—and what they are looking for.

"That's what kids want to see, the younger kids," Thurmond said. "They come to games. They see that black face. It's, like, I can do that. So I see myself as a black athlete. Yes, I do."

More often, Glen Cove's athletes see themselves simply as athletes. Not as black athletes. Not as Hispanic athletes. Not as Asian athletes. Certainly not, ever, as white athletes.

"I don't think of myself as being white," said Nicole Ferrari, a soccer player and member of Glen Cove's track team.

White people rarely do. Color is something to see in other people, and something other people see in themselves.

Some of Glen Cove's white athletes seem to understand this. They know things would change if the tables of race were turned on them. Jamie Dolecki, a three-sport star who graduated last June, said he sees himself as an athlete. But if he was the only white person at an all-black school, Dolecki said, "I'd consider myself the white athlete."

Douglas sees herself as a black athlete. Soon, she will decide whether to continue her career in sports. She hopes to complete post-production on her record soon. She plans to enroll in college in the fall. She might run track. She still says she does not care about the color of her coach but admits, all things being equal, "of course, everyone is going to want to see their own."

And she still thinks about that other coach and his enticing entreaties.

"It's not a bad thing. I see where he's coming from," Douglas said. "He's, like, 'If I was coaching you, we could've, would've, should've been.' You know what I mean?"

Writers' Workshop

Talking Points

1) Note the use of one-sentence paragraphs in the story, starting with the lead. "The pitch was seductive." "But all of its coaches are white." "So the gulf remains." Are they effective? What purpose do they serve? How do they affect the story's pacing?

2) Count the number of sources in this story. What's the benefit of including so many different voices?

3) Study the transitions in this story. Where are they? How are they crafted? Which ones work best?

Assignment Desk

1) Research the demographics in your school district of the student population, the teaching staff, coaches, administrators, and support staff. Does the coaching staff reflect the diversity of the student body? What stories does your analysis suggest about stereotypes and career tracks?

2) "More often, Glen Cove's athletes see themselves simply as athletes. Not as black athletes. Not as Hispanic athletes. Not as Asian athletes. Certainly not, ever, as white athletes." Is this true in your community, your local high school, your newsroom?

Alone in their success

MAY 20, 1999

Young, gifted and black—that is Danielle Simmons. Graceful and athletic, she was on the volleyball and track teams and was named Glen Cove High School's top female athlete. She also was a varsity cheerleader, played softball outside school on a traveling team and acted in drama club productions.

Smart and confident, she took honors and Regents classes before graduating last year.

By either measure—athletic or academic—Simmons was a success. But her achievements, by and large, took place in dramatically different worlds: The playing field often looked nothing like the classroom.

In sports, Simmons mingled with kids from a variety of backgrounds, kids who were pulled together by their love of competition. In classes, she often was isolated, the only black student in a sea of white faces. For Simmons, it was an emotional seesaw—camaraderie on teams, loneliness in the classroom.

"I barely ever talked to anyone in the class, and the only time I became close with people was if we played a sport together," Simmons said about her time as the only black student in an honors math class. "I was really uncomfortable with it…I went to class, did what I had to and got out."

Her experience was not unique. Although some black athletes sitting alone in upper-level courses said they do become friendly with white classmates, others suffer a sense of separation. For these athletes who, like Simmons, make friends easily with teammates in the various sports they play, the contrasts between sports and academia could not be drawn more sharply.

Black honors students who do not play sports also can be isolated. But the problem affects athletes in disproportionate numbers: Teachers say the majority of the students of color who take high-level classes are athletes.

"Most of the kids of color in honors and AP [Advanced Placement] classes also play sports," said John Kessler, an AP history teacher who coaches boys and girls tennis and co-teaches Glen Cove's popular "Minority Experience" class.

Choosing to be "the only one" in a classroom takes courage—the kind of fortitude often possessed by successful athletes. But embracing relative isolation also means dealing with a host of pressures within the classroom.

To basketball player Cliff Davenport, being the only one means feeling that all of the white kids in a Regents class are smarter and that he has to work extra hard just to prove he belongs there—a reverse of the basketball stereotype that expects blacks to be better than whites.

To football and lacrosse player Chris Thaw, being the only one means having white classmates tell him that he has changed their view of the capabilities and interests of black students in general.

Sharon Lopez, a black volleyball player who was Glen Cove's valedictorian in 1995, said being the only one meant the unwanted role of official black spokesperson.

"It is tough because you feel like you're the voice of every black person when things come up," Lopez said. "You know there's no other voice besides mine."

Sometimes the very material being studied in class exacerbates a black student's sense of difference and reinforces her separateness. Theneshia Dixon, who plays soccer and runs track, takes Regents classes—usually with only one or two other black students. In American history, Dixon said, whites and blacks often have opposing points of view on topics such as racism.

"A lot of those white people do not feel there's still racism because either they are ignoring it, they're pretending it's not there or something, I don't know," Dixon said. "And then we would think there is and it would be a minority because there's only two or three of us in the class."

The tension is dynamic and reverberates from a simple discovery kids stumble on as early as middle school: Where sports blends kids from different backgrounds, classes sometimes keep them apart.

"Classes definitely have the hugest thing to do with

how people separate," said Sarah Bellissimo, a white soccer and softball player who takes Regents and honors classes. "In my classes, it's always the same people."

Glen Cove officials say they do not do statistical breakdowns by race of their honors classes. But, as assistant principal Jim Brennan admitted, "It would be an interesting statistic."

The numbers would show that in Glen Cove, as in high schools across the country, the honors track is heavily white.

"Of course, there's still in a sense tracking here in the high school and tracking, of course, sometimes goes along racial lines where that rare minority individual happens to be in honors classes," said Thom Ruckert, an honors English teacher and former lacrosse coach who co-teaches the "Minority Experience" class with Kessler. "We still, I'm afraid, fall into that trap. Athletics is more of an equalizer than the educational system is. Now if we had all heterogeneous classes, we'd have a whole different story."

Sheryl Godine, one of the few black teachers at the high school and assistant to the coordinator of special education, said there is some hope that new state regulations requiring all students to pass Regents exams eventually will produce classes every bit as diverse as Glen Cove's sports teams. But she punctuated her hope with a sigh.

"Will that split still occur? I'd like to say no, but I believe yes, it will continue," Godine said.

"All you have to do is walk into class."

Ricky Johnson, a football and basketball player, said he is the only black student in his two Advanced Placement classes. Thaw is the only black student in his honors American history, physics and honors English classes; two other black students join him for Spanish and pre-calculus. Simmons had numerous honors classes in which she was the only black student.

Often, a black student joins an honors class composed of white students who have been taking the same classes together since middle school.

"I know they probably have been in class together since the beginning, so me being in there, they probably didn't feel the need to say, 'She needs to be a part of us,'" Simmons said.

The bottom line, she said, is either you stay a loner or make friends. Simmons did some of both. Again, athletics provided a point of contrast.

"You can be in a classroom all year, that doesn't mean you're going to be friends with them," Simmons said. "In sports it seems like you go through everything together. It's like a family."

A strong student who began taking honors classes in eighth grade, Simmons also excelled in sports. Though she was short and had small feet, she was fast and fluid with a powerful build. For her, high school athletics was about choices—spring track over softball, cheerleading over basketball (for her last two years, anyway).

By senior year, Simmons was captain of both the volleyball and track teams. Her shopping trips for team supplies with track co-captain Lauren Jensen approach the stuff of legend. Coaches still marvel at Simmons' work ethic and leadership abilities.

"She was one of the most influential people I've had," former volleyball coach Walle Johanson said. "She had the ability to bring a variety of people together for a common goal. She was able to lead them through deed and through her verbal ability…She went the extra step and it influenced a lot of people to do the same thing."

There were awkward moments, as when the captains of the otherwise all-white cheerleading team instructed the team to buy tights of a certain brand and color. They were meant to be skin-tone tights. They were white. To gales of embarrassed laughter, Simmons pointed out that the tights were not going to work for her.

More important to Simmons were her friendships, most notably with fellow cheerleaders and track team members Melissa Castro and Nicole Ferrari. She and Castro, a Peruvian emigré, grew very close—like sisters, both said. Simmons and Ferrari acted in a school play together. Ferrari, who is of Italian heritage, invited Simmons to her house to hang out before the cast party, a memory Simmons recalled with an exclamatory, "Wow!"

Simmons smiles easily, a big smile that starts in her

eyes and blooms outward. That's the smile she was likely to flash on a warm spring afternoon on Glen Cove's asphalt track, as she helped a white teammate with her stance in the starting blocks.

"You kind of draw that friendship on an out-of-school basis, which is better than school," Simmons said. "It's just a whole other level of friendship."

Highly-achieving black students such as Simmons are not the only athletes who find the contrast between sports and academia perplexing. Many of Glen Cove's white athletes agree.

"A lot of these people that I've grown up with, I don't know what they're thinking, I don't know anything about them even though I know who they are," said Julia Schneider, a white AP and honors student who plays soccer and was on the cheerleading squad with Simmons.

Frustrating as the situation might be, the difference for many whites is that the emotional toll on them is minimal.

"It's just the way it is," said Keith Hansen, a senior who plays basketball and baseball. "I don't go in looking like we need more black people in here, we need more Spanish people. I just go in and do what has to be done, and if there's a black person in there, all the better."

Black honors students can be frustrated further by what they sometimes perceive as the unwillingness of their white peers to reach out to them—a jarring juxtaposition to their experience in sports, where teammates often go out of their way to help one another.

"It's not that hard, if they were to come up to us and just speak to us," Johnson said. "A lot of people judge a book by its cover. People see me, they're like, 'Oh, he's a tall black kid with dreads, I'm not speaking to him.' Why? You don't know me not to speak to me."

The converse also can be true. Many students of color who are the only ones in their classes are afraid to ask for extra help or even ask a question for fear of looking stupid and having that attributed to one's color. Godine, who also is moderator of the African-American Culture Club, recalled a meeting last fall in which black students spontaneously formed a tutoring network because they were too embarrassed to talk to their teachers or fellow white students.

"It's very tough," Godine said. "And sometimes that one kid may not have the inner strength to be able to remain in that high-level class because he or she may feel uncomfortable." Sometimes, sports makes the task easier. For many gifted black students isolated in their classes, it is a way to find common ground with each other.

"For the high-achieving student of color," said Mount Holyoke College psychology professor Beverly Daniel Tatum, "sports is the place where they can connect."

Kim Smith, a junior who is on the basketball and track teams and in honors and Advanced Placement classes, said the only time she sees her friends who are not in her honors classes is during lunch or in the hallways—unless they are on the same team.

Some highly-achieving black students struggle with a different form of isolation—the accusation from some fellow black students that they are "acting white."

Black student-athletes easily recite the circumstances that expose them to grief. Nothing, they agree, provokes the charge more readily than taking upper-level classes. But, Thaw said, minefields are everywhere.

"White friends. White music," Thaw said, smiling while shaking his head in frustration. "Walking a certain way. Talking a certain way."

The judgment can condemn or ostracize. Athletes already coping with isolation must now deal with rejection. Others who might join them in honors classes feel compelled to stay away.

Highly-achieving white students can be subject to peer pressure as well. But the charge of "acting white" uniquely affects students of color and can be part and parcel of the high cost of accomplishment, particularly black athletes such as Danielle Simmons.

"There's so much peer pressure and it's like a domino effect that drags the kids down," said Brian Simmons, one of Danielle's older brothers and a Glen Cove city policeman. "It's very frustrating. Extremely frustrating…To me, it's a race problem that we haven't yet programmed our children to [reject]."

The dynamic also is infuriating to community leaders

such as Albert Granger, the first black city councilman in Glen Cove. "Why are you [accused of] trying to be white? Just because you speak properly and you're doing well in school?" Granger said. "It's the most insidious, disgusting thing. I hate it, hate it, because people will never get better unless they educate themselves."

For the student of color who stands accused, the result is a host of pressures that only adds to the strains that characterize adolescence. "[This] is a very stressful time in their life and a very difficult problem," said Hector Garza, director of the Office of Minorities in Higher Education at the American Council on Education, "because all of a sudden they are having to prove their identity and having to disprove that they are wanting to be white."

Danielle Simmons said she felt that a substantial part of the black community did not like her or respect her accomplishments, an observation she followed with a dismissive shrug.

"I get a lot of positive feedback from the white community, which is awkward," Simmons said. "You would think that more people of my own race…would be more or less happy for me."

The criticisms stung, especially those from students she saw as potential peers—the ones, she said, who "have the brains to be in honors classes but think, 'Oh, if I'm in that class they might think that I'm trying to be white.'"

Danielle was not the first member of her family to be singled out. Older brothers Brian Simmons and Michael and Clyde Riggins, all outstanding student athletes, heard the same remarks. All three knew exactly how Danielle felt—rejected, by the prejudices of some whites on the one hand and by the judgments of some blacks on the other.

"You're black but you're not accepted. You're not white and you're not accepted. You're down the middle and it hurts like hell," Brian Simmons said, "because you're a person without a race, a person without an identity, no one wants to accept you and that's not a good feeling at all."

Parents such as Cathy Potter—whose son, Ricky Johnson, often is castigated for his friendships with white teammates—encourage their children to put the criticism in perspective.

"There are good black kids but it's the ones that are not doing good that are saying this to him," Potter said. Her advice: "Ignore them."

But bucking the tide is difficult, said Godine: "You have to be strong in front of the white folks and you have to be strong in front of the black folks. It takes an indomitable spirit and many of these kids just don't have that."

Simmons has been sorting out these kinds of mixed messages for a long time.

As a child, Simmons would accompany her mother to a housecleaning job in a white neighborhood in Glen Cove. Kids her own age would hurl racial epithets and tell the pair to go back to their own neighborhood, a mixed area known as The Landing. When her mother would not let her hang out on The Hill, the predominantly black section of town, Simmons found some black children began keeping their distance, too.

By the time she reached high school, her antennae were finely tuned. As a member of the track team, Simmons delighted in introducing black runners from other schools to a girl she called her relay squad's "true African-American"—South African native Amber Abrams, who is white.

Playing certain sports can help mitigate the stigma. "If you are, on the one hand, at risk for being labeled a nerd or an Oreo because of honors classes," said Tatum, the psychologist, "but yet are a good athlete or successful member of the football team or the basketball team, that sort of balances that."

Other sports only make it harder.

Lacrosse, tennis, golf, swimming, hockey—all are considered "white" sports by many students in Glen Cove. When Thaw tried out for lacrosse, he said some of his black classmates were shocked.

Simmons took up cheerleading partly because she wanted to destroy the perception in the high school that cheerleading was a white activity. To Simmons' surprise, she said some black classmates expressed respect for her choice.

Last September, she went off to Hampton, a predominantly black college in Virginia. She is majoring in computer science. She twirls a flag for the marching band. She might play softball. She is fiercely proud of what she has accomplished.

Recently, her mother visited, accompanied by three kids from their church. On the way home, the kids said they wanted to be like Danielle and go to Hampton. Danielle finds this encouraging.

So do her brothers. Brian is comforted by the thought of Danielle in the company of many highly-achieving blacks.

A few months before heading off to Hampton, a few minutes before the start of another track practice at Glen Cove, Danielle stopped to reminisce. It was early April, the time of year when darkness still comes too soon and the warm promise of early afternoon turns quickly to evening's chill.

Outside, baseball players laden with equipment trundled across the grass to their diamond. Danielle watched them pass by. She talked about wanting to go to Hampton, about making friends with her teammates at Glen Cove, about trying to get through classes, about being like so many athletes of color who walk a fine line between acceptance and isolation.

She let her thoughts drift back a few years, back to eighth grade, back to the time when she was moved into honors classes.

"I was the only black person in my class at all," Danielle said. "So you're either by yourself, or you make friends."

If only it were that easy.

Writers' Workshop

Talking Points

1) Note the word choice in the verbs used by the writer: "The tension...reverberates from a simple discovery," "a big smile that starts in her eyes and blooms outward." Discuss their effect.

2) The writer concludes the story, and the series, with this paragraph: "If only it were that easy." Why does the writer use this for a conclusion? Is it an effective summary?

3) Review and outline the series. Discuss whether the organization was effective. Study the transitions from day to day. Which worked best?

Assignment Desk

1) The writer says he was surprised by students' openness in discussing the issue of race. How can you encourage greater openness with those you interview?

2) Research the breakdown by race of students in honors programs. Is there a pattern of academic tracking? Using this story as a model, write a story based on your reporting.

A conversation with
Michael Dobie

ALY COLÓN: What was the genesis of this project?

MICHAEL DOBIE: The paper had decided it wanted to deal with the issue of race and sports. This was a departmentwide project. We were going to come at it from different angles over the course of a couple of years, and they knew they wanted to do something with the high schools at the early stages. They didn't know for sure what they wanted to do, so that part of it fell on me. I think they came to me because I had extensive experience covering high school sports. When they gave it to me, I was pretty excited about it because I saw a lot of opportunities. The one thing I did not want to do right from the start was be in a position of going to a lot of experts, a lot of adults, and asking them what they saw, what kids felt, what kids were telling them. I thought the only way to do this was through the eyes and ears and mouths of the kids themselves. That really informed this entire project from beginning to end.

Was the race coverage orientation specifically in sports?

This was something sports felt it wanted to do. It's something that Steve Ruinsky, the sports editor, has brought to the section: a big picture look that gets away from the nuts and bolts of game coverage and really looks at the issues. I've done a number of these issue-oriented type projects, so it was a good fit. We had looked previously at things such as the female athlete triad in sports, at hazing, eating disorders among male athletes. So I think this is sort of a natural outgrowth of that kind of curiosity. I should say one other thing that also plays into this. The demographics on Long Island are changing and have been changing for some time. There's been quite an influx of Hispanics from Central and South American countries. They're the fastest-growing segment of the population on Long Island. We

were looking for ways to address not only that con-
stituency but how roles were going to change. How the
newcomers were going to fit into life here; how that was
going to change lives of people that already were here.

**Did you get any sense from Steve as to what the cat-
alytic idea was for him?**

I think *Newsday*, as a paper, has just been very committed to diversity in general. That goes from hiring practices in the newsroom down to what and who you cover.
It's been a topic of a lot of debate. We've had workshops
on developing a "Rainbow Rolodex." It's just a very
pervasive concern. Let's face it, race is a topic that's on
everybody's minds, even if it doesn't progress beyond
that point. So I've got to give Steve a lot of credit for
saying we want to examine this. I'm not sure that everybody knew all the directions I was going to go into
when we did this, but they were very supportive from
beginning to end.

   As far as myself, there are not a lot of writers in
sports who like to tackle large projects, and who can
live with not seeing themselves in the paper for months
on end. A project like this is 95 percent reporting and 5
percent writing. While the writing is very intense, it's a
much smaller percentage of the time involved.

**Was there trepidation on the part of the paper about
this topic, and any trepidation on your part about
what it might mean to tap into a volatile topic like
this?**

I didn't sense any trepidation on the part of the paper in
the beginning or through most of the process. There was
some nervousness during one segment of the series
where I had done a lot of writing about what it meant for
black students to be accused of being white. That was an
explosive situation, and that part of the story was difficult to write. Part of it was a logistical concern that I not
write just about the experience of being a black student
in all-white classes, for example. They wanted to make
sure that I was writing about what was unique about
black student-athletes since this was in the sports sec-

tion. Some of the very strong things that I had ended up on the cutting room floor because they didn't fit into a sports perspective. My trepidations probably were the normal ones in not knowing what kind of resistance you might find from people, not knowing whether people were going to want to go after the messenger instead of the message, not certain if people were going to share what was really in their hearts or not. I also viewed it— for all those reasons—as a tremendous challenge. So I think more than trepidation, it was excitement that I was most filled with.

Did you do anything, or had you done anything prior to this, to prepare yourself?

I think the experience that was the most guiding one was eight years of covering New York City's public and Catholic high schools, being out in those schools, talking with the kids, listening to them, watching them. I had never discussed issues of race in the kind of depth that this project was going to require. I knew that it was going to be a whole different ball game. I did a little bit of reading before I got into talking with the kids. But I really resisted doing too much of that. I did more of that once I was into it for several months, and the reason for that is this: I thought it was very crucial that I go into this with as few preconceptions as possible. I wanted to make sure my questions were not motivated at all by what I expected to find. I didn't want to prejudge anything and I felt that the best thing to do would be to get right into it and start talking to kids, knowing that I had the luxury of time. I did prepare a list of questions to start off with, something I used to help guide me through the early stages and then flow from there in whatever direction the kids were going in.

How did you come up with the initial questions that served as your guide?

With kids, you start asking them about the little factual things in their lives. That gets them talking about deeper issues and allows you to riff off in different directions. Just simply asking them about their parents' backgrounds, where they came from, how they ended up in this particular town of Glen Cove, who their friends were on other teams, what sports they play—that type of thing. You begin to get a sense of who they are and what they care about, what's important to them. I made it a point to be around the school for a couple of weeks before I started asking any questions so I could take a look at who sits with who in the cafeteria, who talks to who on the sidelines at a baseball game, what's the composition of parents in the stands at a softball game.

Then from those kinds of observations, I was able to craft some questions. I was struck, for example, at the beginning about the fact that this was a very diverse high school in its student population, but all the coaches were white. So that was obviously something that I was going to ask the kids. And there would be things that would be happening in real life outside Glen Cove that would spark discussions, whether it was the multi-ethnic Yankees cruising to yet another World Series win and what they thought about that or the home run chase between Sammy Sosa and Mark McGwire. That provided some grist for conversation. But I guess you could say I proceeded slowly with the kids to build up their trust at first and then went from there.

You said that once you did get into it and knew you had time, you did more preparation. Were there any particular books or people that you turned to?

I thought Beverly Daniel Tatum (*Why are All the Black Kids Sitting Together in the Cafeteria?*), a psychologist, was very helpful with the perspective of what it was like to be a minority in a variety of settings. Also I read Lawrence Otis Graham. He writes a lot about racial issues. I'd also read several authors who wrote about immigration patterns earlier in the century and about the role that athletics played even back at the turn of the century in assimilating, or not assimilating, immigrants into society here.

I'd wanted to put what was going on now into a historical context. I ended up using a lot less of that than I thought I might. But it was just good for me to know that this is not necessarily a new phenomenon, particularly with the Hispanic immigrants in Glen Cove, but it was something that has recurred throughout the century with each new group that's come in.

Also, I'd read an article called "Unpacking the White Knapsack" that gave me a lot of insight into some of the aspects of life for people of color along these lines. You know, one of the things that was mentioned in it is that a white person can walk in late to a meeting and it will be assumed that they're simply late. When a black person walks into a meeting late, it might be ascribed to their race rather than to circumstances. It's a subtle but profound change in your thinking when you realize that that's the way life is. That helped me in approaching a lot of the kids in this story. It was things like that that really helped me junk preconceptions I had.

Did you feel a need to stifle, or address, or be alert to your own prejudices, stereotypes, or biases you may or may not have been aware of?

I didn't find myself confronting any biases or prejudices that I hadn't known about. My parents were always very good and very clear about treating people as people. It's something I think that I've always done. Certainly working in the high schools in the city, you're not going to survive if you do anything else.

There were some things that did surprise me: some of the things the kids were willing to talk about, some of the things they thought. I was surprised by the extent to which the kids were so willing to address these topics. It wasn't very difficult to break down defenses in a lot of cases. Predictably, the adults were a lot more wary. You could see the wheels turning. The kids were much more without subterfuge, without artifice. Some were. Some were very nervous. But for the most part, the kids were open. It was very clear they had thought a lot about this topic. They had seen a lot, experienced a lot, and were pretty eager to share their experiences.

How did you feel about being a white writer asking these kinds of questions? What did you try to do to address that?

I was very concerned about that in the beginning, wondering if I would be viewed in different ways by the kids, obviously depending on whether they were students of color or not. One of the reasons I tried to be around an awful lot, even if I wasn't going to be talking to anybody on a particular day, was so I would become more a part of the scenery, a constant in their lives. And I also wanted to make sure our interviews were much more conversations than interviews. A give and take, make it natural, allow the conversation to drift, go into tangents, kibitz, talk about whatever they wanted to talk about that day, whether it was a tough test they had just taken, or boy did you see that game last night—that type of thing. I think, for the most part, that worked.

I found the students of color, in general, to be very receptive. There was no element of distrust that I could see. I think part of that is because the teaching staff is almost entirely white. I think they had had role models along those lines, and when I started asking questions, they could tell that I wasn't there to indict anybody. I wasn't there to fan the flames, or turn this into an explosive issue. I think they all warmed up to the fact that I wanted to know what they felt, what they saw, and what they thought. Certainly you can turn those situations around with the tone of the questions you ask, and I think they picked up correctly on the tone that I had.

What about the white students?

I think some of the white students, a very small percentage of them, were more suspicious. When you go to do a story about race, I think the assumption sometimes is going to be that whites are going to come in for more criticism or that you're going to be pointing a finger at them. And sometimes it took awhile to break down barriers. There were a couple of kids that I never did get through to. There were a couple of kids who absolutely refused to even sit down and talk, which probably said more about them than they intended.

What do you think, as a reporter, were the most valuable things you did to get the most responsive and honest answers?

I think being there and being willing to listen to the kids, as simple as it sounds, was probably the most important thing. I think kids have a lot to say and we don't often stop to listen to them. I probably don't stop to listen to my own kids as much as I should on things like this, and that was a real education for me. And I think the other thing probably was being honest with the kids at all times—no matter what they might want to know—because I think kids respect that.

Was there anything you did that you'd recommend journalists not do?

This is probably an aside—I don't think there was anything I could have done about it—but there were some parents along the way who seemed to think this series was going to put their kid's name out there in bright lights and help them win college scholarships. I'm not sure that they quite understood the direction I was going in. One thing I might try, if I tackled this again, is getting the kids even more in a non-sports setting. Going to their houses, getting them outside the school. But that was part of a debate that I really wrestled with—we all wrestle with from time to time—but in particular on this story.

Whenever we show up, we intrude on a scene. I never want to feel like I'm impacting on the story in any way. So I wanted to be around a lot to have the novelty of me being there wear away. That's something I was very conscious of with kids: the whole idea that we can thrust ourselves into a situation and somehow alter the situation just by our presence.

In dealing with the story, how did you decide how you would break it up?

Trying to decide how to marshal all this stuff was a very difficult process. You're talking about 120 interviews, several hundred hours' worth of tapes, and on top of that all the observations just from watching games, practices, classes, kids in the cafeteria, and kids in the hallway. How we came up with this was a lot of collaboration and give and take between Steve and myself. We spent literally about three or four weeks writing and rewriting outlines before I even got to the writing stage. Then what we set down as the outline, and what I used to guide me when I started writing, was not what we ended up with in all cases, either.

The first day story was a prime example. We had decided that a narrative was going to be the best way to handle the story of these five kids who formed friendships pretty much exclusively through sports and then maintained them—they were all football players—as the football season unfolded. I initially wrote it that way. Then there were some suggestions on the editing end that, no, we really didn't want that. It went through several permutations. It went over to news side. Editors there had a crack at it, and sure enough, what we ended up with was the structure I had originally proposed, which was the narrative. And I think it absolutely worked the best. But the process of organizing was probably the most frustrating part of this entire project.

How did you actually approach the work?

I talked to all the kids with a tape recorder present when we sat down to do formal interviews, not off-the-cuff stuff outside the locker room. I transcribed all those interviews and then printed them out because I like to see interviews on paper. Then, when I had all the interviews, I went through and read them all and took a lot of notes about what the different kids were saying, and then organized those notes into themes. When I took a look at all those themes—and there may have been 30 or 40 different types of topics—I began to see certain things that leapt out as topics that were more important and others that receded into the background. The structure emerged from there. It seemed natural to start with the idea of friendship in sports because I think that's one of the things that we hold very dear about sports: that sports cross all barriers. Sports are supposed to be one of the great melting pots in our country. What we discovered was that, while it can be, it's not always the case. And introducing the notion that there is a lot of gray in what is often considered a black-and-white issue seemed to be a pretty good place to start.

When you actually started going to the schools, how did you make a decision about where you would go, who you would talk to, and what you'd be watching?

At the start, there were some general topics I knew I was going to want to handle just from previous experience: whether sports helps friendships or not; how the kids felt about all the coaches being white. I knew from the start that sports played some role in assimilation for immigrants. I didn't know to what degree, and to what degree in this particular community. I also knew I'd be dealing with the idea of stereotypes and expectations. Then there were other things that came up that were rather unexpected. I think the clearest example of that was at the end of a two-hour interview with one white athlete. He casually mentioned he had black friends on other teams, and he could call those black athletes the "n-word" and they would not mind because he was a friend of theirs through sports. That was something I hadn't been prepared to hear. So that opened up a whole new line of questioning for me, which ended up in a sidebar.

How did you decide to pursue that?

That was a source of great debate when we did do the sidebar: whether or not we were going to print the word. We decided we were going to use it once in a quote from the athlete, and then refer to it from then on as either the "n-word," or in a more general way. As soon as he mentioned that, I realized that this was potentially a very inflammatory topic. It was one that I had to go back to parents on, parents of these athletes who may not have been aware their kids were doing that. Some were and some weren't, incidentally. And it was something you had to talk to athletes—white and black—about. Surprisingly to me—maybe this is where my preconceptions kicked in—the black athletes that I spoke to, for the most part, said, "Yeah, it would be all right. He's our friend and it's okay." That was one place where, if I had a preconception, it certainly was shaken. I think for me the biggest lesson here is that there is no one answer, there is no one experience. There are many different stories, and many different experiences, and painting with any wide brush gets to be a little dangerous.

I'm curious as to how you chose the people you featured.

I think I focused more on the kids who were from multiethnic sports than I did from the kids who played sports that were not. There are some sports that are so-called "white sports," where the teams are predominantly white.

Which ones are those?

Well, certainly golf is considered that way. Lacrosse historically has been that way. Girl's soccer at this high school has been that way. I think a lot of the richness came from teams where there were many different ethnic backgrounds represented—football, girl's volleyball, the two basketball teams, and track. I knew going in that I would be focusing on those sports. I did rely on some recommendations from coaches and teachers about who the sharpest kids were on those teams, because you want kids that have thought about this, that aren't going through life with blinders on. In talking to the kids about one another, you begin to get a sense of who else on the team you really need to speak to, for a variety of reasons. Whether it was a particular experience somebody had, or just their role on the team, or the fact that perhaps they're on two or three different teams and have some different experiences on each team.

As journalists we often say that we're representing other people's points of view when we write. But we are not objective. We have filters. We have our own perspectives. We have our own biases. And we work at addressing those things as professionals. We use certain tools we hope will drive us closer and closer to the core of what the people are saying, and reflecting that back in its most authentic way.

What did you do to help yourself be true to your view of what the kids were saying and what do other reporters need to do?

I think one of the things that I did consciously was to talk to an enormous number of kids—not just to two or three. I'm very distrustful of using the slice-of-life approach to stand for much larger circles in general. I know that's something that we do in journalism. I wanted to apply that approach here but make sure that there was an overwhelming amount of material so I could be convinced that what I was seeing, or what I thought I was seeing, was genuine. Of course, wrinkles inevitably would come up along the way, which made this a more difficult process. It'd leave me thinking that the subject of race is one that's built on shifting sands, and you've got to check your footing all the time. I think that was part of what motivated me to try to expand the web as far and as wide as possible. It's entirely conceivable that if my desk hadn't put some sort of time constraint on this, I could still be talking to the kids in Glen Cove to make sure what I thought I saw was what I was in fact seeing.

Also, I spent a lot of time just driving around the town, going to Pribls Beach, eating in the Boston Market, eating at the ice cream stand, hanging out in the library reading newspapers, driving through neighborhoods—a lot of driving through neighborhoods—just to try to get a feel for the people and the geography. I know it helped in some ways as far as increasing the level of assurance that I had about the stuff that I was seeing and writing. Taking in a Little League game, taking in a youth football game, it just gave me a better sense. Frankly, it also helped me be a lot more casual with the kids when they mentioned something. I didn't have to ask a bunch of questions about what they were talking about. It was a lot easier to make connections as though I was someone who had been around for quite some time.

How much time did you spend reporting and writing?

I had made a couple of brief visits in February 1998 to set up the whole thing. The real earnest reporting started in April. We had decided to keep this to a calendar year. The idea was that this is a year in the life at Glen Cove, so the reporting wrapped up by the end of December.

The month of January 1999 was spent doing the outlines. The next three months solid was writing and
rewriting and rewriting and rewriting.

How did that work?

I think there were times when I was too close to the subject material. I think having an editor at that time was
critical. You know, most of the time when I work—
when I'm doing features, or columns, or whatever it
is—I really do work on my own, send in the story, and
there's often little feedback about it, not very much give
and take. This was marked by an inordinate amount of
give and take. Although I may have fought it at times, it
was give and take that I really needed. Sometimes when
you're in the middle of the forest, it's a little difficult to
see your way out. I'm thinking particularly of the first-
day story, which I thought was the most contentious day
to produce, perhaps because it was the first day and we
wanted to make sure that we started off strongly and on
the right foot.

It must have gone through eight or 10 rewrites from
top to bottom, all the way through. The structure
changed several times—I mean the entire structure
changed—until we ended up back where we started,
with a better version, incidentally, more refined and
more focused. That was a process that I really hadn't
been through before.

I think the fact that this came from someone else
might have made the process more difficult because
there may have been preconceptions in other people's
minds about the kinds of things that I would be doing.
Then when they saw the writing and it was different
from what they originally had conceived, that created
some difficulties. For example, the news side editors at
one point were under the impression that this entire series was going to be a narrative. It was going to be a year
in the life of Glen Cove athletes from the first day I was
there until the last day I was there. That was not my in-
tention from the beginning. Somewhere, the line of
communication on that broke down. Once we got past
the first day, the other days wrote themselves much
more easily.

What advice would you give to reporters when they want to work with the editor on a project like this?

We all have egos. We all tend to think that we're right probably more often than we are. It's important, I think, for a writer to have a strong ego. You need to be firm in your convictions. But you also have to know that there are moments when either you're not going to be right, or you're not going to be as right as you could be, and that someone else's perspective is not necessarily incorrect. I found that to be the case. I fought some things tooth and nail. I was shocked, and still am shocked, about some things that ended up being thrown out, things that I was absolutely certain were going to be essential parts of the story. Some went for philosophical reasons, some for production reasons. But I think you really need to be open to that kind of feedback, especially on a big project like this. When you do spend so much time on a topic like this, you get very, very close to the material. Sometimes you do need to step back. Sometimes you're not able to do that and you really need somebody else to nudge you along. That's a very difficult thing to learn. I'm not even sure that I've learned the dance yet. But I did learn a couple of new steps this time, perhaps.

Now what advice would you give to editors in this kind of situation?

Trust your writer. That's something that comes, not only out of this project, but from other stories I've worked on as well. Let me move off that first point to something else that I wanted to say, which I really think is important. Making sure the writers and editors keep in touch, constant touch, is critical. There were some times when I might have gone several weeks without touching base. My editor didn't know what I was doing at the time. Frankly, that was fine with me because I like to operate on my own. It turned out that it probably would have been far better had we been in constant communication. Then the editor could have helped me look down some avenues that I hadn't thought of. There were some very interesting questions I hadn't thought of that were asked based on what I was telling the editor. Have a firm ego, but not so you are blind to the idea that other people can make some very substantive contributions early in the process, too. I think I probably would have benefited from just alerting the editors to my progress as I went along a little more regularly than I did.

Was there anything else that your editor did for you that you think other editors should emulate?

Given the nature of the subject matter, the most valuable thing he gave me was time. Had he put a limit of three months of reporting, and a month of writing, it would have done a disservice to the project and to the topic. I'm extremely grateful for the fact that he let this unfold naturally. I think I had to be in pace and in rhythm with the school and the kids and the school year, and not rush this through. I think the more I stayed around, the more layers of the onion I was able to peel away, and I had a stronger sense of the kids. I mean they've been living this for 17, 18 years. It would be folly to think you could go in for a month or two and uncover the truth of race and sports. So I think I'm probably more grateful than anything for the time and the resources. The other thing to mention is allotting the amount of space that they did in the paper to do this.

What was the length on this series?

I think the target on the first day—and the targets also changed, as they became aware of what I had—ended up on the first day in the vicinity of 3,500 to 4,000 words for the main story. Then each succeeding day we wanted to be a little bit shorter, a little bit tighter. I believe on the last day we were in the vicinity of 2,000 to 2,500 words.

How did you accomplish that?

I think clearly the best thing is to be as focused as possible. Have as clear an idea of what you really want to do. And be very, very rigorous about cutting out any of the fat. Now there's a difference between fat and texture, of course, and this kind of story just cries out for texture because it's just loaded with gray areas. So that was difficult. In this case, some of the things that ended up being cut, I'm still upset they weren't in there. Other things I realized it was appropriate to cut. One of the things about projects, and about this project in particular, that was fascinating is that in the beginning and through the reporting process you're trying to widen the net as much as you can. Then when you get to the writing process, you have to focus in as tightly as you can. And those two acts are often in violent contradiction.

Is there anything we haven't touched on that you think is important for journalists to know?

This series reminded me about what the essence of journalism is to me, which is getting people to trust you to tell their stories. To me there's no more special gift that someone can give me as a journalist than the trust to tell their story. And I think everybody, everybody has an interesting story to tell. My job is always to find that story. At bottom, this is all about people. People love to read about people. They love to find out about other people. So even when there are big issues you're confronting, I think we always need to tell the story through people.

The New York Times

Somini Sengupta

Finalist, Diversity Writing

Somini Sengupta has been a reporter for *The New York Times* since 1995. She covers social services for the metropolitan desk. Born in Calcutta, India, and raised mostly in a suburb of Los Angeles. she is a graduate of the University of California at Berkeley, a former waitress, radio producer, and community organizer. She previously worked at the *Los Angeles Times*.

Sengupta tells the poignant story of Chinese mothers in New York who ship their babies back to China. Her empathetic reporting and vivid writing illuminate the heartbreaking choices these women make in their search for a new life in a new world.

Squeezed by debt and time, mothers ship babies to China

SEPTEMBER 14, 1999

She spent her days at home with her newborn son, knowing that every day she did not work was another day without money to pay back her $20,000 smugglers' debt. She spent her nights awake, hushing the baby so he would not disturb her husband or the three other restaurant workers who shared their three-room apartment in northern Manhattan.

She named the boy Henry, and for four precious months, she nursed him, even after friends warned that she would soon have to let him go.

On the second Thursday in July, the woman, Xiu, finally did. Wrapping a tiny gold bracelet around his wrist, she placed her son in the arms of a friend of a friend, who, for $1,000, agreed to take him to China.

Xiu's mother is raising him there now, along with the 10-year-old daughter left behind last year when Xiu joined her husband in New York. She plans to bring Henry back when he reaches school age. But until then, she remains here, waiting to be a mother to her child. For weeks after Henry was shipped off, she would hear him cry at night.

"It seemed like she just gave up the baby to a complete stranger," said Sara Lee, a social worker at the Chinatown clinic of St. Vincent's Hospital and Medical Center, interpreting for Xiu one recent morning. "It's really killing her. She said no words can express her sadness."

Xiu's story has become increasingly common among the city's newest Chinese immigrants. Working long hours in garment factories for paltry pay, lacking affordable child care and the safety net of an extended family, growing numbers of Chinese immigrant women—a great many of whom, like Xiu, are here illegally—are sending their infants to China, according to doctors, nurses, social workers and labor organizers.

It is impossible to determine just how widespread the practice is, but it appears to involve hundreds of babies

a year in New York, if not more. At the Chinatown
Health Center, 10 to 20 percent of the 1,500 babies delivered last year were sent away, according to Celia Ng,
the nursing coordinator there. And at the St. Vincent's
Hospital Chinatown clinic, according to Ms. Lee, one-
third to one-half of the women who seek prenatal care
say they plan to send their babies to China.

Most of the mothers are married. Some of their pregnancies, though not all, are planned. And many give
birth knowing that soon, they, too, may end up sending
their babies away.

The children, American citizens by birth, are usually
raised by grandparents. The expectation, though hardly
a guarantee, is that the children will be summoned back
when they are old enough to begin school. It is a reunion
that often comes at considerable emotional cost to parents and children, in the opinion of doctors and social
workers.

Their story is another example of the way families
have been and continue to be fractured by immigration.
Men and women from all over the world come to the
United States, leaving children with relatives back
home until they gain a foothold. And some immigrant
parents send their American children, particularly teenagers, to the old country, to save them from troubled city
streets.

Sending infants to the old country is not unique to the
Chinese. But social service agencies working in other
immigrant communities say that while it is not unheard
of, the practice is still uncommon, usually limited to
cases of extreme hardship. Among Dominicans, for instance, it is usually young, single mothers who send
their children to the homeland, social workers say.

It is the combination of the large debts owed to their
smugglers and the long hours they must work that has
made this practice increasingly common among Chinese
immigrants. There is an additional cruel dilemma: having left China and its rigid one-child policy, they are
finally able to have larger families without fear of penal-
ties or recrimination. But as poor, illegal immigrants
here, they say, they are hard pressed to take care of their
young.

That more of these mothers are sending their babies

to China, people who work with them say, reflects the tougher working and living conditions facing Chinese immigrants today. With the threat of factories' moving abroad driving down wages, and a steady supply of cheap, illegal immigrant labor, mostly from Fujian Province in southern China, a new generation of garment sweatshops has blossomed across the city in recent years, according to garment workers' advocates and those who study Chinese immigration. Wages have fallen, and it is increasingly common for garment shops to require employees to work weekends.

"A lot of people simply have no time for their children," said Joanne Lum of the Chinese Staff and Workers Association, who works with garment workers in Chinatown and the Sunset Park section of Brooklyn.

Since her son was sent home, Xiu has returned to work. She sews women's pants six days a week and sends home $200 each month. At least every other week, she calls home. Every time, her daughter, Kei Wan, asks her to return home.

Kei Wan's chances of coming here any time soon are slim at best, her mother said, since she would have to be smuggled in at great expense.

This was not the picture Xiu had in mind when her husband summoned her here. They had been apart for eight years, she raising their little girl in a small town in southern China, he working as a cook at a Chinese restaurant in Manhattan. When Xiu finally arrived, she brought with her little more than nervous dreams: to work hard, save money, and raise a bigger, more prosperous family than she could imagine doing in China.

In a matter of months, Xiu became pregnant. And that is when she learned of this unforeseen tangle in the immigrant life. "It's not easy," she said, fingering the pictures of her children she keeps in a plastic picture album, "to be a mother here."

It is not illegal to send these American-born children to China. They are American citizens and can travel on American passports. Their couriers are legal residents and so are allowed to travel back and forth.

But while social workers and others say the practice is well known and widespread among New York's Chinese immigrants, that is not to say that the mothers are eager to discuss it. Workers at clinics across the city said they knew of many cases, but only a few mothers agreed to speak to a reporter, and would give their first names only. None agreed to be photographed.

Certainly, most Chinese immigrants do not send their babies away. They manage by staying home, imploring an elderly relative to baby-sit or paying for child care. Day care costs at least $20 a day in Chinatown, a large sum for a garment worker like Xiu, who, in a six-day workweek, takes home less than $300.

A couple of years ago, Ms. Lee saw a flier in the clinic bathroom. For a fee—the going rate is $1,000, plus air fare—someone was offering to take babies to China. Around that time, she noticed an increase in the number of women who sent their babies to China. So she made it a part of her practice to ask all her prenatal patients what they planned to do after giving birth.

Today, she tells each one how painful it can be for a mother to send an infant away. It is hard on fathers as well, though they are more likely to have been separated from their children for many years. She explains how difficult it can be when the child finally comes back, but as a stranger.

"I can't imagine being separated from my kids," said Ms. Lee, whose own children are 1 and 3. "But they have a problem, no matter what."

Zhu, a single woman from Guangdong Province, says that sending her child home is the only way she can imagine surviving in this country. Just before her first child, Thomas, was born last month, Zhu, 36, gave up her job as a home health aide in Brooklyn. Since then, she has lived on her savings, but they will soon be exhausted. So when the Lunar New Year rolls around in February, Zhu, unmarried and alone in New York, plans to take Thomas to China, where her own mother will raise him for a few years, until she can afford to have him by her side once more.

Fortunately for Zhu, she is a legal immigrant. She can take Thomas to China herself. When she can afford it, she can even visit.

That good fortune is beyond Xiu's reach. The other day, the two mothers sat next to each other at the Chinatown clinic run by St. Vincent's Hospital, Xiu keeping her eyes on baby Thomas sleeping against his mother's belly, Zhu admiring the pictures of Xiu's children.

They were talking of the choices they had made, and Xiu was wiping away irrepressible tears.

How hard it was, she said, to walk into the clinic that morning and see babies in their mothers' arms. How hard it was, she said, when the woman who took Henry home called to say that he had cried incessantly on the one-and-a-half-day journey. At least, she said, she had nursed him for the first four months of his life. She would feel so guilty otherwise.

Would it have been easier, she wondered aloud, if she had been younger? A quick rebuttal came from Angel, 33, an immigrant from Guangdong. Five years ago, when she was 28, her husband sent their daughter back home. It wasn't any easier, she said.

At the time, Angel said, she had no choice. She had a good job at a photography shop in Chinatown, and her boss had agreed to let her take a month off after the birth. There was no one to watch the baby all day, nor money for a sitter. Barely 4 weeks old, the baby was sent away.

Three years later, when Angel brought her back to New York, the little girl seemed as miserable as her mother had been when she sent her away. She sat on the sofa in the living room of their apartment in Woodside, Queens, and cried quietly.

A small, sprightly woman who looks half her age, Angel still cries at the memory. It has brought her one lesson. She says she is not planning on any more children.

Lessons Learned

BY SOMINI SENGUPTA

If the worn tenet of many writing workshops is to write what you know, then my story (for that matter, most of my stories) audaciously violated that wisdom. I knew nothing about the lives of the Chinese immigrant women I wrote about—those who, for reasons I could not relate to—chose to send their newborn babies back home.

I was an outsider to their world, by race, language, and most importantly, by experience. The women in the story had risked life and limb to come to this country. Most of them owed giant debts to their smugglers. They hunched over sewing machines 60 hours a week and brought home $300. They did not hire nannies. They were not surrounded by elderly kin to share child-care duties; they did not have partners who were willing to temporarily become stay-at-home dads. They had become pregnant, some by choice, others not, and they had shipped their babies off to the other side of the world, to be cared for by relatives until, they felt, they could take care of them here.

Some of the obstacles I faced were the usual ones. It was difficult to find women who agreed to be interviewed, impossible to find ones who agreed to be photographed. Their illegal immigration status, their fear of being in a strange country, fully visible and yet under the radar, was of particular concern. The women had nothing to gain from speaking to me. I had nothing to offer them but questions that were no more than salt on a wound.

A few things I could relate to, I suppose. I am an immigrant, though raised in this country since childhood and in my heart, an American. I understood something about fear: My parents' eyes held it for years. I was sensitive to how easily things could get lost in translation. And in these interviews, conducted with the help of a social worker who served as an interpreter, it was difficult to gauge the color of their grief. Perhaps, the subtle calculations of their choice did get lost in the exchange.

There were other obstacles, too—namely, avoiding the judgment that could be heaped on their choices. Why did they have children if they knew they couldn't raise them? Were there cultural dispositions? Did the Chinese, known worldwide for their preference for boys over girls, dump their daughters more readily? (My interviews suggested that baby boys and girls were shipped off.)

But the challenge that loomed largest was the one that often does. It was the task of striking a balance between the dual, sometimes seemingly contradictory imperatives of writing a newspaper story: Do you try to empathize with your subject, or do you tell her tale dispassionately?

I think this is somewhat of a false choice. I felt passionately about this story, as I do, blessedly, about many stories I write. In this case, I wanted desperately to understand how these women made their choices, at what cost, with what hopes for the future. How did they cope with the absence? What was it like at night? Did their babies invade their dreams? Did they feel guilty? What elusive promise held them aloft? Through their stories, I wanted to understand—and help my readers to understand—the larger question of how immigration at the turn of this century plays out in families, how these grand movements across continents alter the most intimate relationships.

For me, storytelling is about getting under other people's skin, quite literally. That, I think, is the reporter's gift and responsibility. Perhaps then, it is useful to empathize with a subject, to step into her shoes, no matter how morally ambiguous that subject might appear. Then, I think, it is my responsibility to write as dispassionately and sensibly—which is to say, without judgment—as possible.

In the end, this doesn't just serve the story. It teaches me things about my own world. Sure, I was a stranger to these women's peculiar loss, but I was no stranger to loss. Two months before this story appeared, my best friend disappeared while hiking up a mountain, never to come back. This was the first feature story I wrote after his presumed death.

How to write a good story in 800 words or less

BY ROY PETER CLARK

Most of the good stories we tell can be told in 800 words or less. Let me try one. It involves my father, Ted Clark, who used to have the annoying habit of sucking on ice cubes, which he was doing one day, sitting in his recliner in front of the television set. My mother was in the basement doing the laundry, when she heard a great thump above her. She rushed upstairs and found my father unconscious on the bathroom floor. She called 911 and the paramedics arrived, but not before my father had recovered, seemingly unharmed. It turned out that an ice cube had lodged in his windpipe, cutting off his air supply, knocking him out as he staggered toward the bathroom. Fortunately, his body heat melted the ice cube, restoring the flow of oxygen and saving his life. He's never sucked on an ice cube again.

It took me 128 words to tell that story. If I measure the story another way, by Approximate Reading Time (ART), I can say that the story is about 42 seconds long. I think any discussion of story length should measure a story not just by the number of words or column inches, but how long it takes the average person to read it.

I found this gem in a collection of radio reports from the great Edward R. Murrow of CBS News. The date is April 12, 1951:

> Western Union has delivered about sixty thousand telegrams to Congress and the White House, most of them in favor of General MacArthur. Republican Senator McCarthy, of Wisconsin, says, "It was a victory for Communism and shows the midnight power of bourbon and Benedictine." In Los Angeles, a man smashed a radio over his wife's head in the course of an argument about MacArthur's removal. Reports say it was a table model.

A table model, rather than a console! In other words, the man was kind enough not to strike his wife with a big piece of furniture. This report of 71 words can be read aloud in about 25 seconds. My rough calculations reveal that it takes the average person about 33 seconds to read 100 words.

Let's round that off to 200 words per minute. That means that my new 15,000-word serial narrative would take a reader about 75 minutes to read. That ART is good to know as I consider with my editors whether to publish it as a special section, in four daily parts, or over a greater number of days. Maybe each of my chapters can be very short, say 800 words or less, requiring only four minutes of my reader's time.

If you want to write shorter, or if your editor wants you to, I've got some tips that I've gathered from the best wordsmiths in the business. You can write short without sacrificing your news values or your literary sensibilities. That's the good news. The bad news is that you can't do it alone. Well, maybe that's also good news.

1. Find models of short writing from every genre and medium. Let the writers of those works become your teachers.

Start off with three story collections—all published by Norton. The first is called *Radios: Short Takes on Life and Culture*, by the late writing professor of Florida State University, Jerome Stern. These are printed versions of public radio commentaries. A typical one is about 350 words. Then check out *In Short: A Collection of Brief Creative Nonfiction*, edited by Judith Kitchen and Mary Paumier Jones. For some real fun, enjoy Jerome Stern's edition of *Micro Fiction*. Among the shortest stories is this 53-word nugget by Amy Hempel:

> She swallowed Gore Vidal. Then she swallowed Donald Trump. She took a blue capsule and a gold spansule—a B-complex and an E—and put them on the tablecloth a few inches apart. She pointed the one at the other. "Martha Stewart," she said, "meet Oprah Winfrey." She swallowed them both without water.

2. Know from the beginning whether you're writing a sonnet or an epic.

One of my favorite sonnets begins Shakespeare's *Romeo and Juliet.*

> Two households, both alike in dignity,

In fair Verona, where we lay our scene,
From ancient grudge break to new mutiny,
Where civil blood makes civil hands unclean.
From forth the fatal loins of these two foes
A pair of star-crossed lovers take their life;
Whose misadventured piteous overthrows
Doth with their death bury their parents' strife.
The fearful passage of their death-marked love,
And the continuance of their parents' rage,
Which, but their children's end, naught could
   remove,
Is now the two hours' traffic of our stage;
The which if you with patient ears attend,
What here shall miss, our toil shall strive to mend.

That's 14 lines, 106 words. Never was there a summary of complex news more carefully crafted or more beautifully expressed. Perhaps a reporter for the *London Globe* would have written it this way:

"A pair of teen-age lovers died Thursday, the result of a failed plot to bring their warring families together. Romeo Montague and Juliet Capulet, both of Verona, were pronounced dead from what appeared to be self-inflicted dagger wounds. 'This is the most woeful story I've ever heard,' said Escalus, prince of Verona and chief law enforcement officer. 'I hope the families learn from this terrible tragedy.'"

In his sonnet lead, Shakespeare includes the basic elements of news telling, usually referred to as the Five W's and H. We know the Who: a pair of unlucky lovers; the What: they took their lives; the Where: in fair Verona; the When: right now; the Why: an ancient feud. Of course, the How is about to be experienced: the "two-hours' traffic of our stage," the narrative of the play.

Shakespeare wrote short poems and long plays. Like other writers, he was guided by knowing from the beginning the technical limits of his genre. There's nothing inherently wrong with the 5 W's or the form of writing called the inverted pyramid. Just remember to keep it short.

3. Thaw out the 5 W's and H.

This advice comes from editor Rick Zahler at *The Seattle Times*. The traditional version of the 5 W's freezes those story elements into informational ice cubes. If you thaw them out, the narrative begins to flow. Who becomes Character. What becomes Action. Where becomes Setting. When becomes Chronology. Why becomes Motive. How becomes Narrative. One of the great reporters of his day was Meyer Berger of *The New York Times.* Berger was the master of the short human interest feature. Just before his death in 1959, he wrote a story, about 1,200 words, on an old, poor blind man who was once a classical musician. Then he wrote a sequel:

Eight violins were offered the other day to Laurence Stroetz, the 82-year-old, cataract-blinded violinist who was taken to St. Clare's Hospital in East Seventy-first Street from a Bowery flophouse. The offers came from men and women who had read that though he had once played with the Pittsburgh Symphony Orchestra, he had been without a violin for more than 30 years.

The first instrument to reach the hospital was a gift from the Lighthouse, the institution for the sightless. It was delivered by a blind man. A nun took it to the octogenarian.

He played it a while, tenderly and softly, then gave it back. He said: "This is a fine old violin. Tell the owner to take good care of it." The white-clad nun said: "It is your violin, Mr. Stroetz. It is a gift." The old man bent his head over it. He wept.

In 145 words, Berger turns a traditional Who ("the 82-year-old, cataract-blinded violinist") into a real character, brimming with human emotions.

4. Remember the basics of storytelling.

Tom Wolfe argued that the tools of fiction writing could be adapted for nonfiction, as long as the reporting was deep and careful. Those tools include setting scenes, using dialogue, drawing details that define character, and revealing the world through various points of view. Although we associate these tools with long forms of journalism, such as the narrative reconstruction of events, they can work in short forms as well. Notice the miniature scene created by Meyer Berger above. A nun enters the room with the violin. He plays. She engages in dialogue with the blind man. He weeps.

5. Turn the pyramid right side up. Or use the hourglass.

We think of the inverted pyramid as one of the Great Wonders of the newspaper writing world, and it is; but alternative forms of news narrative have always co-existed with it. George C. Bastian wrote this in a 1923 textbook on editing: "Two Important Types of Narratives—Most news stories, and indeed most news paragraphs, begin with their climax, or most important and most newsy feature, and then proceed to detail and amplify. Some, however, notably those resembling the short story form of writing, begin with details and reserve their climax until the last. These two types of stories may be compared to two triangles, one resting on its base and the other on a point." Professor Bastian might have added a third form in which the two triangles are joined at their points, forming a structure that looks like an hourglass. Many stories lend themselves to an informational beginning, with the key facts stacked in the order of importance. But the story can then take a turn ("Police and witnesses gave the following account of what happened.") with the bottom of the story rendering a chronological version of events.

6. Experiment with the forms of short writing that already exist: the headline, the tease, the photo caption, the brief, the "brite," the notes column.

There is no more underdeveloped writing form in American journalism than the photo caption or cutline. Here Jeffrey Page of *The Record* in New Jersey shows the storytelling potential of the form. Frank Sinatra has just died, so imagine a one-column photo of him. It shows Sinatra from the waist up. He's wearing a tux with a black bow tie. He's got a mike in his hand. He's obviously singing.

If you saw a man in a tux and black bow tie swagger on stage like an elegant pirate, and if you had been told he would spend an hour singing Cole Porter, Gershwin, and Rodgers and Hart, and if when he opened his mouth you heard a little of your life in his voice, and if you saw his body arch back on the high notes (the ones he insisted you hear and feel and live with him), and if his swing numbers made you want to bounce and be happy and be young and be carefree, and if when he sang "Try a Little Tenderness" and got to the line about a woman's wearing the same shabby dress it made you profoundly sad, and if years later you felt that his death made you a little less alive, you must have been watching this man who started as a saloon singer in Hoboken and went on to become the very definition of American popular music.

How can you write a 198-word caption without using the dead man's name? Jeffrey Page explains: "I know, I know, it violates every damned rule. Screw it. They keep telling us to take chances, right? So I did....If you're a U.S. paper, and especially if you happen to be in New Jersey, you don't have to tell people that they're looking at a picture of Sinatra and not Mother Teresa."

7. Think of chapters, segments, vignettes, slices of life.

Even a very long work, such as the Bible, can be divided into books, chapters, and verses. Sometimes little drips of writing can turn into puddles, into streams, into rivers. But the process can work the other way around. Consider this paragraph from an essay titled "Proofs," by Richard Rodriguez:

You stand around. You smoke. You spit. You are wearing your two shirts, two pants, two underpants. Jesus says, if they chase you throw that bag down. Your plastic bag is your mama, all you have left; the yellow cheese she wrapped has formed a translucent rind; the laminated scapular of the Sacred Heart nestles flame in its cleft. Put it in your pocket. The last hour of Mexico is twilight, the shuffling of feet. A fog is beginning to cover the ground. Jesus says they are able to see in the dark. They have X-rays and helicopters and searchlights. Jesus says wait, just wait, till he says. You can feel the hand of Jesus clamp your shoulder, fingers cold as ice. *Venga, corre.* You run. All the rest happens without words. Your feet are tearing dry grass, your heart is lashed like a mare. You trip, you fall. You are now in the United State of America. You are a boy from a Mexican village. You have come into the country on your knees with your head down. You are a man."

Although this is only one of 11 such vignettes in the piece, it can stand on its own as a brilliant 150-word essay on the tensions between freedom, opportunity, and servitude.

8. Focus, focus, focus.

This is the central act of the writing craft. Ultimately, we focus all other parts of the process. We focus the idea or assignment. We focus the reporting. We focus the lead. We select to support the focus. The focus is the cornerstone for building a structure. We revise to eliminate that which fails to support the focus.

Good questions help us find the focus and keep the story short. What is this story about? What do I want my reader to learn? What's the heart or nut of the story? What is the news? What is the point? What is the theme? What's the most important question answered by the story? Can I describe the story in a single paragraph? A sentence? Six words? Three words?

A humorous radio commentary by the late Jerome Stern makes fun of the way famous athletes and celebrities talk about themselves in the third person: "Meryl Streep," says Meryl Streep, "resents her loss of privacy." After a wicked inventory of such atrocities, Stern suggests that common folks should take up the habit: "We owe this to ourselves. We're as good, we're as complicated, we're as important. These celebrities, they have fame, fortune—should they have all the proper nouns, too?

"In naming ourselves we create ourselves, we are the stars of our own sweet universe."

All 350 words of his essay lead to that one, final exquisite point.

9. Turn lumps of coal into little diamonds.

Accept the challenge of transforming a routine assignment into something special: an obituary, a spelling bee, a high school graduation, daylight-saving time, the new phone book.

Famous for his long narratives, Ken Fuson was assigned to do a quick hit on the first day of spring. This piece appeared the next morning on the front page of *The Des Moines Register*:

Here's how Iowa celebrates a 70-degree day in the middle of March: By washing the car and scooping the loop and taking a walk; by daydreaming in school and playing hooky at work and shutting off the furnace at home; by skateboarding and flying kites and digging through closets for baseball gloves; by riding that new bike you got for Christmas and drawing hopscotch boxes in chalk on the sidewalk and not caring if the kids lost their mittens again; by looking for robins and noticing swimsuits on department store mannequins and shooting hoops in the park; by sticking the ice scraper in the trunk and the antifreeze in the garage and leaving the car parked outside overnight; by cleaning the barbecue and stuffing the parka in storage and just standing outside and letting that friendly sun kiss your face; by wondering where you're going to go on summer vacation and getting reacquainted with neighbors on the front porch and telling the boys that yes! yes! they can run outside and play without a jacket; by holding hands with a lover and jogging in shorts and picking up the extra branches in the yard; by eating an ice cream cone outside and (if you're a farmer or gardener) feeling that first twinge that says it's time to plant and (if you're a high school senior) feeling that first twinge that says it's time to leave; by wondering if in all of history there has ever been a day so glorious and concluding that there hasn't and being afraid to even stop and take a breath (or begin a new paragraph) for fear that winter would return, leaving Wednesday in our memory as nothing more than a sweet and too-short dream.

So, it turned out, Ken Fuson could write a short story. Now about that sentence: a single, glorious, 280-word catalog of vernal ecstasy.

Smart editors who crave short writing must find a place in the newspaper where such stories can flourish. Writers need and deserve praise—and good play—to encourage them to turn their epic hands to an occasional sonnet, and maybe, on one glorious day, a haiku.

(This essay on short writing is about 3,000 words long. The Approximate Reading Time is 15 minutes.)

Annual bibliography

BY DAVID B. SHEDDEN

WRITING AND REPORTING BOOKS 1999

Aamidor, Abraham. *Real Feature Writing*. Hillsdale, N.J.: Lawrence Erlbaum Associates, 1999.

Alexander, S.L. *Covering the Courts: A Handbook for Journalists*. Blue Ridge Summit, Pa.: University Press of America, 1999.

Berner, R. Thomas. *The Literature of Journalism*. State College, Pa.: Strata Publishing, 1999.

Bunton, Kristie, et al. *Writing Across the Media*. Boston: Bedford/St. Martins, 1999.

Halberstam, David, and Glenn Stout, eds. *Best American Sports Writing of the Century*. New York: Houghton Mifflin, 1999.

Hicks, Wynford, et al. *Writing for Journalists*. New York: Routledge, 1999.

Kessler, Lauren, and Duncan McDonald. *When Words Collide: A Media Writer's Guide to Grammar and Style*. Belmont, Calif.: Wadsworth Publishing, 1999.

Lanson, Jerry, and Barbara Croll Fought. *News in the Next Century: Reporting in an Age of Converging Media*. Thousand Oaks, Calif.: Pine Forge Press, 1999.

Leiter, Kelly, et al. *The Complete Reporter*. 7th ed. Needham Heights, Mass.: Allyn & Bacon, 1999.

Levin, Mark. *EXP3 Journalism: A Handbook for Journalists*. Lincolnwood, Ill.: NTC/Contemporary Publishing, 1999.

Paul, Nora. *Computer-Assisted Research*. 4th ed. Chicago: Bonus Books, 1999.

Rich, Carole. *Writing and Reporting News: A Coaching Method.* 3rd ed. Belmont, Calif.: Wadsworth Publishers, 1999.

Scanlan, Christopher, ed. *Best Newspaper Writing.* St. Petersburg, Fla.: The Poynter Institute, 1999.

Scanlan, Christopher. *Reporting and Writing: Basics for the 21st Century.* Fort Worth: Harcourt College Publishers, 1999.

Sher, Gail. *One Continuous Mistake: Four Noble Truths for Writers.* New York: Penguin Arkana,1999.

CLASSICS

Atchity, Kenneth. *A Writer's Time: A Guide to the Creative Process, From Vision Through Revision.* New York: W.W. Norton & Co., 1996.

Bell, Madison Smartt. *Narrative Design: A Writer's Guide to Structure.* New York: W.W. Norton & Co., 1997.

Berg, A. Scott. *Max Perkins: Editor of Genius.* New York: Berkley Publishing Group, 1997.

Bernstein, Theodore M. *The Careful Writer: A Modern Guide to English Usage.* New York: Atheneum Books for Young Readers, 1977.

Blundell, William E. *The Art and Craft of Feature Writing: The Wall Street Journal Guide.* New York: Dutton/Plume, 1988.

Brady, John. *The Craft of Interviewing.* New York: Knopf, 1977.

Brande, Dorothea. *Becoming a Writer.* Los Angeles: J.P. Tarcher; Boston: distributed by Putnam Publishing, reprint of 1934 edition, 1981.

Brown, Karen, Roy Peter Clark, Don Fry, and Christopher Scanlan, eds. *Best Newspaper Writing.* St. Petersburg, Fla.: The Poynter Institute. Published annually since 1979.

Cappon, Rene J. *The Associated Press Guide to News Writing*. Paramus, N.J.: Prentice Hall, 1991.

Clark, Roy Peter. *Free to Write: A Journalist Teaches Young Writers*. Westport, Conn.: Heinemann, 1995.

Clark, Roy Peter, and Don Fry. *Coaching Writers: The Essential Guide for Editors and Reporters*. New York: St. Martin's Press, 1992.

Dillard, Annie. *The Writing Life*. New York: HarperCollins, 1999.

Elbow, Peter. *Writing With Power: Techniques for Mastering the Writing Process*. 2nd ed. New York: Oxford University Press, 1998.

Follett, Wilson. *Modern American Usage: A Guide*. Revised by Erik Wensberg. New York: Hill & Wang, 1998.

Franklin, Jon. *Writing for Story: Craft Secrets of Dramatic Nonfiction by a Two-Time Pulitzer Prize Winner*. New York: Dutton/Plume, 1994.

Garlock, David. *Pulitzer Prize Feature Stories*. Ames, Iowa: Iowa State University Press, 1998.

Goldstein, Norm, ed. *AP Stylebook*. Cambridge, Mass.: Perseus Publishing, 2000.

Gross, Gerald, ed. *Editors on Editing: What Writers Should Know About What Editors Do*. New York: Grove/Atlantic, 1993.

Harrington, Walt. *Intimate Journalism: The Art and Craft of Reporting Everyday Life*. Thousand Oaks, Calif.: Sage, 1997.

Hugo, Richard. *The Triggering Town: Lectures & Essays on Poetry & Writing*. New York: Norton, 1992.

Kerrane, Kevin, and Ben Yagoda. *The Art of Fact*. New York: Scribner, 1997.

Klement, Alice, and Carolyn Matalene, eds. *Telling Stories, Taking Risks. Journalism Writing and the Century's Edge*. Belmont, Calif.: Wadsworth Publishing, 1998.

McPhee, John. *The John McPhee Reader*. William L. Howard, ed. New York: Farrar, Straus & Giroux, 1990.

Mencher, Melvin. *News Reporting and Writing*. 8th ed. New York: McGraw-Hill, 1999.

Metzler, Ken. *Creative Interviewing: The Writer's Guide to Gathering Information by Asking Questions*. 3rd ed. Needham Heights, Mass.: Allyn & Bacon, 1996.

Mitford, Jessica. *Poison Penmanship: The Gentle Art of Muckraking*. New York: Farrar, Straus & Giroux, 1988.

Murray, Donald. *Shoptalk: Learning to Write With Writers*. Portsmouth, N.H.: Boynton/Cook, 1990.

Perry, Susan K. *Writing in Flow: Keys to Enchanced Creativity*. Cincinnati: Writer's Digest Books, 1999.

Plimpton, George, ed. *Writers at Work: The Paris Review Interviews*. Series. New York: Viking, 1992.

Ross, Lillian. *Reporting*. New York: Simon & Schuster Trade, 1984.

Scanlan, Christopher, ed. *How I Wrote the Story*. Providence Journal Company, 1986.

Sims, Norman, ed. *Literary Journalism in the Twentieth Century*. New York: Oxford University Press, 1990.

Stafford, William, and Donald Hall, eds. *Writing the Australian Crawl: View on the Writer's Vocation*. Ann Arbor, Mich.: University of Michigan Press, 1978.

Stewart, James B. *Follow the Story: How to Write Successful Nonfiction*. New York: Simon and Schuster, 1998.

Strunk, William, Jr., and E.B. White. *The Elements of Style*. 4th ed. Needham Heights, Mass.: Allyn & Bacon, 1999.

Talese, Gay. *Fame & Obscurity*. New York: Ivy Books, 1971.

Wardlow, Elwood M., ed. *Effective Writing and Editing: A Guidebook for Newspapers*. Reston, Va.: American Press Institute, 1985.

White, E.B. *Essays of E.B. White*. New York: HarperCollins, 1999.

Zinsser, William. *On Writing Well: An Informal Guide to Writing Nonfiction*. 6th ed. New York: HarperCollins, 1998.

— *Writing to Learn*. Reading, Mass.: Addison-Wesley Educational Publishers, 1997.

— *Speaking of Journalism: 12 Writers and Editors Talk About Their Work*. New York: HarperCollins, 1994.

ARTICLES 1999

Bonner, Paul. "Serial Fiction 'Ain't Done Yet' in NY Times Regional Group." *Editor & Publisher* (April 3, 1999): 28.

Bucqueroux, Bonnie, and Sue Carter. "Interviewing Victims." *Quill* (December 1999): 19-21.

Cleaveland, Janet. "Copy Editors Want to Help Tackle Credibility." *The American Editor* (May/June 1999): 25.

Foreman, Gene. "As Copy Desk Work Grows, Credibility Ebbs." *The American Editor* (February 1999): 22-23.

Frank, Russell. "You've Got Quotes!" *Quill* (October 1999): 18-22.

Fry, Don. "Keep Your Sentences Fit and Active." *The American Editor* (March/April 1999): 22.